EXODUS '43

EXODUS '43

John Goldsmith

Coward, McCann & Geoghegan
New York

First American edition 1982
Copyright © 1981 by John Goldsmith
Previously published in Great Britain under the title
Exodus Genesis.

Library of Congress Cataloging in Publication Data

Goldsmith, John, 1947–
    Exodus '43.

    1. World War, 1939–1945—Fiction. 2. Denmark—
History—German occupation, 1940–1945—Fiction.
I. Title.
PR6057.O44E96 1982   823'.914   81-19468
ISBN 0-698-11129-X   AACR2

Printed in the United States of America

FOR
ANTHEA

Acknowledgements

Although this is a work of fiction, in which all the characters are imaginary and bear no relation to real people, living or dead, it is based entirely on fact. There is nothing in it that either did not happen or could not have happened and the action is set against real events in the history of Denmark between 1939 and 1945. The gathering of those facts entailed many days of research in Denmark, many interviews with men and women who were personally involved in the Danish Resistance and in the rescue of the Danish Jews, and much delving into archives. To all those who helped and advised me in this work, whose patience and kindness smoothed my path, and whose hospitality was always generous and often overwhelming, I owe a deep debt of gratitude. I would like in particular to thank Major Flemming Muus D.S.O. and his wife, and Mr Jens Lillilund, all three heroes of the Resistance; Mr Jørgen Barfod, Mr Henning Gehrs and Mr Bjarne Maurer of the Resistance Museum; Mr Arne Melchior, member of the Danish Parliament and son of the Rabbi Marcus Melchior; Captain Jesper Gramm-Andersen, curator of the Royal Life Guards Museum; Mr Henrik Henriques of the Henriques Bank; Mr Leslie Rubinstein of the British Embassy, Copenhagen, and his wife; Mr and Mrs Winkler Kromann, whose encyclopaedic knowledge of Copenhagen and Danish history and culture was invaluable; and Mr and Mrs Dan Daniels for their unfailing hospitality. Above all I would like to thank my brother-in-law and sister, Mr and Mrs Peter Tann, who first introduced me to Denmark and the Danes. But for them this book would never have been written.

MENDEZ and ABRAHAMSEN FAMILIES

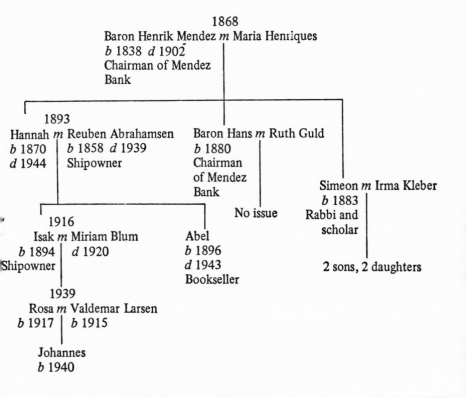

1868
Baron Henrik Mendez *m* Maria Henriques
b 1838 *d* 1902
Chairman of Mendez
Bank

1893
Hannah *m* Reuben Abrahamsen
b 1870 | *b* 1858 *d* 1939
d 1944 | Shipowner

Baron Hans *m* Ruth Guld
b 1880
Chairman
of Mendez
Bank
No issue

Simeon *m* Irma Kleber
b 1883
Rabbi and
scholar

2 sons, 2 daughters

1916
Isak *m* Miriam Blum
b 1894 | *d* 1920
Shipowner

Abel
b 1896
d 1943
Bookseller

1939
Rosa *m* Valdemar Larsen
b 1917 | *b* 1915

Johannes
b 1940

LARSEN and TØLLER FAMILIES

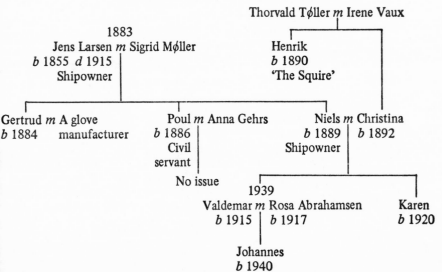

Thorvald Tøller *m* Irene Vaux

1883
Jens Larsen *m* Sigrid Møller
b 1855 *d* 1915
Shipowner

Henrik
b 1890
'The Squire'

Gertrud *m* A glove
b 1884   manufacturer

Poul *m* Anna Gehrs
b 1886
Civil
servant
No issue

Niels *m* Christina
b 1889 | *b* 1892
Shipowner

1939
Valdemar *m* Rosa Abrahamsen
b 1915 | *b* 1917

Karen
b 1920

Johannes
b 1940

Prologue

An incident in Copenhagen, October 1943

The No. 9 tram clattered down Jagtvej and Rosa clung to her strap, swaying a little with the motion of the car, staring past the pale, washed-out faces of the people pressed closest to her, towards the window. It was dark outside and she could see her own reflection in the glass, opaquely, as in a photographic negative. She avoided her neighbours' eyes, just as they avoided hers, obeying the unwritten etiquette of the late-afternoon scramble for home. The tram drew up at the stop by the cemetery and there was some discreet pushing and jostling as people got off and on. Rosa shifted slightly to make more space round her and she heard a woman mutter: 'Oh God, not again.'

She twisted her head round and looked down the car, through the restlessly moving forest of heads and shoulders, to the far end. There were two of them. Wehrmacht, thank God, not Gestapo; even so she felt a premonition of disaster. This was all part of the new campaign in the hunt for Jews – random checks on trains and buses and trams, and in cinemas and restaurants.

The two soldiers were moving slowly up the car towards her, checking identity papers. One of them looked middle-aged, a sergeant probably, and the other was little more than a boy. He appeared tense and nervy.

She turned her face away. What could she do? Impossible to make a run for it, madness, in fact, to display any sign of distress. There was nothing wrong with her papers, but what about her appearance? All round her were grey-white faces, light blue eyes, and corn-coloured hair. She caught a glimpse of herself in the window: dark complexion, black hair, black eyes. Suddenly she felt as conspicuous as an olive on a white table-cloth. Gradually, as the two soldiers moved nearer and nearer, she became aware

11

that the etiquette of the tram was being abandoned. People standing or sitting near her were covertly looking at her. They know, she thought, they know what I am.

And then she became aware of something else. The people in front of her, between her and the Germans, were bunching together. The man next to her was pushing her arm, gently but firmly. She began to shuffle towards the back of the car, people making way for her, standing aside, helping her, encouraging her with little nudges.

There was a wall of bodies now between her and the Germans and the sergeant had noticed it. The young one too. He knew. He had sensed it — a Jew on the tram.

A strange silence descended. The sergeant was staring at the people and the people were staring back, steady stares — without hostility, without fear. The sergeant seemed to decide.

'Enough,' she heard him say. 'Come on.'

But the young one hesitated. He was fingering his gun, peering down the car. Rosa averted her face. She heard the sergeant rap: 'Come on. Move yourself.'

She looked up. They were moving back down the car, they were getting out. As the tram jerked forward there was an outburst of talk and some laughter. The man standing beside Rosa said:

'Bloody animals.' Then: 'You should be in hiding. You shouldn't be on the streets.'

A woman behind her said:

'Here, take my seat dear. You look as pale as a ghost.'

Rosa sat down. Another man said:

'I can help you. I'll give you somewhere to hide. I know people who can help you.'

'No, no,' she said. 'You're very kind. I — I have a place.'

The tram stopped again. Suddenly she knew she had to get out, get away from all the staring faces; she felt that the whole world was gazing at her. She pushed her way down the car. People stood back to let her pass. There was babble all round her, strangers exchanging Jew-stories. She jumped off the tram and began to walk. There was no strength in her legs. She stopped to rest for a moment in the doorway of a shop. She found she was sweating, as if she had been running. She walked on, grateful for the darkness. If only it would rain, then people would scurry by, their heads bowed against the wind, or masked by umbrellas, and they wouldn't be able to look at her. She didn't want anyone to look at her.

Part One
1939

1

'Home,' Rosa said, and the Captain smiled and replied: 'Yes, not that you can see much of it.'

It was true. The night air was soft and warm but the cold water of the Sound exuded a fine haze. She wandered off the bridge, out onto the deck, and leaned on the rail. In a few minutes they would be docking – always a delicate manoeuvre – and it was better, more tactful, if the owner's daughter was out of the way.

Through the mist she could see the string of lights along Langelinie pier, a series of diffused glows. She glanced at her watch. Three o'clock. They were nine hours behind schedule. Would her father be there to meet her? Probably not. He hated turning out in the middle of the night. But no doubt he'd laid on a car.

She felt the vibrations in the deck change as the *Odessa's* engines were reversed and her mood changed with them. She walked over to the port side as the ship slowly came round to present her stern to the dimly lit wharves and warehouses of the Abrahamsen yards, now discernible through clear patches in the mist. She had been excited, almost exalted, but now she was keyed up. She hoped her father would not be there. She did not want to face him yet, she did not want to hear the news of grandfather – yet. She wanted to let herself quietly into the flat and tiptoe to her own bed and wake up in the morning as if she had never been away. For a moment she wanted the *Odessa* to go on throbbing quietly through the night, through the mist.

The note of the engines, having risen to a pitch, was dying. There were shouts from the crew as they threw lines to gesticulating figures on the dock. And suddenly she was exhausted.

It was a strain chatting and joking with the stevedores, always so unnaturally lively at this dead hour, most of whom she had known all her life; and a relief when dear old Sørensen, the supervisor, said: 'There's a young gentleman, with a car, to meet you, Miss Rosa.'

It vaguely occurred to her that the information had been oddly phrased, but she picked up her overnight case – her trunk would be sent up to the flat in the morning – and walked out of

16

Sørensen's office with a polite 'Good night'.

She recognized the car at once – the neat two-seater parked by the wall of the Old Cotton House – but for a second she failed to connect it with Valdemar. Then she saw him climb out of the car and walk eagerly towards her. Her immediate reaction was irritation. She hadn't wanted to face her father – but Valdemar ... He must have sensed it because he stopped a few feet from her, smiling awkwardly. It was obvious that he could think of nothing to say and all she could think of was:

'Val – how long have you been waiting?'

'Hours,' he said.

'But how did you know when we'd dock? I mean we've been delayed.'

'I didn't know,' he said with a shy smile.

They began strolling towards the car. He took the case from her but made no move to embrace her or kiss her.

'I got chatting to the driver your father sent and persuaded him to go home to his wife and family.'

'But Val you're crazy. Father's bound to find out.'

'Don't worry. The driver hasn't got a clue who I am.'

'But the others – someone must have seen you.'

He shook his head, said solemnly 'I promise you, I've handled the affair with incredible discretion', and grinned. She grinned back. She couldn't help it. Then his arms were round her and he was hugging her tightly.

'You look marvellous,' he said.

'I feel hideous.'

He released her, kissed her lightly, and slung the case into the dickey. They got into the car.

'I'll take you straight home. You don't mind if I spend the rest of the night gazing up at your darkened window?'

She laughed. 'You're completely mad.'

'True. But then so are you, remember. Or has a month in England changed you?'

She looked away for a second then said: 'Not really.'

Old Johan, the night watchman, peered through the high wire-mesh fence that separated the Larsen from the Abrahamsen yards. His stick was hooked to the mesh and his hands gripped the wire. He had watched the *Odessa* come in and had seen that

17

little Rosa Abrahamsen come down the gangway. Then he had prowled round to check that the car which had been parked all night by the Old Cotton House was still there. He had not recognized it as young Mr Valdemar's car – he hardly ever saw the boy these days – but had been curious about it and about the long vigil of the man inside it. When he saw Valdemar, and recognized his tall figure and white-blond hair, saw him walk towards that girl, talk to her, put his arms round her, he had felt outraged, then shamed – as if he was peeping at some obscene act – and finally frightened.

Absently he wiped moisture from his eyes. There was a brief roar from the car, and a dazzle of light as it swung round and away. He was left staring at the blackened wall of the Old Cotton House, through the wire-mesh, through the barrier that divided Larsen property from Abrahamsen property and, irrevocably, Larsen from Abrahamsen.

Suddenly Old Johan wished he had stayed in his snug cubby-hole, had seen nothing. He unhooked his stick and limped away into the shadows. He would have to tell Mr Niels, have to: sixty years of loyalty demanded it. Yet there was also his loyalty to Valdemar, Valdemar who'd been like a son to him. That bright little face, that eager voice piping: 'Tell me a story, Johan. Tell me the story of the wicked orphan boy.'

Old Johan was suddenly angry. Had Valdemar forgotten that story? It had been his favourite, he'd been forever demanding it. Old Johan had always told it as a fairy tale: Abrahamsen was the poor orphan, without a penny in his pocket or a shirt on his back and Valdemar's grandfather, old Mr Jens Larsen, was the kindly benefactor who takes him in, gives him a job, and sends him to the West Indies to make his fortune. And the orphan boy shows his gratitude by cheating his friend out of half his property, blotting out his name from the Old Cotton House wall, and putting up a new sign, with his own name on it, over the kingdom he has usurped.

'Was the orphan boy punished?' little Valdemar would ask, his face tight and cross.

'No,' Old Johan would reply. 'He became a very rich man and built a fleet of merchant ships. He became as rich as his benefactor.'

'I hate him!' little Valdemar would shout.

Old Johan paused by No. 7 warehouse and looked back at the Abrahamsen yards, once Larsen property. How could Valdemar have forgotten that hate? What was he doing hugging and kissing the wicked orphan boy's granddaughter? What would his father, what would Mr Niels say?

Jensine, the maid, brought Rosa her breakfast in bed at eight o'clock as usual — thin slices of ham and cheese, fresh bread, butter, bilberry jam, and coffee. A few minutes later her father came in. Isak Abrahamsen looked spruce and scrubbed and an unusual brightness in his eyes signalled to Rosa that he was moved.

'Ah, you minx,' he said, 'what time did you get in?'

He hugged Rosa tightly.

'Three this morning, thanks to the gross inefficiency of R. Abrahamsen & Son.'

'I sent a car — but old Sørensen tells me you made other arrangements.' He added: 'I had to speak to him on the 'phone first thing.'

'It was just a friend.' Rosa said.

There was a short silence, then Isak said lightly: 'Anyone I know?'

'Oh no.'

That at least was true, Rosa thought.

'How's Grandfather?' she said.

Isak did not answer immediately. He sat down on the edge of the bed and looked away.

'Bad,' he said after a moment. 'I don't think it's going to be very long.'

'I'll go and see him this morning.'

'Yes. It'll cheer him up. He fretted all the time you were in England.'

He paused, seemed to decide something, then said: 'I may as well warn you. Mother says that his mind is — wandering.'

'*Grandpapa?*'

She had known for months that her grandfather was very ill, probably dying, and she had learned to accept it, but the thought

19

that his mind might be going – that marvellous, incisive intelligence which, for as long as she could remember, had been the standard against which she measured others – frightened her. Isak saw the shadow in his daughter's eyes. He said:

'Apparently it's all to do with his illness. And it's only what mother says. He seems perfectly lucid to me.'

'I'll go this morning.'

'Will you come on to the office afterwards? We'll have lunch together. We'll go to the *Arena*. I want to hear all about England.'

It was Rosa's turn to look away.

'Well, it's a bit difficult, Father. I've arranged to meet someone else for lunch.'

'I see. Your "friend", I suppose.'

There was another silence, then Isak said: 'You might have thought.'

'I know, Father, but——' She didn't finish. Instead she smiled tentatively, and immediately a light was switched on in her black eyes, a light full of wry humour, affection and – complicity.

Isak smiled back, in spite of himself. So that was it, he thought; she's in love.

'Perhaps you'll introduce me.'

'Perhaps.'

'And dare I hope that you'll be able to dine with me this evening?'

Rosa laughed. She put out her hand and squeezed her father's wrist.

'Of course.'

Suddenly Isak leaned forward and hugged her again.

'It *is* good to have you back, Rosa.'

He rose swiftly. He hated emotional display.

'I'm off to the office,' he said. 'Give my love to the old people. Tell them I'll look in this afternoon.'

At the door he paused.

'It's not one of your red-hot Bolsheviks, is it?'

'No, Father,' said Rosa dryly. 'Quite the opposite.'

'Well, praise God for that.'

Rosa and her father lived, with the dour, devoted Jensine, in a cavernous and opulent block of late nineteenth-century mansion flats in Fridtjof Nansens Plads. Her grandparents lived in an equally ornate and gloomy pile on the corner of Grønningen and Toldbodvej, opposite the English Church, a ten-minute walk away. Between the two lay The Citadel, whose tidy ranks of seventeenth-century barrack-blocks lay sunk in the centre of what was now a park.

It was Rosa's favourite place in Copenhagen, her playground and garden as a child, her place of refuge and introspection as an adolescent. She walked slowly, savouring the crisp heat of the June morning, the familiar tang of the sea in the air, the familiar shimmer of the Sound, and it was in keeping with the parish-pump atmosphere of the city – so different to the teeming strangeness of London – that she soon came across someone she knew. Arne Katz was leaning against a tree and staring moodily down at the red roofs of the barrack-blocks. He was in an old open-necked shirt and baggy flannels and Rosa thought he looked more boyish than ever. Coming up softly behind him, she said:

'Planning the Revolution, Arne?'

Arne jumped and swung around.

'Rosa!'

He blushed, and his eyes flicked away.

A year ago, when Rosa had still been a member of the Communist Party, and a devout believer in the doctrine of Free Love, she had decided that she would sacrifice her virginity to Comrade Arne, the son of a prosperous stockbroker. Arne's over-eagerness and her highly developed sense of the ridiculous had combined, with the result that she had remained intact, but Arne's pride had not.

'How's your grandfather?' Arne asked to cover his confusion.

'I'm on my way to see him now. How are you, Arne?'

'Oh, so-so. My father's thrown me out. I'm living in a sort of slum, off Vesterbrogade.'

'Well, you can hardly expect him to nurse a viper in his bosom.'

'Is that why you left the Party? Parental pressure?'

He said this almost angrily.

'Not entirely. I just thought it was about time I started growing up.'

'I may be going to Moscow later this year, if there isn't a war.' Arne said defiantly.

'Well, they're digging shelters in the parks in London.'

'I won't fight.'

21

'I don't suppose you'll be asked to. I don't suppose any of us will.'

Arne was in the mood for political controversy; she escaped before he could get started.

As she came out of the park by the English Church she met Mr Cohn, who was standing outside his little barber's shop in Toldbodvej. Mr Cohn, once described by Isak as the foremost pessimist in Denmark, was soaking up the sunshine with an air of profound gloom. He greeted Rosa with the suspicion of a smile, and pressed her hand as he shook it.

'I don't like what I hear about the old gentleman,' he said.

'I'm going to see him now.'

'Give him my best wishes. Remember me to him. Forty-five years I've had the privilege of cutting his hair − a very fine-textured hair. You've been away?'

'I've had a month in England.'

'Ah yes. I don't like what I hear from that quarter. I smell a war.'

'Well, I don't suppose it will involve us.'

'I don't know. We've got a good King on the throne, that's one thing.'

Rosa began to edge politely away.

'I won't keep you,' Mr Cohn said. 'Remember me to the old gentleman.'

There was a third encounter, although it was hardly that, before Rosa reached her grandparents' flat. She was waiting to cross Grønningen when a long, black Chevrolet, with a chauffeur at the wheel, slowed down to let her pass. She glanced at the man sitting in the back of the car and recognized him immediately as Niels Larsen, Valdemar's father. He smiled at her as she stepped off the pavement, obviously having no idea who she was.

She crossed the road but did not go into the flats straight away; she stood and watched as the Chevrolet drew up in front of the offices of the Larsen Shipping Company in Bredgade. Niels Larsen got out of the car, a big, solid figure in a dark blue, double-breasted suit. Valdemar described him, with bitterness, as the most respectable man in Copenhagen; well, he certainly looked the part.

She found her grandmother sitting alone in the sepulchral dining-room, cutting a pear with a tiny silver knife. There were

22

touches of silver everywhere in the room – with the silver-grey of Hannah Abrahamsen's hair, and random glints from the heavy tureens and *tazzas* set out on side-boards crusted with ormolu.

Rosa kissed her grandmother. The flesh of her cheek felt soft and loose.

'Your grandfather will be so pleased to know that you are back,' Hannah said.

'How is he? Can I see him?'

Hannah had been told that morning by Dr Blum that her husband would probably die within the next twenty-four hours. But children – Rosa was still a child to her – had to be shielded from such knowledge. She paused before she replied.

'He's not well at all, I'm afraid,' she said. 'He's so thin. He hardly eats as much as a bird.'

'Father said something about his mind——'

'Your father has no business to tell you such things. Reuben is very ill. He tires easily, and when he is tired he sometimes sounds a little odd in his talk. That's all.'

But Rosa pressed the old lady. She wanted to be prepared, properly prepared, for seeing her grandfather.

'Odd in what way, Grandmamma?'

Hannah shifted in her chair and fiddled with the core of the pear, the least composed and yet the most natural movements that Rosa had ever seen her make.

'He seems to be having a lot of dreams, nightmares – he calls them visions – and he remembers them and insists on telling me about them. It's really nothing to worry about.'

'What sort of visions?'

'I don't know – a lot of nonsense about the Germans, and the Jews, and the pogroms in Russia when he was a child. You mustn't let him upset you.'

'Can I go and see him now?'

Hannah nodded and put her hand – dry and soft as her cheek – on Rosa's arm.

'Don't worry him with a lot of politics, will you Rosa?'

A year ago Rosa would have given her grandmother a lecture on the need to face realities, now she just smiled. She walked down the dim, thickly carpeted passage to her grandfather's bedroom and knocked very lightly on the door. When there was no response, she opened it gently, in case the sick man should be asleep.

But he was not asleep. He was sitting on the edge of the bed, totally absorbed in the task of lifting a glass of milk from the bedside table and bringing it to his lips. So intense was his concentration on this act that he had not heard Rosa's knock on the door and was not aware of her presence or of her eyes on him.

Rosa was shocked by the old man's appearance. He was skeletally thin. His striped pyjamas hung on him in grotesque drapes.

His skin was blotched with round, reddish sores, and it was yellow-brown, as if stained with tobacco. But what struck her most was that his hair was as neatly cut and brushed, and his beard as trim, as if he were about to stroll forth to the office or to a reception at the Palace. Did Mr Cohn come in every day to barber him? Did her grandmother, or the nurse, attend to him? She suddenly realized that it must be Grandpapa himself who was responsible for the well-groomed hair and the tight, neat beard. It was the only part of himself that he could preserve from the wrecking process of his illness, and he had preserved it with all the tenacity and perfectionism of his nature.

He managed to lift the glass from the table. His whole body trembled with the effort of drawing it up and towards his mouth. His head bent down and his lips touched the rim, then, as head and hand tilted back so that he could take a sip of the milk, Rosa could almost feel for herself the terrible labour.

He swallowed the milk. His neck was so emaciated that when his throat muscles moved it was like some agonizing convulsion.

Rosa's eyes began to sting. She closed the door softly, ran across the passage, and shut herself in the linen room. She leaned against the shelves of scented sheets and pillow-cases and for the first time for many months let the tears come. Part of her – the part that was her grandfather – wanted to wail and howl; but the part that was her father and her grandmother remained in control. From a pile, she took a handkerchief, one of her grandmother's little silk things embroidered with the arms of the Mendez family, and dried her cheeks.

The door suddenly opened. It was the nurse, prim and grim in her starched uniform, and astonished. Rosa was instantly in command of herself and the situation.

24

'I'm going in to see my grandfather,' she said. 'Please don't disturb us.'

She swept past the nurse and went into Reuben's room. He was lying back in the bed, his head supported by a mound of pillows. His eyes were closed. He opened them and said:

'Rosa!'

His voice was surprisingly strong. She bent down and kissed him, pressing his shoulders gently.

Old Reuben began to cry, letting his tears flow without shame or embarrassment and smiling as he cried. Rosa handed him her sodden handkerchief. He took it and said:

'Rosa, *you've* been crying.'

'No.'

He laughed, painfully, with wheezes in his lungs, but with something of the dry richness she had always known.

'There's no crime in weeping, though I seem to be the only one in the family who thinks so.'

Rosa was about to say something but Reuben stopped her.

'Don't ask me how I am. It's a ridiculous question. Dr Blum asks it every morning. "You tell *me*," I say, or, better still, just jot it down on the back of your bill.'

Rosa laughed and drew up a chair to the side of the bed.

'I suppose Hannah's warned you that I'm losing my mind?' Reuben said in his disconcerting way.

'She says you've been having visions.'

'Is that what she calls them? Well, perhaps she's right. She doesn't understand, though. Or she won't allow herself to understand, as usual.'

'Try them on me.'

Reuben took her hand. Rosa made an effort not to recoil from the strangeness of his touch — like a spider on her wrist.

'No,' he said. 'Tell me about England. It seems they've woken up at last — probably too late.'

'Tell me about your visions first.'

'No, no'.

'Please, Grandpapa.'

He seemed to retreat into himself for a moment, then he said quietly:

'Do you believe in dreams, Rosa?'

25

'Believe in them in what way?'

'Do you believe that dreams can tell us something?'

'I believe they can tell us something about ourselves.'

'I'm not talking about Freud and all that nonsense. I'm talking about a glimpse of the future, perceived through a dream. Do you think that's possible?'

'I don't know.'

'I do. Or I think I do. I have always dismissed such ideas as obviously false. I still do in a way. Yet I'm not sure. What am I to make of a dream that comes back, night after night, always slightly different yet always essentially the same?'

'What sort of dream?'

'It's difficult to tell you. The very nature of dreams makes them almost impossible to describe.'

He closed his eyes for a moment, then:

'It always starts in the same place, in the catacombs beneath Odessa. I'm hiding down there, in that maze of dark tunnels, hiding from something that's happening in the city above. I have a feeling that I am not safe, because I know that the stone of which the city is built was quarried from these very tunnels and I have a terror that my every footstep is echoing in the stones of the houses and that all the people know that I'm down there. I know what they're thinking: "rats in the cellars". At any moment I expect them to appear with lanterns and sticks. Then – somehow – there are horsemen pounding through the catacombs, and the catacombs have become streets. I know the horsemen. They're the Black Hundreds, the Jew-haters. They carry flaring torches, and crosses, and portraits of the Tzar on banners. It's me they're hunting. I'm certain of it. But they gallop past me. They don't even look at me.'

He stopped, exhausted.

Rosa was alarmed by his pallor.

'Grandmamma made me promise not to tire you,' she said.

He let out a little wheeze of a laugh.

'What does it matter?'

'You must rest.'

'I do nothing else but rest. I want you to hear the last part of the dream.'

Again he closed his eyes, and seemed to gather himself.

'I am running through the streets and gradually I become

aware that this is not Odessa but some great city I do not know. I turn a corner into a vast square. It's full of people – thousands of them. They seem to be formed into long lines and they are shuffling slowly forward. They carry cases and bundles. The children are crying. The men and women stare at the ground. I realize that they are all Jews and that they are being driven out of the city. And I know that somewhere in this huge multitude are my own family – Hannah, you, your father. But still the most important thing is to find out where the horsemen have gone, so I run away from the square. And there, in and amongst the unfamiliar streets and alleys, is a place I know. It is Fioldstraede. I am in Copenhagen.'

A spasm of coughing stopped him. Rosa begged him not to continue but he waved away her protests with a fluttering gesture of his hand. The coughing subsided.

'I recognize the Cathedral and the top of the Round Tower rising behind the old houses. There is a little crowd in front of my son Abel's bookshop. I recognize some of them without knowing who they are. Familiar faces, Danish faces, the sort of faces you see every day in Strøget. One of them picks up a brick. I know that he's going to smash the window of Abel's shop. I know that I should talk to them, reason with them, but I cannot move, I cannot speak.'

His lips were grey and scored with whitish cracks; he moistened them with his tongue and gave a little shrug.

'Well? What did you make of it?'

Rosa considered her words carefully.

'I think you've been lying here for weeks with nothing to occupy your mind but the papers. You've read all the stories about the Jewish persecutions in Germany and Italy and they've got mixed up in your mind with your childhood and have been giving you nightmares.'

'So much is obvious. But there is more to it than that. I've told you what happens in the dream but I can't describe the atmosphere of it – especially the last part.'

Rosa was silent. Reuben looked at her.

'I know', he said, 'it means nothing to you. Thank God, you have never known what it is like to be an alien in your own country, to be marked out from all your neighbours because you are a Jew. You do not know what it is to be a Jew.'

27

There was nothing Rosa could say. He was right.

'I must explain to you, my darling. It's important for you all.'
There was an urgency in his voice now.

'I've never told you why I left Russia and came to Denmark. I've never told your father or your uncle. I want you at least to know.'

He gathered himself again.

'I was seventeen. My mother and father were dead – killed in an anti-Jewish riot. I had very little money and no idea where I should go. All I wanted was to get out of Odessa. I bribed an official to give me a passport and took a berth on the first ship leaving Russia.'

His voice trailed away and his eyes closed. Rosa thought, and hoped, that he was drifting into sleep. But his eyes opened and he continued:

'On the ship I met a man who was very kind to me. He was a Dane – an engineer who had been working in Russia. He was cultivated and widely travelled and I told him all about myself. One day he mentioned casually that he too was a Jew. I was astonished. I had taken him for a Gentile. I questioned him – and my questions seemed to puzzle him. I realized that he came from a country where the distinctions between Jew and Gentile simply didn't exist. At that moment I decided to go to Denmark. The ship I was in was bound for Turkey. In Constantinople there was trouble about my papers. I had to pay another bribe to get out of the country. I had no money left.'

'What did you do?'

'I walked.'

He closed his eyes again.

'I walked through Bulgaria. I crossed the Transylvanian Mountains. I walked through Rumania, Hungary, Austria, and Germany – through the heart of Europe – to get where I wanted to go.'

'But how did you live?'

'I worked. On farms and in factories. And when there was no work I begged for my bread.'

He opened his eyes and smiled.

'Does that surprise you? To learn that your rich grandpapa was once a beggar in the streets of Prague?'

She nodded.

'I was a pedlar too. I would buy cheap jewellery and trinkets and coloured handkerchiefs in the cities and sell them to the peasants in the countryside. I suppose I have had every kind of Jewish experience, from street vendor to philanthropist. My whole life in Copenhagen has been an attempt to forget all that, to put it behind me. I abandoned my religion, my class, my origins. For the first time in my life I felt a free man. But I wonder if a Jew can ever really forget, can ever really escape? I wonder whether there is anywhere in this world that he can be truly safe?'

'There's here,' Rosa said.

'So I have always believed. I have constructed a whole life on that belief. But now I am not so sure.'

'But Grandpapa, it's only a dream.'

'Yes. But I think it's more than that. I think it is a very special kind of intuition. Pour me a glass of water, would you Rosa?'

She quarter-filled a glass and handed it to him. She made as if to help him drink it but he said:

'No, no, I can manage.'

She looked away as he sipped the water. She did not want to see the convulsions of his throat. He handed the glass back to her.

'I was in Africa once,' he said. 'A business associate took me on safari into the bush. One morning we came across an immense herd of deer – okapi or eland, I don't remember what. There were thousands and thousands of them, grazing on the plain. There was a kind of pattern to the way they moved about. Then suddenly the pattern changed. It was as if an invisible signal was passing from animal to animal – a danger signal. Some of the deer were a long way from the main herd, but even they sensed it. The deer began to cluster together and drift away. My guide nodded sagely and said: "Lion." We watched and waited. Ten minutes must have passed before we saw the lions. By this time the deer had moved away towards the horizon. I asked my friend how it was that the deer had scented the danger so early, and he explained about the herd instinct – the instinct, he said, that man had lost.'

He was silent for a moment. Then he went on:

'I think he was wrong about that. I think there are some men in whom that instinct is still alive – we call it intuition. I have always had intuition. I have always been able to feel the way events will shape.'

'Supposing you're right, Grandpapa – what can we do about it?'

He did not answer for a long time. He stared at the ceiling. Then he said:

'There lies the tragedy, my darling. What can the hunted Jew do but seek a refuge – as I did? And when the last refuge has been closed – what can he do then?'

It was not a question that required, or even admitted of an answer. Rosa tried a different line.

'What were your parents like?'

Reuben smiled.

'I don't remember them very well. That part of my life seems infinitely remote. My father had long, plaited hair that hung either side of his face and he was constantly worried about his bowels. My mother spent all her days cleaning the house, fighting a battle against a non-existent tide of dirt. She was constantly worried about *my* bowels.'

He chuckled and then changed tack, with a flash of his old suddenness.

'You promised to tell me about England.'

Rosa began to tell him: about the new offices in London, about English friends and business acquaintances, about the apparent inevitability of war. But after a few minutes she realized that her grandfather was asleep.

She stood up quietly and put the chair back in its proper place. She leaned over and kissed him lightly. Then, as softly as she could, she left the room.

3

'When the Germans invade he may well be proved right,' Valdemar said.

He lit a cigarette and offered the packet to Rosa. The little student restaurant was crowded and foggy with smoke. Rosa had walked from her grandparents' flat to her rendezvous with Valdemar. She had passed through Amalienborg, and paused for a moment by the equestrian statue of Frederik V in the centre of the octagon, to look at the four little palaces. She had crossed

Kongens Nytorv, the hub of the city, and looked at the notices outside the Royal Theatre. She had strolled along Strøget, absorbing the gossip, the chatter, the greetings.

The atmosphere of her grandfather's dream had lingered in her mind, but soon evaporated in the bright sunshine. She had tried to imagine what his mother and father could have been like and had tried to conjure up a mental picture of Reuben himself, trudging along a white, dusty road through a Transylvanian forest with a bag full of flashy bracelets and necklaces.

She had studied the faces of the people in Strøget, trying to think of these cheerful, tolerant fellow-countrymen as potential persecutors. It was nonsense. Yet a certain lingering disquiet had remained and had made her want to discuss it with Valdemar.

'The Germans didn't invade us in the last war,' she said. 'We were neutral. We're still neutral.'

'But there's a difference. In 1914 we were neutral and strong. Now, thanks to the Social Democrats, we're neutral and weak. With the whole of Europe about to explode, we're actually *reducing* our armed forces. It's insanity.'

Rosa laughed.

'There speaks the military man. It's not soldiers we need, it's diplomats.'

'There speaks the ex-Communist.'

Rosa smiled, but Valdemar was earnest.

'We need a strong army to protect our neutrality,' he said.

'But if we started re-arming we'd only provoke the Germans.'

'We'd gain their respect. We'd make them think twice about invading.'

'What on earth makes you think they want to invade us? What would be the point?'

'The point would be to add another province to Hitler's Aryan empire.'

'Nonsense, Valdemar. You're a typical soldier. All you can think about is war. You *want* war.'

'Well, Germany's run by soldiers. What do you suppose they want?'

'They don't want war with Denmark.'

'A typical Danish attitude. You remind me of my father. He's got his head buried so deep in the sand he'll end up with his nose poking out in Australia.'

31

Rosa laughed again: 'I'm glad your father and I have something in common.'

There was an edgy silence which Rosa broke.

'Valdemar, do you ever think of me as a Jew?'

The surprise in his face answered the question for her.

'Well,' he said, 'I know that your family's Jewish but——'

'It doesn't make any difference?'

'What difference should it make? Your family's religion is not the problem.'

'No.'

Valdemar took the plunge.

'What are we going to do, Rosa?'

'I don't know.'

'I think we should tell them — and to hell with it.'

'No. Not yet.'

'Why not?'

'Grandpapa's dying. I can't start a family row now.'

Valdemar stubbed out his cigarette and lit another.

'I've got three months' leave,' he said. 'I'm thinking of going up to Skagen. Will you come?'

He took her hand.

'We'd be alone. It's wonderful up there. Please.'

'It depends on Grandfather. I can't go anywhere until——'

'No. I see that.'

Suddenly Rosa saw him as often, lying alone in her strange bed in London, she had thought of him: as lover and companion. After the revelation of that first time, soon after they'd met, the revelation of his gentleness and his instinctive knowledge of what touches, what movements, aroused her, their meetings had been infrequent, covert, but increasingly important to both of them — alarmingly important, given their circumstances. Her trip to London had been tacitly accepted as a kind of test. It had taken just that brief journey in his car, from the docks to the flat, to make her sure that he was indispensable to her.

She dropped her hand below the level of the table and laid it on his thigh. He shifted on the banquette seat and said:

'But tonight? Sven's away. We can use his place.'

'I can't Val. I've got to have dinner with my father.'

She sensed his frustration and withdrew her hand, but he replaced it.

'Tomorrow?'

She thought of her grandfather. She took her hand away, firmly this time.

'I don't know, Val. It's difficult.'

'It's impossible.'

He saw the light go out of Rosa's eyes and felt angry with himself. For God's sake, her grandfather was dying, but he hated that frozen look in her eyes. It cut her off from him. She was looking away from him, stirring a spoon round and round in a half-empty cup of coffee and suddenly he was angry with her. Why should her sudden remoteness trouble him? Wasn't it what he preferred?

Rosa looked up. The light was back on.

'Of course I'll come to Skagen,' she said. 'I'll tell my father exactly where I'm going and what I'm doing. We'll clear the air. It's just that we can't do it yet.'

The thought of Rosa at Skagen, at the cottage in the dunes, his private paradise, dispelled Valdemar's anger. He kissed her, and she squeezed his thigh.

'I've got to go now. I'll see you when I can. You understand.'

'Of course.'

He watched her weave through the packed tables, and noticed how the men glanced up at her, and followed her dark, trim beauty with their eyes.

It was hard to believe that he was to share Skagen with her; harder to believe that the prospect of sharing himself, or anything that was his, with another person, should so excite him.

Rosa and her father never had their tête-à-tête dinner. When Isak left his office in Toldbodgade and went to his parents' flat, two minutes away, he found Dr Blum there. Reuben had lapsed into a coma. It was only a matter of hours now.

Isak sat by his father's bed, holding his cold, spindly hand, listening to his fight for breath. Half an hour later Rosa joined him. They spoke very little; from time to time the nurse looked in, and at six Hannah, who had been resting during the afternoon, put her head round the door to tell them that dinner would be in an hour and that they must both eat.

The curtains were drawn in the dining-room, shutting out the pale evening light. With the six silver candelabra set out on the

33

long table, shedding a buttery glow, the high forbidding room came into its own. The portraits of Hannah's forebears, distinguished people painted by undistinguished artists, were transformed into kindly presences. The cold glitter of silver and ormolu became a reassuring lustre.

They sat at one end of the table; Reuben's traditional place, at the head, was empty. They spoke very little, and paid less attention to what they ate.

Hannah said: 'Dr Blum has promised to come at nine.'

Isak said: 'The nurse seems to be very competent.'

Rosa said nothing.

She was the first to leave the table. Isak stayed behind to talk to his mother. He asked for her permission to smoke and lit one of his fat, pungent cigars.

'What are you going to do, Mother?' he asked. 'Had you thought?'

'I shall go to Rosenhus. I won't want to stay here. It's too big. And noisy.'

Isak nodded. Rosenhus was a home for elderly, genteel Jewish ladies in Charlottenlund, a charitable institution of which his mother had been President for many years. It was by far the best solution; Hannah would be cared for like a Dowager Empress. Trust her to have it all worked out.

He poured himself a glass of wine and looked at his mother. Such calm, he thought, such control; I wonder what she feels?

'I telephoned Abel,' Hannah said. 'He has promised to come.'

'Good.'

Silence. Isak sipped his wine and let the fragrant smoke of his cigar fill his mouth and nostrils. What *does* she feel?

Rosa sat by her grandfather, amazed at the stillness she felt inside her, puzzled by her own detachment. She felt as detached as the poker-faced nurse opposite, and just a little guilty at the thought that by allowing him to talk to her at such length that morning she might have precipitated this crisis.

Reuben's breath was now coming in a series of short, high, rhythmic rasps. It sounded exactly as if someone were sawing a tree. The door opened and she expected to see her grandmother or her father, but it was her Uncle Abel. As always, he looked pudgy and dishevelled, his long, curling red-grey hair wilder than ever.

Abel went over to the bed, bent down, and kissed Rosa. He put out a hand to touch his father but withdrew it.

'My God,' he murmured. Then, in a low voice, he said to Rosa: 'Come outside.'

Rosa hesitated. She wanted to stay with her grandfather, but there was something urgent in her uncle's appeal. She rose and went with him.

'Come into the music room,' Abel said. 'Mother and Isak are talking in the dining-room.'

The music room was stuffy and unaired. Abel rolled himself a cigarette. His hands were trembling.

'How long has he been like that?'

'He went into a coma this afternoon. I was talking with him this morning. I think it's going to be very quick.'

'I saw him yesterday,' Abel said, almost defensively. 'We talked. He was wonderful. I hadn't really talked to him for years.'

He choked and seemed to be about to weep, but controlled himself and lit his cigarette. It was loosely packed and misshapen; little red threads of burning tobacco floated to the floor.

'How are you, Rosa? You haven't been to see me.'

'I've only been back a day.'

'I saw you in Strøget with your handsome young man, but, of course, I did not want to intrude.'

Rosa smiled.

'Ah, Uncle Abel – did I steal him from you?'

She had first met Valdemar in her uncle's bookshop in Fioldstraede. Abel laughed. His niece was the only member of his family to whom he could talk with any freedom; it was always a relief.

'There was never any chance,' he said. 'Valdemar is distressingly normal, as I am sure you have discovered.'

Away from the sights and sounds in the bedroom, Abel was recovering his usual quick, cryptic spirits. Then Rosa said:

'I must get back to grandfather.'

'I don't know that I can stand it,' Abel said.

'Go and talk to Grandmamma.'

'I *know* I can't stand that,' he replied with a sharp twitch of a smile. 'I'll come with you.'

At nine o'clock Dr Blum arrived. He examined Reuben briefly,

35

while Hannah, Isak, Abel, and Rosa waited outside. When Dr Blum said that he would stay, they knew that the end could not be far off. During the next twenty minutes Reuben's fight to breathe became frantic. Rosa held one of his hands, Hannah the other. As Reuben's breaths grew tighter and shallower, the pace of the sawing grew steadily, regularly faster. Abel stood by the window, fiddling with the tassels on the curtain, a glaze of sweat on his skin. Isak stood behind his daughter.

The sawing suddenly ceased. From Reuben's lungs came a sound, familiar to the nurse and the doctor, but appalling to the others; partly a liquid gurgle, partly a dry rattle, mostly a sigh, and wholly terrible.

For a long moment nobody moved. Then Abel blundered out of the room as if it were filled with smoke. Dr Blum touched Hannah lightly on the shoulder and she rose and went with him. Isak took Rosa's arm. The nurse stepped forward; there were things she had to do. As they were about to leave the bedroom, something extraordinary happened. The nurse, that silent, efficient, apparently emotionless woman, began to cry.

Hannah, dry-eyed, stared at the woman.

'Come along,' she said to the others, gesturing them to the door – a party of children who had to be shooed away from an unpleasant scene in the park. In fact she seemed to want to hurry them out of the flat. She would not hear of Rosa's staying the night and when Isak began to talk about the arrangements she told him that all the necessary arrangements had been made. Isak, Abel, and Rosa left together. Dr Blum had preceded them, and Hannah was left alone with the nurse, whom she sent to bed.

She went into Reuben's bedroom, to sit for a while beside the body of her husband. The nurse had laid him out (what a distasteful phrase, she thought) and covered him with a sheet. She pulled the sheet back. The skin of his face looked taut and drawn, as if someone had stood behind him and stretched it tight over his bones, yet there was an extraordinary calm, almost a beauty, about his features.

Beauty! Her mind went back forty-six years, back to the West Indies, to the heat and dust of St Thomas. She was walking with her mother along the quay at Charlotte Amalie – a Danish baroness and her daughter on a tour of the world; and what a safe, comfortable world it had been in those days. Her mother

36

was talking about the decline of the cotton trade but she was paying scant attention because towards them was walking a tall young man with black curling hair and a close-cropped beard. He was wearing a white suit and a wide-brimmed hat and he looked beautiful. She was twenty-three, unmarried, untouched by love, untouchable, so she thought. That evening he sat next to her at the Governor's table. His voice, with its lilting Russian cadences, fascinated her; he transformed the flat monotones of Danish into something rich and musical. When her mother discovered that he was going back to Denmark on the same ship, she warned her: 'Don't consider him, Hannah. He hasn't a penny. He's little better than a clerk.'

Beauty! She had never known it before. The warm, purple nights, the lisp of the waves against the hull of the ship, his voice in the darkness telling her of his dreams, convincing her that her love and her money could make them a reality. Yes, he had seduced her into the one act of rebellion in her life, the one gamble, the one risk. It was something for which, even after the gamble had paid off, and the risk had been justified, she could never quite forgive him. She could not forget that she had introduced the son of an Odessa pawn-broker into a line which, if only ennobled in the last century, and then only with a German barony, could nevertheless boast a score of eminent bankers, statesmen, and scholars. Worse, she had introduced into her own polite and prosaic life a man whose passionate intelligence and sensitivity frightened and baffled her. It didn't matter that he had become as rich, and as respected as any Mendez; the taint was there. It was there in her son Abel, a dealer in second-hand books, a shop-keeper, and, though she had only the vaguest notion of the nature of his degeneracy, a degenerate.

Yet there was still some vestige left in Hannah, some tiny trace, of the passionate and reckless. She suddenly wanted to lie down on the bed beside Reuben, and rest her head on the pillow next to his for the last time. The instant the thought occurred to her, she suppressed it. Everything fastidious and prim in her nature revolted against such a monstrous idea. To lie by the side of a corpse!

She rose, switched off the light, and went to her room. She took out a pen and writing-paper, and began to draw up a list of those who should be invited to the funeral.

4

Reuben Abrahamsen's death was widely reported in the Danish press. He had been an important man. There was a long obituary in the *National Tidende*. Niels Larsen read it over his breakfast and derived a certain grim satisfaction from the elegant half-truths, masquerading as accuracy. It confirmed his deepest suspicions about the objectivity of the press, even in so distinguished a journal as the *National Tidende*.

As he read the paper he ate his porridge, and ate it with more than his usual relish. Winter or summer, his breakfast never varied: hot, thick porridge with cream and sugar, black coffee, and a little cheese on black bread. It was a balanced and substantial meal, as balanced and as substantial as himself. He folded the paper and offered it to his wife, who was sitting opposite, absorbed in a French literary magazine of advanced or, as Niels thought of them, pretentious and subversive ideas.

'Read old Abrahamsen's obituary,' he said. 'There's hardly a line of truth in it.'

Christina Larsen looked up.

'I'll read it later,' she said.

Niels sighed. The magazine had a garish abstract design on its cover which he found offensive, ugly, and in some way disturbing.

'I must say I'm glad the old crook is dead,' he remarked.

Christina looked up again, slightly startled this time: the statement was so uncharacteristic of her husband.

'You shouldn't gloat over a man's death – whoever he is,' she said.

'Nonsense. It would be hypocritical to pretend otherwise.'

'It's not like you to take that attitude,' Christina said, and resumed her reading.

Niels sniffed crossly and rose from the table.

The sunlight, streaming in through the three open French windows, tempted him into the garden. He consulted his pocket-watch. He had five minutes before he need start for the office; it was a glorious morning and he had decided to go by bicycle. He walked across the broad, stone-flagged terrace, through the formal parterre of low, clipped beech hedges and roses, and onto the lawn. The billiard-table perfection of the grass did not fail to give him the usual sense of satisfaction, yet still he felt at odds with himself. Christina was right, it was unlike him to exult over a man's death – even Reuben Abrahamsen's. And there lay the whole perplexing problem of the Abrahamsens: he hated them, but at the same time he disliked and mistrusted the emotion they inspired in him. It was not in his nature to hate; he regarded hate, or indeed any other extreme, as wasteful and destructive.

The lawn sloped down to a strip of white, sandy beach and beyond was the Sound. There was not a hint of wind and the water shimmered and glinted with a Mediterranean blue. The peace and beauty of it had a calming effect.

He turned to see his son Valdemar striding down the lawn towards him, dressed in an old towelling bath-robe.

'Good morning, Father,' he said. He did not stop, but walked out onto the little wooden jetty that projected a few yards into the sea.

Niels watched him as he threw off the bath-robe and paused, for a moment, to let the sun play on his body. He experienced a moment of pride in having sired such a perfect specimen, the sort of pride a sculptor might feel in having carved a finely-proportioned statue; at the same time he felt a little bewildered and angry at the distance, the silence, that had grown between him and his heir. There were times, and this was one of them, when Valdemar seemed to embody all the qualities of a statue – coldness, remoteness, mysteriousness – and there seemed to be no trace left of the flesh-and-blood boy he had loved with such strength.

Valdemar dived cleanly into the sea and began to swim with powerful strokes. Now Niels felt a twinge of envy. Once he too had revelled in the icy embraces of the Sound, hacking a bathing-pool out of the ice in mid-winter and exulting in the shock as he plunged into it, and the wonderful glow on his skin when he came out. He was conscious of his breakfast sitting in his ample stomach like a dumpling. He felt suddenly bloated and old.

He walked back to the house in a thoroughly bad temper. He noticed that the flag was flying from the old mast in the centre of the lawn and remembered that it was his daughter's birthday. He also remembered that she had come in very late last night and as he re-entered the dining-room he asked her what she had been up to.

Karen was sitting at the table wanly toying with a cup of coffee.

'Oh, just a party at Anne-Marie's,' she said in the casual tone that meant either that she was telling the truth or that she was practising the most accomplished duplicity – Niels could never quite decide which.

'But you didn't get in until four in the morning.'

'Sorry, father, I didn't mean to wake you.'

'Well you should tell whoever it was that drove you home not to churn up my gravel with his back wheels. Who was it, by the way?'

'Oh, just a friend of Anne-Marie's.'

Niels glared at her. There was nothing to be read in her pretty, pale face – never was.

'I trust you'll be in a fit state for your party tonight,' he said.

'Don't worry. I have amazing stamina.'

Niels sniffed and stalked out of the room. His children baffled him, both of them. Valdemar was virtually a stranger, wrapped up in his army career, totally uninterested in, indeed almost contemptuous of, the business. Still at least he had a job of work to do. What did Karen contribute? She worked only when it suited her, or, more accurately, when she had over-spent her allowance, and then only in that over-priced dress shop of Anne-Marie's. She was out at all hours, seemed to live solely for pleasure – he didn't know what she got up to. He sometimes suspected that she was not a virgin; there was something very knowing about her. But her behaviour at home was always dutiful, suspiciously dutiful when one remembered that at the age of five she had stolen all Christina's jewelry and distributed several thousand kroner's worth of diamonds and emeralds among her schoolfriends.

This sense of bewilderment and frustration remained with him as he pedalled sedately from his house in Hellerup into the centre of Copenhagen. It was only when he reached the office that his temper improved. Here at least he was in control and could forget about his troublesome offspring. He did so, very successfully, until noon when there was an unexpected interruption. His secretary announced that Old Johan was asking to see him.

Niels, who was drafting a letter to his London agents, did not in the least wish to be disturbed; but he could hardly refuse to see Old Johan.

The old man limped into the room and Niels shook his hand.

In spite of his age and his withered leg Old Johan still cut a fine figure. He sat down painfully and accepted a cigar.

'What can I do for you, Johan?' Niels said. 'You've not come to tell me you're retiring?'

A look of apprehension flickered in Old Johan's eyes. Did Mr Niels want him to retire? The next words reassured him.

'I'll be retiring before you do.'

Old Johan smiled and then frowned.

'I've been a long time thinking whether I should say what I'm going to say,' he began. He paused for a moment. 'You'll probably tell me it's none of my business, you may even know.'

'Know what, Johan?'

Old Johan told him, haltingly at first, then so fluently that Niels could almost see Valdemar's car by the Old Cotton House wall, could almost see his son take that girl in his arms. He let Old Johan talk without interrupting him and when the old man had finished he said, with his usual calm:

'You were quite right to tell me, Johan. I had no idea this was going on.'

'I don't understand it, Mr Niels. I don't,' Old Johan said.

Niels gave him a handful of cigars and ushered him out. Then he sat at his desk and tried to analyse his own reactions as clearly and as unemotionally as possible.

What emerged was a feeling of profound repugnance combined with a fear, hardly rational yet very potent, that Isak Abrahamsen was in some way plotting to steal his son and heir from him, as his father, Reuben, had stolen half the Larsen fortune.

But what was he to do? What could he do? Stop it. Yes, but how?

He must tackle the problem as he would tackle a business problem. Immediately he felt happier. He must first of all establish the facts of the matter; only then would he know how to act prudently. Until then he would say nothing. That was the way to succeed in business, that was the way to succeed in life: careful reconnaissance, a cautious approach, a compromise; this was the pattern that governed all his dealings – and he was a very successful man.

In spite of such comforting resolutions, Niels could not enjoy the

41

family dinner he gave that evening to celebrate Karen's twentieth birthday. Half an hour before his guests arrived he performed the ritual that, in normal circumstances, was, for him, the most pleasurable part of the evening: priming and lighting the line of iron braziers which were placed at intervals by the side of the semi-circular drive leading up to his house.

He was a hospitable man, and the flickering fires of the braziers, and the lesser glows of the candles in the portico and the ground-floor windows, symbolized something very important to him: the light and the warmth that he hoped his guests would find within his house. They were also, of course, a tradition – and Niels loved traditions. It pleased him to think that the flaring braziers were a direct link, a visible link, with the feasting and wassailing of his Viking ancestors.

But tonight there was no pleasure in it. Even the contemplation of his house, whose white stone seemed to glow in the dusk, did not give him the usual sense of stability. It had been built by his grandfather on land originally bought by his great-great-grandfather and this long history of proprietorship normally afforded him as much satisfaction as the house itself – a copy, slightly Scandinavianized, of a villa at Cap d'Ail designed for a Russian prince. But tonight he felt that something threatened the continuity of ownership, the dynastic tradition represented in the stone and mortar.

It was the same at dinner. The food was succulent, the champagne and claret excellent, so excellent that for once he did not regret Christina's ban on the more traditional beer and *snaps* for gala occasions. (Her grandmother had been French; she had never got over it.) The table was a dream of silver and flowers and candles, the servants were, for once, models of discreet efficiency, yet he could not enjoy it.

There seemed to him to be an air of impermanence about an occasion which was supposed to be, at least in part, a celebration of the most enduring element in life – the family. He could not rid himself of the irrational notion that none of these people would be here next year.

He caught Christina's eye. She was looking at him enquiringly. He switched his attention from his plate to what had inevitably become the focal point of the table, the chair at the far end in which Christina's brother, Henrik Tøller, was sitting and from

42

which he was holding forth in his usual demagogic style. Squire Tøller's visits to Copenhagen were rare; he preferred the seclusion of his South Jutland estate. Niels had always been grateful for this – he found his brother-in-law's vivid personality more than a little irksome. Squire Tøller picked up a slice of bread in his fingers.

'This is Denmark,' he declared. 'Here is Hitler,' he said, opening his mouth wide.

Then he tilted his shaggy head back and dropped the bread into his mouth.

'Nazism,' he went on, 'is Prussianism with a different face. Instead of a lot of Junkers with heads like billiard balls and bellies like barns, we have a pack of backstreet cut-throats with faces like sewer-rats and a pistol under each armpit. But they still want the same old thing, a German empire stretching from the Arctic to the Mediterranean – and probably beyond.'

He turned to Poul Larsen, Niels's brother.

'As for you politicos – I can't decide whether you're deaf, blind or both. But we'd all be better off if you were mute.'

Poul Larsen wished to protest, but twenty years as Permanent Extra Secretary to the Cabinet Office, twenty years of practising the art of political compromise, had robbed him of the power; so he merely demurred.

'I think you exaggerate,' he said in his precise, lawyer's voice. 'Germany will respect Denmark's traditional neutrality. There is nothing for anyone to fear.'

'The official view,' said Squire Tøller. 'Do you know that in Schleswig any child caught singing a Danish nursery rhyme is whipped?'

Niels was only too familiar with his brother-in-law's extreme anti-German views. The Tøllers had lost their estates in Schleswig after the 1864 war against Prussia, and they had lost three sons in the defence of Dybbol. Ancient history to him, but to Squire Tøller a fresh wound.

'You're living in the past, Henrik,' he said. 'You're still fighting the battles of the nineteenth century.'

'Why not? They still have to be won.'

'It's absurd.'

Valdemar, who had been silent as usual, suddenly looked down the table at his father.

'If it's so absurd,' he said quietly, 'why are you still waging war against the Abrahamsens after fifty years?'

Niels almost gasped. He felt like a man who, walking down a street, is suddenly attacked without warning or provocation. How dare Valdemar, of all people, raise the issue of the Abrahamsens?

He heard his wife murmur '*Touché*' and Squire Tøller say: 'People are always very quick to bury *other* people's hatchets for them.'

Karen saved the situation:

'The reason I can't stand Germans is that they're all homosexuals,' she said.

Under cover of the others' laughter Niels was able to retreat into silence.

But the shock of Valdemar's words remained with him into the small hours. He could not sleep. There had been something almost violent in his son's softly spoken question, as if it were the opening skirmish in a war, as if Valdemar intended to embroil his family in a war in the same way that Germany, according to Henrik, wanted to embroil Europe.

It was the last day of the *shivah*. Isak sat on a low stool in his mother's dining-room and wondered what on earth he was doing there. Next to him, his brother Abel seemed to be totally absorbed in himself, meditating about God knew what. The five-day growth of stubble on his face made him look more than ever unkempt and seedy: custom apparently forbade a man to shave during the *shivah*.

On the other side of the room Hannah was engaged in placid conversation with her stout brother, Baron Hans Mendez. The gilt-framed glass over the centre sideboard was draped with black cloth; candles for the dead flickered on the long table.

Isak was oppressed by a sense that it was all a sham. At the same time he could not escape from the feeling that to conform to these peculiar traditions was, in some obscure way, right. Until the day of his father's funeral he had hardly set foot inside a synagogue. He had never received any instruction in the Jewish faith, in spite of pressure from his uncle, the Rabbi; he had only the vaguest notions about the dietary laws; yet at his father's death he had gone along with the ritual without question. It was a puzzle.

A knot of people came into the room: Uncle Simeon and his wife (bearing an overloaded tray of food), the Micheelsens, friends of his mother – and Rosa. Rosa seemed to bring with her into the room light and laughter, even though she was dressed in her dreariest clothes and her face was pale and, he thought, a little strained. She walked over to him and smiled.

'This thing's making my scalp itch,' he whispered, scratching his head just below the rim of his skull-cap. He suddenly felt that he must look a fool and that Rosa, who stood at an even greater distance from things Jewish than he did, must find him so too.

'I suppose you think it's all absurd,' he said.

'No. No, I think it's rather wonderful.'

He wanted to challenge this but Rosa said: 'I must go and talk to Grandmamma.'

Uncle Hans strolled over. Even in his dark mourning suit he contrived to look extremely smart and thoroughly baronial. He stopped by Abel and nodded. There could hardly be a greater contrast between two men, Isak thought: his brother shabby, fleshy, and decidedly unsavoury; his uncle perfectly turned out, almost dapper.

'And how,' Baron Mendez asked Abel, 'is the book trade?' The very blandness of his tone implied disapproval.

'Flourishing,' Abel said, with one of his curious sideways smiles. 'And how is the usury business?'

The Baron, who regarded the chairmanship of the Mendez bank as a sort of hereditary princedom, started.

'The times are uncertain,' he said, 'but don't worry. I doubt if you will have to rely on the profits of the second-hand book business for a living.'

His nephew needed to be reminded of the source of his financial independence.

'The antiquarian book business, Uncle Hans,' Abel said. 'Quite a different thing. Not nearly so sordid.'

Isak was amused by this exchange. He understood his younger brother's character no better than the Baron, but it pleased him to see Uncle Hans's patrician poise rocked a little. Uncle Hans had never been able to disguise the fact that, as the direct descendant

45

of Israel Mendez, one of the original Sephardi Jews invited to trade in Denmark by King Frederik III in 1657, he regarded the Abrahamsens, and all later immigrants, as vulgar.

The Baron abandoned Abel and turned to Isak. He approved of Isak; Isak had all old Reuben's shrewdness and acumen without his peculiarities of temperament.

'Your mother takes it very bravely,' he said. 'She tells me she is going to Rosenhus.'

'It's what she wants.'

'I suppose it's for the best.'

Isak suspected that the Baron did not entirely approve of his sister's living in an institution, however grand. The Baron changed the subject.

'The news looks ominous,' he said. 'Reminds me of the summer of '14.'

'Yes.'

'You'll have problems if there's war between Germany and England.'

'I suppose so. But we've branched out, you know. Manufacturing, building development.'

The Baron showed a little animation at last. He pulled up a chair and sat down. A long discussion about business and investment was just what he felt like. It was, in fact, almost all he ever felt like in the way of conversation.

Abel wanted to talk to Rosa, but on his way over to where she was standing, chatting with the Micheelsens, he was intercepted by his uncle Simeon. Abel had long been aware that Uncle Simeon regarded him as a natural ally in the Abrahamsen family. Uncle Simeon was a scholar, whose *Commentary on the Dalalat al-Ha'irin of Maimonides* had gained him a certain reputation internationally, and he assumed that Abel, who was undeniably bookish, and moved in what Simeon imagined were 'literary circles', was a kindred spirit. At family gatherings he invariably pounced on Abel and attempted to initiate intellectual conversation. He had even presented his nephew with a copy of the *Commentary* and Abel, who did not read a word of Hebrew, had been at a loss to respond to the gift in a way that would not offend the earnest Rabbi.

'Hannah bears up well,' Simeon said in a low voice.

'Yes, she does.'

46

'I wish she had told me sooner – about your father's condition. I had no idea that it was so serious.'

'I don't think any of us quite realized.'

'I wish I had seen him. I feel I could have been of some use.'

Abel suppressed a smile and a desire to ask his uncle if he had hoped for a deathbed conversion. Instead he said: 'We are all so grateful for what you've done.'

Simeon sighed. 'Hannah has had a telegram from the palace.'

'I believe so.'

'Ah well, your father was a very remarkable man. Very remarkable.'

Abel smiled to himself. Uncle Simeon had always been completely baffled by Reuben; Reuben had regarded Simeon as a complacent bore. Once Abel had overheard an exchange between them. 'God is necessary to you, as a theologian,' Reuben had said, 'in the same way that a stable banking system is necessary to me as a businessman. Why bring worship into it?' Simeon had smiled and replied: 'That sounds far too clever to be true.'

Abel nodded to his uncle and said: 'I must go and have a word with Peter Micheelsen.' Simeon made a gesture to detain him, but Abel edged firmly away.

Later, Isak and Rosa walked back to their flat, choosing the leafy road through The Citadel. The sun had gone down but the last of its light flushed the sky mauve. Rosa was pensive and monosyllabic; she had decided to tell her father about Valdemar and the trip to Skagen, but did not know how to begin. Isak solved the problem for her by broaching the subject of the summer holiday himself.

'I'm thinking of going up to Hornbaek for a few weeks. Will you come?'

Isak owned a summer house at Hornbaek, on the coast, north of Copenhagen.

'I'm sorry, Father. I've – I've got other plans.'

'What other plans?'

'I'm going up to Skagen.'

Some of Rosa's tension transmitted itself to her father.

'I suppose it would be naive of me to ask whether you're going alone?' he said.

'I'm going to stay with a friend.'

'*The* friend?'

'Yes.'

'And I suppose you would think me a complete fossil if I asked you his name?'

Now that the moment had come, Rosa hesitated.

'I suppose you think I won't approve of him,' Isak said, lightly enough. Then with an edge: 'Do you really care if I approve or not?'

'It's Valdemar Larsen.'

Sheer astonishment stopped Isak in his tracks.

'What?'

He stood under a street lamp, looking like a child startled by a sudden bang.

'Where on earth did you meet him?' was his first question.

'At Uncle Abel's.'

'Good God,' Isak said stupidly, 'is he a bibliophile?'

'He collects books on military history.'

Isak walked on, more slowly, then he stopped again.

'I don't know how I feel. I don't know how to react. Do you mean to marry him?'

'I don't know.'

'Has he asked you?'

'No.'

'How long has this been going on?'

'A few months.'

Isak strolled on. Suddenly he laughed, harshly.

'My God you must have been discreet. In an overgrown village like Copenhagen——' He laughed again. 'What does Niels Larsen say?'

'He doesn't know.'

'Well, when he finds out he'll—— He hates me, you know.'

'I know.'

'A thing like this – It might drive him into showing a genuine human emotion for the first time in his life.'

'What about you, Father?'

Isak was instinctively evasive.

'Oh, *I'm* human enough.'

'I didn't mean that. Are you furious?'

'Probably.'

They walked on to Fridtjof Nansens Plads in comparative

silence. As they were about to go into their block Isak suddenly asked:

'Rosa, if you *did* want to marry Valdemar Larsen and if I was against it, I mean really against it, would you still marry him?'

It was Rosa's turn to be evasive.

'He hasn't asked me,' she said.

They walked across to the elevator, and waited a moment for the machine to rattle down from one of the upper floors. As it arrived Isak had a sudden impulse to hug his daughter. He put his arms round her and squeezed her fiercely. Rosa responded, pressing her face against his jacket, transported for an instant, by his touch, back to childhood. She felt that he was telling her that he would never let her go, never cut her out of his life, whatever happened.

A disinterested observer, a private detective, perhaps, engaged at so much per day, plus expenses, to observe the movements and habits of Niels Larsen and Isak Abrahamsen, would have found many more similarities than differences between the two men.

After all they were both independent shipowners of considerable substance. Larsen's business was preponderantly local – coasters and small freighters operating in the Baltic and the North Sea, with old established links with England and Holland. Abrahamsen's was a worldwide enterprise; he had big tankers trading in North America and the Far East. Larsen specialized in refrigerated storage and shipping – meat, bacon, furs – and Abrahamsen had for some time been ploughing his profits into shore-based enterprises – building and light engineering.

They both had offices near Amalienborg, within a minute's walk of each other; their warehousing and dry-dock facilities were adjacent; they both bought their clothes at Brdr. Andersen, their wines from Kjaer & Sommerfeldt, and their cigars from Paul Olsen.

Even if the professional observer had known all about the old conflict between the two families, and had noted now delicately and discreetly the two men avoided each other, he would still not have been surprised to have found them lunching in the same restaurant. Isak was eating with his lawyer, Jacob Meyer, and Niels with Lieutenant Sven Carlsen, his son's closest friend.

Although their tables were at the extreme ends of the room, they had seen, but not acknowledged each other.

Isak had had a day and a night to discover what he felt about Rosa's bombshell. His first reactions had been conventional – she's only twenty-two, too young to know her own mind. It's my fault. I've been too easy with her since her mother died, allowed her too much independence, been too wrapped up in business to worry about whom she was meeting, what she was getting up to. He had never been able to discuss that sort of thing with her. Of course one was aware that a great many of the tabus about sex had been swept away since the war but it had never occurred to him that Rosa——. Yet she was proposing to spend several weeks alone with a man. The implication was inescapable.

Then he had started to think about the other implications. Valdemar Larsen. Larsen. What if they did marry? What if he died? Rosa would inherit, and if they had a child, the child would inherit – a Larsen child. The thought was repugnant. Yet equally repugnant was the thought of disinheriting his only child. And there was something else, something more mysterious and disturbing, an almost physical revulsion at the prospect of that man Larsen's son possessing Rosa, physically possessing her. He had put it out of his mind as far as he could and decided to concentrate on finding a way round the financial problem first, hence his lunch with Meyer.

Niels Larsen was also concerned about financial matters. It was Valdemar's right, his duty, to succeed him in the chairmanship of the family company, as he had succeeded his father. He could not possibly do this if he were married to the daughter of Isak Abrahamsen; *ergo* he must not marry her. It was perfectly simple. All Niels needed was the means to prevent it; to acquire those means he needed knowledge of the situation; hence his lunch with Sven Carlsen.

Carlsen was twenty-five, a year older than Valdemar. He was the son of an Aalborg railway clerk and through brains and charm had achieved a commission in the Royal Life Guards. The first time Valdemar had brought him home Niels had sensed the young man's ambition. Carlsen had naturally been impressed by the house in Hellerup, but Niels had seen something else in his reaction – envy. For a time Niels had suspected Carlsen of having designs on Karen, and via her, on a position in the company, but

50

he had soon been reassured. Karen was not interested in Sven, and Sven was interested only in the possibility of a job at the end of his service in the army. Niels was inclined to give him a job, and had hinted at this more than once; as a result he expected Carlsen to speak to him frankly about Valdemar's affair, and he was not disappointed. Sven told him all he knew, only suppressing the fact that he allowed Valdemar and Rosa to use his flat.

As they were about to rise from the table, Niels saw Isak Abrahamsen approaching. He assumed that Isak was going to talk to someone at a neighbouring table and deliberately turned his back. He was astonished to hear Isak's voice addressing him.

Isak too had been about to leave the restaurant, but as he had passed near Niels's table, some demon in him had told him to go up and confront the man, to administer a jolt to his stolid complacency. But when the moment came to speak he found he had nothing to say but 'Good day'. He said it, and felt rather foolish. Niels Larsen stared at him, then, rising from his chair just so much as was consistent with civilized manners, he returned the greeting. Isak found himself still tongue-tied.

'I should offer you my condolences on your father's death,' Niels said, breaking the silence.

Isak was irritated at having lost the initiative. He retorted, with a smile:

'I don't imagine you've shed many tears.'

'There is a value in preserving the accepted forms of politeness and good manners,' Niels replied. 'Do you have something you wish to say to me?'

'No. Nothing. I apologize for having disturbed your lunch.'

With a little bow Isak turned and walked away. Niels stared after him. Carlsen pretended to drink the last of his coffee, so as to avoid his host's eye. He was in no doubt that what he had just witnessed was the first salvo of the first battle of a war.

6

Rosa awoke an hour or two after dawn. Already the strong sunlight of Skagen, not the hottest but the most intense sunlight she had ever known, was penetrating the bare little room through the slats of the shutters. The horizontal beams were so clearly defined that they seemed like tangible objects, dividing the air into layers. Where they splashed against the wall, the light was so brilliant and concentrated that she felt the rough, whitewashed plaster would soon begin to go brown, then smoke and burn, like a piece of paper under a magnifying glass.

She lay on her back in the old, high bed, her hands clasped behind her head. Beside her Valdemar was sleeping deeply. He was facing towards her, his arms wrapped round the pillow in which his head was buried. The coarse linen sheet lay across his thigh, white against bronze.

He stirred and shifted and the sheet slipped off his thigh. Rosa turned her head to look at him. She felt curiously privileged to be able to observe him like this: he looked so vulnerable. She often felt desire for him; she sometimes felt close to him, especially on those rather rare occasions when he opened up and shared the trivial happenings of his day with her, as she was always bubbling to share her news and gossip with him: but this was a new kind of tenderness.

He moved again. His leg came to rest across hers and his thighs pressed gently against her side. She felt a flutter, the lightest caress, against the skin of her leg. So he was awake. She looked. No. He was still sleeping, dreaming some delicious dream. She grinned.

She began to study the tiny, barely perceptible movements in his body in order to see if, by interpreting them, she could imagine herself into his dream. She put out a hand and held it just under his nose, not touching his face, so that she could feel his warm, regular breaths tingle her skin. She touched his hair, which the sun had bleached to an almost pure white-blond. She touched the prominent ridge of his cheek-bone, running a finger delicately along it. She wanted to lean over and kiss one of his eyes, feel his long eyelashes tremble against her tongue; but at the same time she did not want to waken him. Instead, as lightly as

52

possible, she brushed the backs of her fingers across the stubble on his chin.

His hand closed over hers, reversing it and pressing it against his cheek. Then, in another movement, as natural as sitting down or standing up, as tacit and easy as a kiss, he moved onto her.

'Hullo,' he said.

'Hullo.'

The cottage lay in the dunes two hundred yards from the sea. It was protected by a few stunted pines, gnarled and stooped by years of wind and storm, and behind it lay the marsh, an expanse of tawny heather and bogs through which a stony, sandy track twisted. On either side the dunes stretched for miles. To the north was the little port of Skagen, to the south nothing but a seemingly endless Sahara of white dunes whose peaks and valleys occasionally concealed villas and summer houses. Each season Valdemar had to re-learn the geography of the sands after the winter gales had re-sculpted them.

There were four rooms under the thatched roof of his cottage. The furniture was solid but sparse. Water came from a pump out in the back, and light from tarnished, hissing paraffin lamps. He had inherited the property from a great aunt. There was a legend in the family that it was the original home of the Larsens, from which they had set out to build their fortunes in the late eighteenth century. It was only a legend, but such was Valdemar's love for the place, that there were times he could almost believe it.

Every evening he and Rosa walked the two miles along the beach to Skagen, to dine at Brøndums Hotel. For Rosa this was always the high point of the day; the atmosphere of the place fascinated her. The warm brown panelling of the walls framed scores of canvases by the Skagen artists, the Impressionists of the North, who in the 1890s had discovered, in this remote promontory of vast skies and all-embracing seas, a quality of light that had continued to fascinate and inspire them for a century. The light they had succeeded in capturing in paint seemed to reflect a great glow over the intimate, cluttered, room. At the top of the panelling a frieze of small, square paintings ran round the room, portraits of men and women who had loved Skagen and had spent their lives trying to interpret it — Krøyer, Krogh, the

Anchers (Michael and Anna), Johansen, Adrian Stokes, and so many others. Rosa could not help comparing their strong, intelligent features with the pompous and insipid faces that graced her grandmother's dining-room.

One night she said to Valdemar: 'This place gets into one's blood.'

He loved her for that. He liked Brøndums for its superb food and as a civilized contrast, at the end of a day, to his primitive life of swimming, fishing, sailing, and walking. But it was the primitive he craved; it was the emptiness, the wildness, the desolation of Skagen that brought out the most powerful responses in him. He loved to steep himself in sun, salt water, and silence. He disapproved of the Skagen artists – 'Too cosy,' he said – because his father collected them, and Brøndums reminded him of the house at Hellerup. But he did not see that Rosa's response to Skagen was at one remove from his: she needed the artists to distil the essence of the place for her before she could savour it.

One evening, as they were walking to Skagen, Valdemar drew her away from the beach, into the pine forest.

'There's something I want to show you,' he said.

They came to a sandy dell, fringed with scrub. In the centre of the dell was one of the strangest buildings Rosa had ever seen, a squat, sturdy tower with a sharply pitched roof and steeply stepped gables.

'It looks like the top of an old church tower,' she said.

'That's exactly what it is.'

'What happened to the rest of it?'

'It's buried.'

'Buried?'

'Listen. I'll tell you the story.'

He fumbled for a cigarette and lit it. 'Two hundred years ago Skagen was a green and fertile place. The fattest cows in Jutland grazed in its meadows and the farmers, who were even fatter, were rich enough to buy golden chalices and silver candelabra for their churches. When the fishermen came home from the sea in the evenings they came to orchards full of apples and woods full of game. But then it all began to change. The sea began to throw up sand, mountains and mountains of sand, that invaded the land like an army. The sand marched across the fields

54

carrying salt that poisoned the earth. The crops withered and died, the grass grew coarse and bitter, and the milk from the cows tasted like acid. Eventually the sand reached the walls of the graveyard that once surrounded this church. It climbed over the walls and smothered the graves. The force of it beat down the church door. It poured into the nave, into the vestry, it piled itself in heaps on the altar.'

He paused and drew on his cigarette.

'If someone had raised and buttressed the churchyard wall,' he went on, 'they could have kept the sand at bay. But all the fat farmers had fled, taking their gold and silver with them. Only the fishermen remained; and when they came home from the sea they found nothing but sand dunes, marshes, and roofless houses. In a few years nothing remained of the church but the top of its tower and Skagen was left empty and ruined.'

Rosa put out a hand and touched his cheek.

'I've never heard you talk like that before,' she said.

He laughed shortly.

'As a matter of fact I was quoting someone else. You know Old Johan, the watchman at the docks? Oh, no, of course you wouldn't.'

'You mean that tall, old man with the limp who looks like a Viking?'

'That's right. Well he was born here. He used to tell me the story of the buried church. It was my favourite.'

'But, Valdemar, what you've described was a natural catastrophe, a shift in the sea bed or something. No one could have done anything to stop it.'

'The Dutch have kept the sea out of their land for centuries.'

'But it must have been different here. You can't hold back a million tons of sand with a few dykes.'

'Maybe not. But the point is – nobody tried. At the first sign of danger they packed up their bags and waddled off to find somewhere more comfortable to grow fat in. I should know, because that's precisely what my ancestors did.'

Dusk was coming in, tingeing everything with a blue-black blush. Rosa stood up.

'Come on. I'm hungry.'

'Of course you are,' said Valdemar, stubbing out his cigarette in the sand. 'Let us by all means go and fatten ourselves.'

There was a harshness in his voice. Rosa linked arms with him, but she felt that there was suddenly a distance between them. During dinner at Brøndums he hardly spoke. When she began to talk about the paintings he was sullen, and almost angry.

'They're just the sort of thing my father would collect. They make suffering and desolation look pretty. They're daubs – cleverly done, I suppose – but meaningless.'

'I don't think so. I think a lot of the Skagen group were great artists.'

'Great for what?'

'For exploring the relationship between light and form, for a start.'

'You sound like my mother at one of her artistic soirées.'

Rosa laughed lightly. She wasn't going to let him provoke her. She said, gently:

'I don't understand you, Val. You love the wildness and the desolation of Skagen. What are you so angry about?'

He didn't answer immediately. He fiddled with the pepper mill. Then he said, not looking at her:

'No. You don't understand me.'

The mood lasted all through the next day. Rosa discovered that two people could lie together in the same bed as if they were at opposite ends of the universe. The sun blazed so intensely that sea and sky merged into a hazy bowl of gold and blue. Each individual object – a twig, a blade of grass, the table and chairs outside the front door, the bricks and beams of the cottage – seemed to carry its own inner charge of light.

Valdemar, stretched out naked on the beach, offered himself to the heat like a sun-worshipper. Rosa stayed in the shade, read novels, and tried not to sulk.

The following day, Valdemar was himself again; more than himself. It was as if he had absorbed so much power from the sun that it was overflowing from him in sparks and flashes. When they woke he leaped out of bed, threw open the shutters, and, with a whoop, picked Rosa up bodily. Running, he carried her down to the sea, laughing and kissing away her protests.

He ran her right into the waves. The shock of the icy water paralysed her. For a moment she felt that every cell in her body was frozen. Then she found that her body was coming alive again, was crackling and tingling with energy. Valdemar was swimming out to sea. She swam after him and they ducked and dived like otters, then paddled back to shallower water. Valdemar took her in his arms. The sea was as clear as silica; under its magnification her breasts seemed huge. They half-swam, half-stumbled towards the sand, and lay down in the shallows. Little wavelets lapped and sucked at their legs, providing a counterpoint to their own rhythm.

Later, as they were lying together on dry sand, Valdemar said: 'Rosa, I want this — us — to go on for ever.'

That evening he ordered champagne with their dinner. The man at the neighbouring table, who was eating alone, shot them a disapproving look and raised the newspaper he was reading, as if to shield himself from them. Valdemar caught sight of a headline. He rose and stepped over to the table.

'Excuse me——' he began.

Without a word the man handed Valdemar the paper.

Rosa came up behind Valdemar.

'What's happened?' she said.

Valdemar handed her the paper. The headline on the front page told her that England and Germany were at war.

A gusty wind was whirling the light snow into flurries as Niels Larsen walked up Bredgade towards his office. The cold penetrated his thick overcoat, making him feel naked and unprotected. The feeling was not entirely due to the weather: a fortnight ago one of his ships had been arrested in a German port. A week before that another had hit an English mine-field and had limped into Harwich with the loss of ten lives. He had just come from a meeting of leading owners, chaired by his brother Poul in his room in the Red House. The meeting had been encouraging. Poul reported that the British and the Germans seemed inclined to respect Denmark's neutral position. It was still possible to trade with both the belligerents, but by God the times were uncertain; sterling wasn't worth a light, and the Hamburg importers were cancelling orders left, right, and centre. Still, a prudent man could always steer a middle course – and survive.

The most disturbing aspect of the meeting had undoubtedly been the presence of Isak Abrahamsen. They had ignored each other, but to be in the same room as the man was an unpleasant experience. Niels thought it monstrous that Valdemar should impose additional burdens on him at a time like this. As if he did not have enough problems to cope with without this impossible marriage. Valdemar was waiting for him in his office. He was in uniform.

'Well, Father, I have obeyed the summons.'

Niels sat down at his desk.

'I suppose you know what I want to talk to you about?'

'I have an inkling. You know, Father, you're wasting your breath.'

Niels snorted through his nostrils.

'Have you any idea what this war is doing to business? Do you realize what a struggle it's going to be to keep things going? Why do you want to make it worse for me?'

'I don't. Rosa and I are going to get married. I haven't asked you to concern yourself. It's you who have chosen to do so.'

'Yes. And why do you suppose that is?'

'I have no idea. I imagine that it's something to do with business – as usual.'

The contemptuous tone stung Niels, but he controlled himself. A temper lost, he reminded himself, was an argument lost.

'I know you have never shown any interest in the business, Valdemar. For some reason you seem to despise it, and everything connected with it, even though it provides you with a more comfortable life than most people enjoy.'

Valdemar shrugged dismissively.

'All right,' Niels said. 'But will you at least listen to what I have to say? Will you try to understand my point of view? You owe me that, even if you think you owe me nothing more.'

Valdemar shrugged again. Niels picked up a bulky folder, bulging with thin, yellowing papers.

'This file,' he said, 'contains the story – the *true* story – of how Reuben Abrahamsen started his business. I won't ask you to read it, I just want you to know that everything I am about to tell you is corroborated and fully documented.'

58

'It would be,' Valdemar said.

Again Niels controlled himself. He put down the folder and leaned back in his chair.

'Reuben Abrahamsen first worked for my father in the early 1880s. He was given a job as a clerk but from the first it was obvious that he had exceptional talents. My father recognized this and did everything in his power to help him. Apart from anything else he used his influence to obtain Danish citizenship for him. He promoted him to manager of our offices in the West Indies. It was a time of crisis. My father had already started a new company, because the original West Indies firm was in difficulties. Abrahamsen's job was to salvage what he could. But he did more than that. He proposed a scheme whereby the company could be saved. I won't bother you with the details, it's all here, if you want to read it,' he patted the folder, 'in Abrahamsen's own handwriting. My father was impressed by his ideas; especially when Abrahamsen found a backer, a Danish bank, prepared to invest a great deal of money. The only security they required was my father's shares in the company. He trusted Abrahamsen implicitly and signed over the shares. He placed the affairs of the company entirely in Abrahamsen's hands. In less than a year it faced disaster. The bank foreclosed on its loan and took over the shares. A week later Reuben Abrahamsen announced his engagement to the daughter of the bank's chairman, Baron Hendrik Mendez.

'My father thought this would be the saving of the company. He still believed that Abrahamsen's plans would succeed. He gave a reception to celebrate the engagement; after all, Abrahamsen had been like a son to him. He offered to buy the shares back from the bank. They refused. They sold them instead to Abrahamsen – for a fraction of their true value. The whole thing had been a fraud from the start. There had never been any loan. Abrahamsen had lied and cheated. He had grossly abused my father's trust. He was nothing but a common swindler. And that is the man whose grand-daughter you propose to marry. Can't you see it's unthinkable?'

Valdemar was silent for a moment. Then he said:

'You say this is the true story. There must be another side to it.'

'Naturally. It is here.'

Niels took a sheet of thick blue writing paper from the folder and handed it to Valdemar.

'This is the letter Abrahamsen wrote to your grandfather in his own defence. Read it.'

Valdemar fingered the paper. It was brittle and smelt musty, like a document in an archive. The heavy gothic letter-heading, the copperplate handwriting, and above all the old-fashioned cadences of the words themselves, conjured up a picture of a remote era, long dead.

'Well,' said Niels when Valdemar had read the letter, 'what kind of defence do you think that is? He admits everything.'

Valdemar smiled.

'Yes, he's honest about that. The whole letter strikes me as honest.'

'*Honest?*'

'Yes. And true.'

Niels stood up and walked to the window. He had to move. 'All right,' he said. 'You affect to despise business. Yet you seem quite content to live a life of luxury on the profits.'

'I don't despise business, Father. I just see it for what it is. If the money's there, I'll take it. Why not? But I don't need it. I have my own career.'

'I'm very glad to hear that.'

'Oh, Father – are you going to disinherit me?'

Niels glared at him. This was mockery. He sat down at his desk again. His voice was level, but there was a quake in it.

'I have no choice,' he said. 'I have spent my life building this firm to hand on to you and your children, not to enrich the descendants of Reuben Abrahamsen.'

'You've never even met Rosa. You have no idea what sort of person she is. You reject her just because she's somebody or other's granddaughter. We're all to suffer because you can't forget some shoddy deal in which the family lost a few of their millions in the late nineteenth century. It's pathetic, Father.'

Niels stared at his son. He wanted to hit him, but of course he could not allow himself to be provoked that far.

'What about her father?' he said. 'Have you forgotten him? Do you seriously expect me to admit a man like that into the family?'

'Why not? What's he ever done to you?'

'The files in this office are full of what he's done, or tried to do, to me.'

'Files! Look – your grandfather owned slave ships. He bought

60

and sold human beings like sides of bacon. Do you expect me to hate you for what he did?'

Niels stood up. So did Valdemar. They faced each other across the desk.

'Valdemar, if you marry this girl that's the end of it. You can get out of my house. You'll never have another penny from me.'

Valdemar shrugged and began to walk towards the door.

'Valdemar!'

Valdemar turned.

'It's your funeral, Father,' he said. 'I don't give a damn about your money. You can leave the whole lot to a home for old donkeys. You'll be the one to suffer − and you'll make Mother and Karen suffer too. But you won't make me suffer.'

'Valdemar!'

The office door opened and closed. Valdemar was gone. Niels sat down. His legs were trembling as if he had been running in a race. It had all gone wrong. He had allowed Valdemar to push him too far − fatal. There could be no compromise now; Valdemar had forced him to an extreme, and he was right, there would be suffering; suffering came from extremes.

Hannah Abrahamsen occupied the two best rooms in Rosenhus; a large bedroom with a private bathroom, and a sitting-room with a view over the gardens and the Sound. The rooms were furnished with her own things: her ancestors adorned the walls and family photographs, in silver frames, cluttered every available surface. A small army of devoted or, more accurately, intimidated nurses and servants guaranteed her physical comfort, while the institution of coffee and cakes on Sunday afternoon in her sitting-room, which she had announced during the first week of her residence at Rosenhus, made sure that she did not lose contact with her family and friends.

On a bleak Sunday in late November her son Isak and her brother Simeon were sitting with her. The subject of the conversation was Rosa.

'My objection,' Rabbi Simeon said, 'is quite simple. She should not be permitted to marry outside the faith. I have always opposed mixed marriages.'

Isak looked a little exasperated.

'I'm afraid that's not an argument she's likely to find very persuasive, Uncle Simeon,' he said.

'Whose fault is that? It was you who chose to cut her off from her religion.'

'I was cut off myself, remember.'

He glanced at his mother, who looked distant and disapproving.

'What is a Jew without his religion?' the Rabbi said. 'Only half a man.'

'Thank you, Uncle Simeon,' Isak said, with a smile.

But the Rabbi was earnest.

'Everyone, Jew or Gentile, needs a spiritual side to his life. And Jews have a special duty to keep their faith alive. I have never been able to convince you, Isak, but perhaps I could persuade Rosa.'

'I doubt it.'

Hannah decided to intervene. Simeon's religious zeal had always been something of an embarrassment to the family.

'If it were not for this war making everything so difficult' – she made the war sound like an unseasonable rainstorm – 'I would suggest that you send the girl abroad for a time. She'd soon get over this infatuation.'

'It's not an infatuation, Mother. I only wish it was.'

'Well, what attitude do the Larsens take?' Simeon asked. 'Surely they object as strongly as we do?'

'Oh yes,' said Isak. 'Niels Larsen has cut his son off. And that's only made the situation worse. He's made the boy into a martyr.'

'Ah,' said Simeon. He shook his head.

There was a silence.

'If only Reuben were alive, he'd know what to do,' Hannah said. It was a remark she had been making more and more frequently in the past few months and it irritated Isak intensely.

'Father would have been just as perplexed as I am,' he said shortly. 'She's of age. I have no legal means of stopping her marrying whom she likes. My sole argument is that she will hurt me – all of us – very deeply if she marries this man. But do I have the right to say even that? Why should my pain be more important than hers?'

'You must threaten to cut her off, Isak,' said Hannah. 'That surely would bring her to her senses.'

Isak laughed.

'I have. And I will. But she doesn't give a rap about money, Mother.'

Hannah found this idea so extraordinary that she was silenced.

The door opened and a nurse ushered Abel in. He was dressed in old flannel trousers, a thick pullover, and a shirt without collar or tie. Hannah thought that he looked like a disreputable old tramp. Abel walked over to his mother and kissed her.

'Hello, Mother,' he said, 'I thought I'd look in. How are you?'

He shook hands with his brother and uncle.

'I suppose you're discussing the Great Family Scandal,' he said. He poured himself a cup of coffee. 'The Elders meet and decide. Poor Rosa.'

'Instead of sarcasm, you might offer some constructive suggestions,' Isak said sharply. 'You and Rosa are very close these days, I've noticed.'

'I don't think you'd like my suggestion.'

'What is it?' Simeon asked.

Abel ran his fingers through his hair.

'That we should all dance at her wedding and pretend we're enjoying it,' he said. 'That shouldn't be hard − we're past masters at pretending. In my case, of course, there would be no pretence. I approve of Valdemar.'

'You would,' said Isak.

Abel shrugged.

'You don't give a damn, do you?' Isak said.

'Please let us have no unpleasantness,' Hannah said. Isak and Abel ignored her.

'The way things are going in the world,' Abel said 'you should be delighted that your daughter is marrying into a family of impeccable Aryan origins. It's a form of protection she − and all of us − may find very useful one day.'

'What are you talking about, Abel?' Simeon said angrily.

Abel turned to him. 'If you were to give a little more of your attention to the twentieth century, and a little less to the twelfth, Uncle Simeon, if you'd stop reading Moses Maimonides for a moment and look at any newspaper, you might discover that two hundred kilometres from where we are now sitting a nation ruled by a gentleman called Adolf Hitler is carrying out the most comprehensive persecution of Jews since the diaspora.'

'Abel!'

Hannah's voice was sharp and loud. All three looked at her in astonishment; none of them could remember when they had last heard her raise her voice.

'Abel,' she said. 'How dare you talk to your uncle in that tone?'

Abel was unabashed. It struck him that his mother, like so many head-in-the-sand Danes, reacted strangely to the name Hitler.

'If the family outcast can't tell a few home truths,' he said with one of his taut, bright smiles, 'who can?' He turned to Simeon. 'Tell me, Uncle, that learned Professor you used to correspond with, Dr Zimmerman of Leipzig, have you heard from him recently?' Abel answered for him. 'No. Of course you haven't. And what do you suppose has happened to Dr Zimmerman? I'll tell you. He has been hauled out of his bed in the middle of the night, he has been clubbed and beaten and thrown into a cattle truck, and shipped off, with thousands of others, to rot in a camp. That is what has happened to Dr Zimmerman.'

Simeon's eyes were glowing with anger.

'You are distressing your mother,' he said.

'I hope I am. I hope I am distressing you all.'

'This is wild and irresponsible nonsense,' Simeon said. 'I know what's happening in Germany as well as you do. Whom do you think I pray for every morning and evening of my life?'

'Do you also pray for your fellow Jews in Poland? Have you received any papers from your scholarly colleagues at Warsaw University in the last few months? I don't imagine you have. Are you blind, Uncle Simeon? Can't you see that Hitler means to swallow up one country after another? Can't you see that there isn't a single Jew in Europe who's safe?'

He turned to the others. His sallow skin was shiny in the light of the table-lamp.

'You sit here babbling about Rosa's marriage as if it's the end of the world, when out there, in Berlin, the end of the world – at least the end of your world – is being very efficiently organized by a demented Austrian corporal.'

Simeon got to his feet. His voice was hoarse.

'This is dangerous and pernicious nonsense,' he said. 'We have nothing to fear in Denmark. This is a neutral country. The King himself has told me personally that we have nothing to fear.'

'I hope,' Abel said quietly, 'that the King has not forgotten to inform Herr Hitler.' He turned to Hannah. She looked suddenly very old, and lost, and bewildered.

'Mother' he said gently, 'I'm afraid I have spoiled your party. If you'll excuse me, I must go now. I'll miss my tram.'

Isak stood up.

'I'll give you a lift into town,' he said.

Abel was taken by surprise.

'Oh – well, thank you,' he said. 'Good-day, Uncle Simeon. Good-bye, Mother.'

Simeon inclined his head stiffly.

Isak kissed his mother and shook hands with Simeon.

Simeon said: 'I'll stay a little longer. I think Hannah could do with some reassurance.'

Isak and Abel walked across the gravel to Isak's car. Abel gestured towards the plain, pinkish façade of Rosenhus.

'It's like a gigantic preserving jar,' he said. 'I could almost taste the formaldehyde in mother's coffee.'

They drove through Charlottenlund, into Hellerup, and along Strandvejen. Oblique pillars of rain stood over the grey waters of the Sound.

Isak said: 'You're wrong, you know. All the evidence points to Hitler's respecting our neutrality.'

'Do you really believe that madman's assurances are worth anything?'

'I believe in the general opinion of the business community here. And that is that Denmark will survive in this war as she did in the last.'

'That wasn't the view of one rather intelligent businessman I spoke to.'

'And who was that?'

'Father.'

Isak glanced quickly at his brother.

'What did Father say?'

'I went to see him the day before he died. He told me about a recurring dream he was having – a sort of vision of the future. He painted an extraordinarily vivid picture – you know what a way he had with words. It was quite terrifying. Jews being herded out of Copenhagen, ordinary Danes screaming anti-Semitic slogans.'

'Nonsense. He was a dying man.'

'"Nonsense." That seems to be the catch-word when it comes to discussing these matters. Father may have been dying, but

65

there was nothing wrong with his mind. He had an extraordinary insight you know. He even understood me.'

Abel suddenly changed tack.

'It's me you have to blame for introducing Rosa to Valdemar Larsen, you know. They met at my place. I confess I had taken rather a fancy to the young man myself.'

'I'd rather not hear about that.'

'No, of course not. Odd, isn't it, that two brothers should be so different?'

Isak didn't reply.

'Isak, listen,' Abel said. 'I'm not much of a one for family affairs – I lead my own life – but you can't stop Rosa, you know. She'll marry the boy and they'll be happy. It won't do any good cutting her off. It'll only make you miserable, and you can't afford to be miserable. None of us can. There isn't time. Terrible things are going to happen in the world, things that will make these family squabbles seem petty.'

'It is not a petty matter to me. I don't expect you to understand.'

'Because I have no children? You may be right. But then, on the other hand, perhaps I have a clearer perspective.'

They were turning into Fridtjof Nansens Plads.

Abel said: 'Drop me here. I'll walk the rest of the way.'

'You won't come in?'

'No. Goodbye. Think about what I have said.'

Isak did think about it. He thought about it as the elevator rattled him up to his flat. He thought about it as Jensine took his coat and hat. Rosa was in the drawing-room, speaking on the telephone. As he went in he heard her say:

'I must go. Goodbye.'

She put down the receiver.

'Hello, Father. You look cold.'

'I suppose you were speaking to Valdemar?' he said.

She nodded.

'Rosa, I want to talk to you about it.'

She sighed. 'It's no good, Father. You know it's no good. I may as well tell you. Val's found a flat. I'm going to move in with him.'

'I see.'

Isak sat down.

'Of course, there's nothing I can do to prevent you. I can only stop your allowance, and that I intend to do.'

'Naturally. After all money is at the root of all this, isn't it, Father? Nothing else.'

'Sit down and listen to me, Rosa,' Isak said.

He said it gently and Rosa obeyed.

'I've been thinking things over. Perhaps money is at the root of it, and perhaps that's wrong. But you must see it from my point of view. There are things that have happened – in the past – things I can't forget. Even so, I can't bear the thought of losing you. I can't bear it. I will meet Valdemar, I will even meet his wretched father, I'll give my consent to the marriage, I'll think of some arrangement to take care of the money side. I'll do all this if you will promise to wait for one year before you marry him. You've known him for so short a time; I want you to be absolutely sure. And *I* want to be sure that he will make you happy. I could stand a little pain if I knew that you were happy.'

Rosa began to cry. Isak went over to her, and put his arms round her.

'What is it, my darling? I'm trying to be reasonable.'

Rosa sniffed, and wiped her eyes with the back of her hand. Isak offered her his handkerchief.

'Here,' he said.

She did not take it. She stood up.

'Father,' she said, 'I can't wait a year.'

'Why not? Is it so very much to ask?'

'No. No, it isn't. But you see I can't wait because I am going to have his child.'

Isak stared. The handkerchief fluttered out of his hand. His hand moved. He slapped her face, once, twice. She made no attempt to avoid the blows. There were patches of red on her face. She turned and walked out of the room.

Isak stood, staring at the ground. Mechanically he bent down and picked up the handkerchief, then sat down heavily in an armchair. He heard footsteps in the hall; he heard the front door open and close.

All the pain that had been festering in him for months – the pain of his father's death, the pain of Rosa – boiled into his throat and choked him. He choked and choked until the chokes turned into sobs. He pressed the handkerchief to his face as if to block his

67

tears, but there was no blocking them, no controlling them. Forty-five years of blocks and controls went down before those tears like sluices in a spate.

When it was over, he felt a great relief, as if he had vomited up poison; and he felt a great desolation.

Rosa and Valdemar were married in a civil ceremony a week before Christmas. Their only witnesses were Sven Carlsen, Abel, and Karen who made Abel laugh when she told him: 'My father thinks I'm fund-raising for the Red Cross.' The registrar was suffering from a heavy cold; the ceremony was punctuated by coughs and nasal explosions which reduced them all to a mild hysteria.

Dizzy with *snaps*, they slipped and slithered through the ice-strewn streets, startling the crowds of Christmas shoppers. Karen insisted on relieving herself behind a snowdrift. Abel fell down the steps into his shop. Rosa and Valdemar went back to their dank, cramped flat off Sønderboulevard. It was bitterly cold: there was ice on the inside of the window panes, there was even ice on the brass rails of their bed. It didn't matter.

That same night Niels and Christina Larsen sat, one either side of the fire, in their drawing-room. Niels read a business journal, Christina a novel by Céline. Christina looked up from her book.

'It all seems so old-fashioned and unnecessary,' she said.

'Valdemar forced my hand.'

Christina sighed.

'Well, it'll be a gloomy Christmas.'

Isak was alone in his flat. He had sent Jensine off to see her family in Funen.

The telephone rang, and he felt a surge of excitement as he picked up the receiver. But it was only a friend. Her husband was away, she was giving a little impromptu Christmas party, would he care to join them? He refused politely, and replaced the receiver. He paced the room. He stood at the window, and watched the snow dance and whirl. He listened to trains clattering past on the railway lines by Langelinie.

He went back to the telephone and dialled his friend's number.

Part Two
1940

8

On a grey February afternoon, Captain Aksel Olsen, executive officer of the Special Intelligence department of the Danish General Staff, stood by the window of his office in Proviantgaarden and looked out, through the steamed-up glass and the driving rain outside, at the Parliament building opposite. He was reflecting on the remarkable contrast between the public pronouncements, and, in many cases, the private beliefs about German intentions voiced by the politicians who occupied the Rigsdagen, and the reports of his own agents in Germany. In the Rigsdagen they said that Hitler would honour his commitment to Danish neutrality; in Proviantgaarden, in his own office, there were documents which suggested the opposite. But they were only suggestions — hints, rumours, fragments of gossip. He himself had no doubt that Hitler was preparing an invasion, but without positive proof he was powerless to influence events. The politicians would go on believing exactly what they wanted to believe, and go on saying just what the vast majority of Danes wanted to hear them say, and the question was: how to prove them wrong?

He sat down at his desk and picked up a file. It was the official service record of Lieutenant Valdemar Larsen. He glanced through the details, neatly set out in black ink:

1935 Private, 3rd Life Guard Battalion;

1935–6 Infantry Cornet School, Kronborg and 2nd Life Guard Battalion, Jaegersborg Barracks;

1936–8 Officer School, Frederiksberg Palace, 4th Battalion, and Infantry Training School, Small Arms;

September 1938 1st Lieutenant. Transferred to Special Intelligence, General Staff.

How very little, Olsen thought, a man's official record tells about him. Here there appeared to be a typical young officer, keen, efficient, even slightly dedicated, pursuing a standard course that would lead him, in time, to somewhere near the top. Ostensibly, there was nothing extraordinary about him; yet Olsen knew that Lieutenant Larsen was one of the most unusual young officers in the Danish army: he was that rare thing, a born intelligence agent.

70

For a start he seemed to be completely unconcerned about his personal safety. He had the cold courage which comes either from an almost total lack of imagination, or from a profound, but ruthlessly suppressed cowardice. At the same time he had an instinct for self-preservation; he could smell danger like a wild creature, and avoid it. He was stealthy and cunning, he liked to move in the dark. Above all, he could assume an identity. Give him a role to play and he would sink himself into it, like an actor. No, that was wrong. An actor performed a part; Larsen seemed to have the ability to *become* another person.

Sometimes Olsen wondered whether this capacity did not spring from the same source as his courage: a deep dissatisfaction with his own nature. But it was not his business to analyse Larsen, only to assess his fitness for the present job. On the face of it, he was the perfect choice. The results of his previous tour of duty in Germany had been brilliant: he had established a line of contacts directly into Admiral Canaris's private secretariat. He had a genius for finding people who would supply information out of conviction rather than for money – the most valuable kind. All this was to his credit. On the debit side, there was his unpredictability. Larsen lived on his nerves; he was all tension and animal instinct; routines and procedures meant nothing to him; he was difficult to control, even more difficult to protect. Perhaps this mission should be entrusted to an older, steadier man, someone less complex. Last spring Larsen had been on the edge of cracking up. Three months' summer leave appeared to have sorted him out, but then again, his personal situation had changed.

Olsen picked up the internal phone.

'Larsen. Would you come in for a moment?'

He put down the receiver and began to fill a pipe. Valdemar came in.

'Sit down.'

Olsen lit his pipe, sucking in noisily, wreathing his head with smoke.

'Smoke if you like,' he said, between puffs. Valdemar lit a cigarette.

Olsen flicked his match away.

'I'm pulling Hesselholt out of the *Isted* network,' he said.

Valdemar nodded.

71

'I need someone to replace him. You seem to be the obvious choice.'

'Thank you, sir.'

'I can't order you to go.'

Valdemar smiled.

'You don't have to order me.'

'Things are very different in Germany these days, Larsen. Now that the country's at war internal security is stringent.'

'That doesn't worry me, sir.'

'Perhaps not. But there are other considerations. You are a married man now. I believe your wife is expecting a baby?'

'Yes, sir. I don't see that makes any difference.'

Olsen raised an eyebrow.

'Don't you? There's a very real danger in what I'm proposing. If you were caught I could do nothing to protect you. I have had instructions to avoid what the politicians call "provocations". If certain people had any idea of the extent of our intelligence operation inside Germany there'd be one hell of a row. I'm being frank with you.'

'Thank you, sir.'

'There are other men I could send.'

'I'm the man for the job. I know I am.'

'Possibly you are. But you should think of your wife. You might have to be away for several months. You would have to lie to her about where you are going and what you are doing.'

'I know that, sir.'

Olsen stared at him. Strange fellow, he thought, a cold fish. He felt rather sorry for the wife.

'Very well. I'll brief you in this office tomorrow morning.'

Valdemar stood up.

'Thank you, sir.'

When he had gone Olsen re-lit his pipe. Yes, he thought, a very strange fellow. A touch of the fanatic about him. You'd think that with a father as rich as his he'd be content to play at business for a few years before pocketing a big inheritance. Still, he had a nose for secrets — that was the main thing.

'My God — is it twins?' Abel said in mock horror.

At seven months Rosa seemed to be enormous, almost a caricature of a pregnant woman. Perhaps it was the contrast

72

between her smallness, her fine-boned neatness, and her swollen belly that made it seem so.

'Would you like to listen to the heartbeat?'

'You're teasing me. You know I find everything to do with the process of human reproduction thoroughly distasteful. I can't think how women put up with it. To be made sick, to be hideously disfigured, and finally to suffer tortures of pain – I don't see where the attraction lies.'

'Well there's something to be said for the activity that starts the whole thing off.'

'I wouldn't know anything about that.'

'And there's everything to be said for the end result.'

'Is there now? I sometimes wonder whether children ever do anything but cause worry and pain? Look at me. Look at you.'

'Perhaps we're exceptional.'

Rosa avoided his eye. It was hot in the big, low-ceilinged sitting-room behind the shop. It was late in the afternoon and the shop was closed. Abel's assistant, a tall, blond, handsome, dim-witted youth called The Viking, was sitting at the far end of the room, rubbing wax into the leather binding of a book. Books lined the walls, books were piled on tables and chairs, there were pyramids of books on the floor.

'I saw your father last week,' Abel said.

'How is he?'

'Hurt.'

'And how's Grandmamma?'

'You know Mother. She's convinced herself that you, Valdemar, and the baby don't exist. It's "too much of an unpleasantness" for her.' His imitation of his mother's prim voice was cruelly accurate.

'Why don't you ring your father? Or write to him,' he said.

'Why should I? He didn't even attempt to understand.'

'He loves you very deeply you know.'

'I know. That's why I think it'll work out in the end. I love him too, Uncle Abel, but – it's difficult to explain – it's so marvellous to be away from him, to have my own home.'

'I understand that. Isak never was much good at dealing with the unconventional. That was your mother's forte.'

Rosa had no recollection of her mother, who had died when she was three.

73

'Miriam was a free spirit if ever there was one. I remember when she led a demonstration down at the docks demanding the reinstatement of the Zahle Government. Your grandmother was appalled.'

He chuckled.

'Have some coffee, Rosa,' he said. 'The Viking makes an excellent cup of coffee.'

'No thank you, Uncle Abel. I must be going.'

Abel turned to The Viking.

'Then just one, for me, dear boy,' he said.

The Viking rose obediently and disappeared.

'Does he ever open his mouth?' Rosa said. She had always found The Viking rather sinister.

'Oh yes. At least three or four times a year. He's the ideal companion for an introspective man.'

Rosa smiled and kissed her uncle.

'Goodbye,' he said. 'Look in again soon. Give my regards to your handsome husband. And Rosa — think over what I said about your father. He's an unhappy man.'

Rosa walked up to Ørstedsparken and caught a No. 16. An elderly man gave up his seat to her and several women asked her about the baby. She got off the tram in Absalonsgade and walked through the damp, dismal streets to the flat. It was little better than a tenement, but she and Valdemar had transformed it. A large proportion of Valdemar's pay had been invested in paint, carpets, and curtains.

Valdemar was not back. She opened the door of the stove to let more heat into the sitting-room, then went into the little spare bedroom which was to be the nursery. Valdemar had sold his car and they'd blued some of the proceeds on a beautiful eighteenth-century fruit-wood cot she had found in an antique shop behind the University. She ran her hand along the smooth, polished wood. She had devoted hours of sweat and pots of beeswax to restoring its patina. She felt the baby kick inside her and smiled to herself. She went into the other bedroom, took off her coat, and hung it up in the wardrobe next to Valdemar's suits and uniforms. She paused to feel the rough cloth of his favourite tweed jacket. She buried her nose in it and breathed in his smell — a hint of musk, a hint of tobacco, and a score of other subtle odours that all blended together to form a scent that was uniquely his.

In the early days of their marriage it had been exciting to wake up to his smell every morning in their bed, and to get a sniff of it when he came home from Proviantgaarden in the evening. Now it was familiar – and they had only been married for two months. It seemed so much longer; perhaps because they saw so few people – Sven occasionally, and one or two others, but no family except for Abel and Karen. Valdemar said that he had always hated social life anyway and she, who had loved parties, found she did not miss them.

She was in the kitchen, preparing the fish for their dinner, when Valdemar came in.

He kissed her and patted her belly.

'How's our embryo?'

'He's training to become a professional footballer.'

He smiled. He went to the window, opened it, and picked up one of the bottles of beer standing in a row on the sill where the wintry air kept them cold. He shut the window. There was a hiss from the beer bottle as he prised off the cap. He took a swig, then said:

'Rosa, I've got to go away for a bit.'

'Not another course?'

'No. It's a job. Abroad. I can't tell you much about it.'

'Abroad? Where?'

'I can't even tell you that.'

Rosa started to chop an onion.

'How long will you be away?'

'I don't know. A month, probably more.'

'Valdemar – the baby's due in two months.'

'I know. I'm sure I'll be back before then.'

'What if you're not?'

'I will be. I'm sure I will be.'

She turned and looked at him. There were tears on her cheeks.

'You won't. That's what you're trying to tell me, isn't it?'

'For God's sake don't start crying.'

Valdemar had a horror of tears.

'I'm not. It's the onion.'

She tried to laugh – and failed. Valdemar put his arms round her.

'Rosa, I told you that something like this might happen. I told you before we were married. I'm not just an ordinary officer.'

'Couldn't they send someone else? Don't they know I'm going to have a baby?'

Valdemar felt a little stab of guilt.

'There is nobody else,' he lied.

Rosa pulled away from him.

'I suppose you're going to Germany.'

'I can't tell you anything. You know that.'

'How will I know if you're all right? What if you end up in some Gestapo prison? Am I supposed to just sit here and wait?' Her voice was rising.

'I can get messages through. You'll hear every few days. I promise.'

'What if something goes wrong with the baby? Have you thought of that?'

'There's Doctor Blum. There's Sven.'

'I don't want Blum. I don't want Sven. I want my husband.'

'Rosa,' he said – God, was she going to get hysterical? – 'Rosa, the job I've got to do is important – important for Denmark.'

'Is it more important than the birth of our child? Is it?'

Valdemar did not answer. Rosa turned away and tipped the chopped onion into a frying-pan.

'Go and wash,' she said. 'Supper is nearly ready.'

Later, as they lay side by side in the darkness, Rosa remembered that interlude during the summer at Skagen, that one night when they'd lain in bed not touching each other, not speaking. It had been as if all the intimacy of the long days and nights had never been. She had been slightly sickened by the smell of his body and she had longed for the privacy of her own bed.

It was not like that this time; this time, though the silence and the distance were as great, and she almost felt hatred for him, she longed to inhale the sweet staleness of his skin. She was frightened, she realized, frightened for him. Was he frightened too? Had she made it worse for him? She reached out and touched his thigh.

'I'm sorry, Val. I'm scared, that's all.'

He put his hand on hers.

'Don't be. It'll be all right.'

76

'It's just that you have this other life. I feel I've only got half of you.'

'You've got more than anybody else has ever had,' he said.

She felt for him and began to stroke him. His thighs flexed as he stiffened.

'Make love to me Valdemar,' she said.

'Rosa — the baby.'

'Be gentle. It'll be all right.'

'Are you sure?'

She turned to face him.

'Please,' she said. 'I want you.'

Waiting about — it was the most dangerous thing you could do in Hitler's Reich. People stared at you, and then they began wondering about you because they had nothing better to do. There were informers everywhere — children, old ladies, smartly-suited businessmen, priests: the Germans had become a nation of whisperers. But why panic? If a man could not legitimately wait about in the Hamburg Central Post Office, where could he?

He lit a cigarette and threw the match on the floor. An old man sitting on a bench glared at him. He moved away towards the counter. Trouble was, it was too early in the day. Not enough people about. No queues. He should have come later.

'Herr Nissen.'

He started. The woman at the counter was beckoning to him. Christ, he must get hold of himself — jumping at the sound of his own name. He went over to the counter.

'Your connexion to Silkeborg. Booth 4,' the woman said. 'No smoking in the booths,' she added severely.

'Of course,' he mumbled.

He was about to throw the cigarette onto the floor and tread it out when he remembered the sand-filled pedestals provided. He poked the cigarette into the sand and walked over to the wood and glass booth marked '4'. The air inside was warm and stale. The phone buzzed and he picked up the receiver.

The voice of the anonymous girl at the Silkeborg exchange was instantly reassuring. It was good to hear one's own language spoken again, even if it was only a brief:

'Hold the line, I am trying to connect you.'

Another voice, a familiar one this time: Ole Pedersen, manager of the N.D. Dairy Co-operative in Silkeborg. They spoke for two minutes, a pre-arranged conversation about butter prices and sales prospects in North Germany. At the end, he replaced the receiver. In an hour or so Rosa would get a call from Olsen's office, telling her that he was all right.

He came out of the booth and went back to the counter. The hard-faced woman seemed to take an age to calculate the cost of the call. There were more people milling about now but he suddenly had the claustrophobic's urge to get into the open air. He paid the woman, thanking her politely. He turned and began to walk towards the exit.

'A moment.'

The voice was politely firm, the phrase crisply enunciated – exactly as he had always imagined it would be.

He turned. Two men. One middle-aged. Bulky overcoat, a sort of leathery hat. The other young, thin. His double-breasted suit looked baggy on him.

Valdemar was suddenly cool, almost exhilarated.

'Yes?' he said.

The older man flashed an identity card at him.

'Police. Your papers, please.'

He fumbled for his passport, *Ausweis*, letter of accreditation, and all the other bits and pieces and handed them over. The older man began examining them. His colleague peered over his shoulder.

Without looking up the older man said: 'The purpose of your visit to Hamburg?'

'I have an appointment with Stummer & Koll, the butter wholesalers. You see – on the schedule.' He moved a step nearer as if to help.

'Very good.'

The older man handed the papers back with a dismissive nod and a sharp '*Danke.*'

Valdemar was moving away when the younger one said:

'Herr Nissen.'

Valdemar stopped.

'Yes?'

'Do you know what date it is today?'

Valdemar looked blank for a moment. Then he said:

'The fourth of April.'

'Your travel permit expires on the ninth. It will require renewal if you intend to remain in Germany.'

Valdemar smiled.

'Thank you, but I hope to return home tomorrow or the day after.'

'Very good.'

He made himself pause for a few seconds on the pavement outside, then crossed the road and strolled into the Botanical Gardens opposite. He turned down a path and looked back through a screen of bushes. Were they following him? No. No sign of them. Just a routine spot check, then? Must be. The sense of exhilaration had gone. He felt fluttery and fluid inside.

The walk back to the Altstadt restored his confidence a little. For some reason he felt safer in the Old Town. Perhaps it was simply that he felt that if it came to a chase he could easily lose himself in the maze of alleys, canals, and warehouses.

He had a room in a lodging-house over a shop. The shop was boarded up and defaced with anti-Semitic slogans. It had been a tailors: *E. Zuckermann.* Sometimes Valdemar wondered what had happened to E. Zuckermann. The place was used mainly by prostitutes, male and female. Nobody asked any questions; it was completely anonymous and safe. He let himself into his room. The window looked out onto a narrow canal and the prison-like façade of a tobacco warehouse. There was a permanent stench of mud and rot.

Becker arrived punctually at noon. Valdemar had last seen him in Berlin, three weeks ago. He remembered him as plump and dapper, but now the man looked haggard. He had lost weight; he was still beautifully dressed, but the haunted look in his eyes made him appear almost dishevelled. They shook hands.

'I have the documents,' Becker said. 'But I have to tell you that my friend has been arrested.'

Becker's friend was a minor official in the Abwehr, working in Admiral Bürckner's department. Valdemar didn't know his name, or anything about him, only that he was a prime source of military intelligence.

'When?' he said.

79

'Yesterday.'

'Can he implicate you?'

'No, no, I am sure not. He is not suspected – it is a question of his morals, you see.'

Valdemar did not see.

'You look worried,' he said. 'You must tell me the truth. I may be able to help you.'

Becker was fumbling in his attaché case. He pulled out a sheaf of papers.

'Take them. I know very little. Only that he has been arrested.'

'By the Gestapo?'

'I think so, yes. There is a purge.'

'A purge? What sort of purge?'

'Take the papers.'

Valdemar took them. He sat down at the dirty deal table and looked at the first document.

It was a copy of an official directive from Hitler's private office – 'Distribution: All Service Commands'. It was dated 1 March 1940, and was headed: '*WESERUEBUNG* – TOP SECRET.' Valdemar began to read.

'The situation in Scandinavia requires the making of all preparations for the occupation of Denmark and Norway by a part of the German Armed Forces. In view of our military and political power in comparison with that of the Scandinavian States, the force to be employed will be kept as small as possible. The numerical weakness will be balanced by daring actions and surprise of execution ...'

Valdemar was sweating. He began to flip through the flimsy carbons with one question in his mind: *when?*

He searched for the thread of the story in the stilted language of half a dozen inter-departmental memoranda. They seemed to be concerned with the progress of the Russo-Finnish war. One, dated 13 March, stated: 'In view of the capitulation of the Finnish Government it seems that *Weseruebung* must be postponed, or even cancelled.'

Cancelled? No. What was this? A private report from a Captain Otto Schenk to Admiral Bürckner, dated 2 April. It was headed *Weseruebung*. It read: 'Yesterday, as instructed, I rendered my report on the intelligence aspects of this operation to the Führer personally, and to General Falkenhorst. (See attached

80

schedule.) The Führer complimented the Abwehr on its activities in this regard. In the evening, at a meeting of all the senior officers concerned, from all service branches, the Führer addressed us. He said that the strain of waiting until the start of the operation would be as great as any he had had to endure in his life, but that he had complete faith in victory. This morning at 1100 hours, after a meteorological report, it was confirmed that *Weseruebung* will commence on 9 April.'

Valdemar's hand was trembling. He groped for a cigarette and lit it. He looked at Becker who was pacing up and down.

'Have you read these?' he said.

Becker shook his head.

'I am only a courier.'

'They are of vital concern to my Government.'

'Good, good.'

'I must ask you to tell me everything you know about your friend's arrest.'

'I tell you I know nothing.'

'You said there was a purge?'

'Yes.'

'What sort of purge?'

Becker stared at him. 'Isn't that obvious?'

Valdemar did not wish to appear unintelligent; but Becker had been recruited by Hesselholt, and he knew nothing about him other than that he was an 'idealist', or in other words, did not require bribing.

'Your friend is surely not a Jew?' he said.

Becker laughed.

'No. Nor is he a gypsy or a Bolshevik or a Freemason or a Jehovah's Witness.'

'I'm sorry,' Valdemar said. 'I understand.'

'Do you? Have you ever been in love?'

'Yes.'

'And what would you do if the penalty for loving was torture and imprisonment, or even death?'

Valdemar had no real answer. He said:

'I think your courage is extraordinary.'

Becker laughed again. 'I am a coward. I am frightened of everything. For eight years now I have been frightened. Ever since the Nazis.'

'Is there anything I can do for you? Is there anything my Government can do for you?'

'No, no. I must go. I will not be able to help you any more.'

Becker closed his attaché case, and held out his hand.

'Goodbye,' he said.

Valdemar took his hand.

'Goodbye, Herr Becker and——' he was going to thank him again but suddenly he felt Becker's arm round his waist, pulling him into an embrace. Becker was hugging him tightly. His whole body was shaking as if with ague. He smelt of some sweet, expensive scent. After a moment Becker released him.

'I'm so sorry,' he said, 'I——' He faltered and turned to the door. With his fingers on the handle he looked back and said:

'Are you married?'

'Yes.'

'Then go home to your wife. Get out of this hateful country.'

Before the door had closed behind Becker, Valdemar's decision was made: he must follow him. It was not that he didn't trust him; it was rather an instinctive feeling that Becker was vulnerable. The man was in a state of panic. Ten to one his friend had talked and the police were after him. He quickly stuffed the papers into his briefcase, grabbed his coat, and left the room.

Becker was approaching the end of the street when Valdemar came out of the lodging-house. Becker turned left, to cross the little metal bridge over the canal, and Valdemar spurted, then paused at the corner. Becker was across the bridge, and walking in the direction of Neustadt. There were few people about, but Becker was ridiculously easy to follow: he walked briskly, never looking behind, heading west.

It was when they came into broader, more prosperous streets that Valdemar became aware of the car. It was a black saloon, with three men inside, and it was moving slowly along the kerb, a hundred yards behind Becker. Valdemar paused in a doorway and looked towards the far end of the street. Sure enough there was another black car, parked. The classic pattern. Couldn't Becker see it, for Christ's sake? His only chance was to cross the street – now – and run like hell.

But Becker kept steadily on.

Two men got out of the parked car and began walking towards him. The car behind pulled into the kerb. Valdemar stood in the doorway and watched helplessly: it was like looking at a blind man heading for a hole in the pavement. Becker noticed the two men approaching him. They were only a few yards away. He faltered.

Valdemar wanted to yell at him – no, don't run, your only chance is to bluff it out. Becker panicked. He turned and began to pound back towards Valdemar. He didn't even have the sense to cross the street.

As he came alongside the first car, the driver's door was swung open and Becker ran slap into it. They picked him off the pavement and slammed him against the side of the car.

There was a sprinkling of people about: women with shopping baskets, clerks scurrying back to their offices after their lunch. They all averted their eyes, crossed to the other side of the street, and hurried by. Nobody stopped to stare, not even when Becker let out a high-pitched shriek as a knee thudded into his groin.

Valdemar walked away. He glanced at his watch. Five past one. A train left for Flensburg, on the border, at two. He just had time to catch it.

The station was crowded – German stations were always crowded – and Valdemar thanked God for that. The woman in the ticket office was unsuspicious, examining his travel permit perfunctorily, and it was the same at the barrier: the inevitable Gestapo man, standing in the background, looked bored.

Valdemar chose a compartment full of naval ratings, who would want to talk among themselves and would leave him alone. He settled into the hard seat and pretended to go to sleep. The train set off at a tremendous pace. An express. Something else to be thankful for. They seemed to reach Neumünster in no time. The sailors got off there, no doubt to change for a local train to Kiel. They were replaced by three taciturn businessmen and a middle-aged woman and her daughter, who maintained a low-pitched and virulent conversation about a third party called Frau Kessel. Valdemar closed his eyes again. There was a routine check of tickets and papers ten minutes before they steamed into Rendsburg. The two women joked with the inspector.

Between Schleswig and Flensburg there was an unscheduled stop. The train halted in the middle of the flat, green countryside and waited, panting. A general conversation started in the compartment – dangerous.

'It's always happening these days.'

'I have an important appointment. I shall be late.'

'Last month we had to wait over two hours outside Hanover.'

'The heating broke down and I froze.'

Valdemar kept his eyes shut.

The train started off again. One of the men said:

'That was the cause, then.'

Tentatively Valdemar opened his eyes and looked out of the window. The train was moving slowly alongside a road. The road was packed with armoured cars and Mark II tanks; a Wehrmacht motorized rifle brigade moving north.

Weseruebung.

Valdemar closed his eyes again and began to think. Becker had been in Gestapo hands for over three hours and the probability was that he'd talked. By now they would have searched the room in the Altstadt and found clothes, shaving gear, and his list of afternoon appointments. They'd check, find he'd missed his 2.30 meeting at Stummer & Koll, draw the obvious conclusion, and alert all the railway stations – especially Flensburg.

He decided. He stood up, left the compartment, and walked down the corridor to the lavatory. He had to wait for two minutes before a fat Wehrmacht sergeant came out and lumbered away. Inside the lavatory it smelt of stale cigarette smoke and the sergeant's intestinal gases. Valdemar ignored the smell and got to work. He carefully destroyed his Danish passport in the name of Nissen, tearing it up and pushing the pieces out of the window; his *Ausweis* and other documents went the same way. From the lining of his briefcase he took another set of papers identifying him as Konrad Ritter, a German citizen, an agricultural engineering consultant of Elmshorn. These papers, which were excellent forgeries, and included a medical discharge certificate from the German Army, had cost a lot of money.

There was little he could do to hide the documents Becker had given him. He put them in the lining of the briefcase where the identity papers had been concealed; he might be able to survive a routine search that way and he would easily be able to get rid of the incriminating evidence, if he had to, by throwing away the briefcase.

There was nothing he could do about his appearance; he could only hope that if Becker had given a description of him, it would be as vague and inaccurate as descriptions exacted under torture usually were. With his height, his blond hair, pale blue eyes, and prominent cheekbones he looked German enough. The only thing that made him conspicuous was his youth, combined with the fact that he was not in uniform, but he had that angle covered.

It was dark when the train pulled into Flensburg station. Valdemar waited until the carriages had emptied, then mingled with a stream of people coming off a different train. He joined the long queue at the barrier. The queue was long because two uniformed railway inspectors, aided by three plain-clothes police, were meticulously checking papers. Valdemar was slightly relieved to see that the women were being checked as thoroughly as the men. As he shuffled nearer and nearer to the barrier he waited for calm to descend on him as it had never before failed to do.

There was a man standing a few feet behind the inspectors, observing the slowly moving line. He was abnormally tall, over two metres, and thin to the point of emaciation. This thinness gave his face, which was a young face, a look of age. His hair, cropped short, was almost pure white, but he was not an albino: his eyes were dark blue, and they appeared to have no eyebrows.

Valdemar was suddenly certain that those eyes were seeking him out, that this haggard, young-old giant had been sent to arrest Kaj Nissen. He quickly averted his own eyes and took a pace forward. There were only two people ahead of him in the queue now.

His turn came. He had his papers ready and handed them to the inspector. The inspector glanced at them and gave them to one of the plain-clothes men. Valdemar tried not to stare at the ground. Instead he stared at the Gestapo man's hands. He somehow knew that the giant was watching him, analysing his features and his clothes, comparing them with Becker's description.

The Gestapo man handed his papers back, with a dismissive nod. Valdemar began to walk away. He waited for the crisp: 'A moment.' It didn't come.

Act with complete naturalness, he told himself. His whole body was screaming for nicotine: very well then, stop and light a cigarette. He fumbled in his pocket for his cigarettes and matches. He halted, fitted a cigarette into his mouth and struck a match. He inhaled a deep, dizzying lungful of smoke, threw away the match, and walked on.

'Excuse me.'

The voice was polite and firm. Valdemar stopped and turned.

In the instant that his mind took in the speaker – short, bespectacled, suited – it also registered a movement behind him: the white giant, coming towards them.

As the little man said:

'I wonder if you would oblige me with a light,' Valdemar snapped. He ran. He shouldered his way through a knot of gossiping soldiers and pelted towards the exit. Behind him he heard shouts and a whistle.

The cold of the street hit him, the lights from cars dazzled him. He dived to the left, weaving between parked lorries and cars. He saw the dark entrance to an alley and ran into it. The alley twisted between the backs of factories. Christ, it was blind. No. There were street lights ahead. He slowed down to a walk, he stopped. He listened for sounds of pursuit. He could hear nothing.

His breathing was frantic. There were stabs of pain in his chest. He must calm down. Shit, shit, shit, shit.

The words of the little man mocked him: 'I wonder if you would oblige me with a light.' If he'd given him a light, and walked on, nothing would have happened. He'd behaved like Becker. Christ. What now? They'd comb the town for him. The docks, the customs post, they'd be crawling with police. They'd alert the border patrols. Christ.

He was standing by the rear entrance of a shop, a deep recess filled with dustbins. He stepped into the shadows and tried to think. He was breathing more regularly; the pains in his chest had eased. What the hell could he do?

He had a contact in Flensburg, an address near the Marienkirche. If he could shelter there and somehow get word through to Copenhagen, Olsen would smuggle him out. But would he even make it as far as the Marienkirche without being picked up?

He had a sudden picture of Rosa, sitting alone in the flat, polishing that damned cradle. Or was she already in hospital? Had the baby come? He felt a renewal of panic and a sense of miserable loneliness.

He stiffened. There was someone coming down the alley. He peered cautiously. It was a man in the heavy cap and thick, short coat of a factory worker. He was wheeling a bicycle. Valdemar knew what he had to do. He was cool now. Here was something he had practised many times with Sergeant Andersen. He allowed the man to go two paces past him, then he stepped out behind him and took him in a stranglehold. Total surprise, total paralysis. He kicked his legs from under him, and going down with him, cracked his head on the pavement. The struggling body became a deadweight. The only noise had been the clatter of the bicycle as it fell over.

Valdemar dragged the man into the shop entrance. He was immensely heavy. He checked him quickly − breathing all right, heartbeat strong − then began to manoeuvre him out of his coat. His body smelt strongly of alcohol and fish. Valdemar slipped out of his own coat and into the man's. He put on his cap and felt in the pockets of the coat. Identity papers, tobacco, cigarette papers, some small change, keys. Good. He picked up his briefcase and extracted Becker's papers. He stuffed them inside his shirt. His own coat, and the briefcase, he concealed under the rubbish in one of the dustbins. He stepped out into the alley, picked up the bicycle, and leaned it against the wall. He checked his victim's papers: Hans Zoll. Occupation: worker. Place of work: Geltinger Fish Curing Factory.

He set off full of new confidence. There weren't many people about but most of them seemed to be cyclists dressed very much as he was. Then panic began to set in again. He could not get his bearings. The street lighting was dim, he did not dare stop anyone to ask the way, and his sense of direction was baffled by the uniformity of the factory-lined streets.

He turned left and right and left and right and, to his horror, realized that he was heading away from the centre. There were some soldiers coming towards him, talking and laughing, making it impossible to turn back. He pedalled on. He was in the country now. It was dark and silent and cold, and the light from the bicycle lamp was feeble. He was about to turn round when he came to a cross-roads. There was a sign-post. The lettering was faded but he could read it.

Pattburg.

There was something familiar about the name. Of course. It was the German equivalent of Padborg; and Padborg was in Denmark, a mere three kilometres away, according to the sign. He was right on the border. The road he was on ran parallel to it.

All he had to do was to cycle on for an hour or so, until he was well out of the Flensburg area, then take to the fields.

He had put twenty kilometres between himself and Flensburg when he decided to turn right, off the main road, into a lane that seemed to run in the direction of the border. As few as seven vehicles had passed him on the road. Each time he had been warned of their approach by their lights, and had been able to take cover in the ditch. A fine rain had started, noiseless but penetratingly wet and cold; he didn't care, he was enjoying the adventure.

It happened so suddenly that he almost fell off the bicycle – a light in his eyes and a hoarse order:

'Halt.'

Valdemar recovered his balance and turned his head away from the light, blinking. The sentry was young, about his own age. His drab, green, waterproof cloak was slick with rain. He carried a heavy torch and a machine pistol.

'Where are you going? Show me your papers.'

Valdemar fumbled in his coat pocket.

'My sister, Fräulein Zoll – she lives at the farm up there.'

The sentry glanced at the papers. He looked angry and nervous.

'No, no. Your special pass. Show me your special pass.'

Valdemar stared blankly at him. The sentry's voice rose.

'This is a restricted area. You must have a special pass.'

'Ah – just so – the special pass,' Valdemar said.

He fumbled in his pocket again. His fingers found Herr Zoll's packet of cigarette papers. He drew it out and then let it slip and flutter to the ground.

The sentry instinctively bent forward. Valdemar lashed out. It was a bad blow, poorly aimed – he felt the skin of his knuckles rip on the sentry's teeth – but it gave him his chance. He dived past the sentry and through an open gate into a field. He was halfway across the plough before he heard shots rattle out, and shouts.

He plunged through a hedge, into another field. Mud weighed down his shoes, he slipped and stumbled. He saw a row of bobbing lights to his right and veered into a wood. Briars and low branches slashed at his face, tugged at his clothes. He knew he should slow down; he knew that the noise he was making would draw the pursuit like a trail of aniseed. He crashed on. Out of the wood, across another field, the thick earth clawing at his ankles.

A barbed-wire fence. He scrabbled over it, with a tearing of cloth and jabs of pain. Another field, another fence; there was blood on his face, blood on his hands, blood on his legs. Every thorn and twig and barb in Germany seemed to be clutching at him, pulling him back. The very soil of Germany was hugging his feet and calves, dragging him down.

On and on he ran, blind and stitched with pain. Then agony exploded in his knees. His legs were whipped from under him. He somersaulted into a ditch full of thick, icy water, and lay still, sobbing.

—10—

Silence. Except for the steady drip-drip of water, as leaves and branches collected particles of the misty rain and turned them into fine trickles.

Valdemar got to his feet. He had been brought down by the stump of a tree, half-concealed in long grass. His knees throbbed from two swelling bruises and he was smarting all over from dozens of small cuts and abrasions. His clothes were soaked through, they shrouded his body in chill dankness.

But much worse than this physical misery was the rage he felt against himself. He had behaved like an amateur and an idiot, first at the station, then with the sentry. And the result? He had no idea where he was. He might have run for ten kilometres or one; he might have run in circles like a hare; he might be in Denmark, he might still be in Germany. In his headlong panic he had completely lost his bearings. His only guide was the suggestion of a path in the grass. He decided to follow it, aware that every step might be taking him back into danger.

The path widened into a rough track, rutted by tractor wheels. He sensed that he was approaching a farm and tried to keep to the grass verges so as to minimize noise. The track began to descend. He halted and peered through the murk. Ahead, at the bottom of the gentle gradient, he could just make out the outlines of farm buildings. He crept closer, choosing his ground carefully, aware that the rattle of a loose stone or the snap of a twig would be enough to alert the farm dogs.

It seemed to be a typically Danish farmstead – ramshackle

barns, sheds, and outhouses, huddling round a long, low, single-storey thatched house. He could hear cattle shifting and snorting in the covered yard. But he knew that it could just as well be a German farm. After all the whole of Schleswig and Holstein had been under Danish rule less than eighty years ago.

He found what he wanted in one of the outlying sheds: an old truck thickly crusted with dried mud. He squatted down and pulled out the matches. The flimsy box was damp, and he broke three matches in ineffectual scrapings before there was a hiss and a flare of light. The registration plate was buckled and splashed with mud, but there was no doubt that the number was a Danish one. It was not final proof; he must still be very careful, yet he had a conviction that he was now safe.

He took the lane that ran out of the farmyard and plodded steadily on between the hedgerows. The rain had eased; a few stars had appeared, and a barely perceptible change in the colour of the sky told him that dawn would soon be breaking.

He walked on. The lane emerged onto a narrow, metalled road. He had no particular plan. He must come to a village soon and then he would know for sure whether he was in Denmark or not.

It was the sudden, startling shriek of some nocturnal bird – an owl? – that made him look up, otherwise he might never have seen the tower. Towards the east the sky was silvery grey, and the tower, though it was little more than a ragged pile of stone crowning a hillock, stood out against it in sharp relief.

He recognized the shape of the modest ruin immediately, and it brought back a spate of childhood memories: holidays with Uncle Henrik at Vidlund, creeping out alone at dawn before the household was awake, trekking across the fields to this magic castle where, for an hour, he ruled as king over an imaginary court of warriors, witches, and wizards. Then back to Vidlund, to crackling fires and breakfast. Sometimes he would let Karen come with him on these expeditions. He enrolled her into the order of chivalry he had invented, making her cut a nick in her thumb so that her blood could mingle with his. She hadn't flinched or cried, she had been excited and solemn, and the bond they pledged had been a real one, an enduring one. He cut across a meadow and climbed up to the tower. In this country of gentle rises and shallow valleys, it was the highest point for miles. As a boy he had thought of it as a mountain, dominating the land, and the tower had been an impregnable stronghold; later, he had come to realize that in any place other than Jutland, the hill would be considered a mere knoll and the tower a minor relic of the past, of no interest or importance. Yet, as he stood below the mossy wall, only a few metres higher than himself, it was the child's perspective that reasserted itself: the tower still held mystery and power for him.

He sat in what had once, perhaps, been an embrasure, and lit the last of his cigarettes.

The sun was up, the sky was clearing. There were patches of blue, like freshly washed cloth, and a hint of warmth in the air, a smell of earth and grass. Feathers of mist still hung over the fields, their filmy whiteness a contrast to the dark green of the grass.

Valdemar suddenly had a sense of the generations and generations of quiet, patient men who had toiled on this land, whose grit and sweat had slowly moulded the thin, stony soil into a source of plenty. How many centuries had it taken to turn the barren northern heaths into this soft and cosy landscape?

Cosy. It was a word, and an idea, that normally he despised. He had always argued that cosiness was the vice of the Danes; their complacency, their love of comfort, their mistrust of the heroic, all were the products of a featureless, undulating terrain like this. How could they strive for the heights when there were none? How often had he raged against the paltriness of life in Denmark?

But there was no rage of that sort in him now. There seemed to be nothing paltry about this countryside, rather something very precious; it existed because men had cherished and nurtured it. If the Danes had turned their backs on high ideals, they had at least opened their hearts to tolerance. They might be bland and self-satisfied but they were free. There was still one passion left among a people who had abandoned idealism and forged their swords into ploughshares – a passion for liberty.

A crackle of paper against his stomach reminded him of what he had brought out of Germany, of what he knew. The Germans were coming with swords not ploughshares; they would fill these gentle valleys with corpses; they would bring fire and terror to the farms. There would be an end of cosiness.

He took the familiar path down through the deer forest, with its perpendicular pines and broad, straight rides, and climbed over the stile onto the smooth lawn of Vidlund.

91

The ochrous brick of the old manor house was mirrored in the dark green water of the moat; a family of ducks was busy diving and dabbling. Valdemar crossed over the stone bridge and opened the front door. There was a fire burning in the hall with a huge yellow dog basking in front of it. The dog opened its eyes and its tail thumped on the Persian rug. Valdemar knelt down and tickled its silky ears.

'Hello Barker old fellow,' he said.

He walked down the long, dark passage, lined with antlers mounted on shields, and found Squire Tøller in the great dining-room at the end.

The Squire was pacing up and down, eating a bowl of porridge.

He seemed hardly surprised at all to see his nephew. 'Well, well,' he said, then: 'Watch it, you've got half Jutland on your boots. You'll have Mrs Hansen after you with her rolling-pin.'

'As a matter of fact it's half Germany I've got on my boots.'

'Ah-hah – that's it, is it? I thought perhaps you had been fleeing your outraged father across the fields.'

'Uncle Henrik, I need your help. Will you drive me to the telephone in the village? I've got to get back to Copenhagen as quickly as possible.'

It was one of Squire Tøller's many eccentricities that he refused to have a telephone installed at Vidlund.

'All in good time, all in good time. I want to know what on earth you've been up to,' then, seeing Valdemar's hesitation, 'Oh I don't want you to reveal any State Secrets. Just tell me – did you manage to kill any of the bastards?'

Valdemar grinned.

'I'm afraid not.'

'Pity, pity. Now, some hot coffee – it's muck – and some food.'

'Uncle——

'All in good time. You look half-starved.'

While Valdemar poured himself a cup of hot coffee and fell on the dishes of ham and cheese and freshly baked rolls, Squire Tøller rang the bell. After a minute his elderly house-keeper appeared.

'Ah – Mrs Hansen – here's my prodigal nephew turned up out of the blue looking like something the dog's sicked up.'

Valdemar smiled at Mrs Hansen, who had been the friend and

ally of all those childhood holidays.

'You'd better look him out some clean clothes. Then a hot bath – if the damned boiler's working – and tell Peter to get the car out and see if he can start it.'

'Uncle I haven't got time for a bath,' Valdemar said.

'My dear boy – just look at yourself in the glass.'

The dining-room had been added to the main house by Squire Tøller's French grandmother in the mid-nineteenth century. The walls were lined with mirrors, framed with moulded plaster, in a florid and tasteless imitation of Versailles.

Valdemar surveyed himself: his stolen jacket was in shreds; his legs were showing through gashes in his trousers; his hair was wildly tangled; and his face was filthy.

'I see what you mean.'

He found that he was shivering. The idea of a steaming bath seemed like paradise.

Squire Tøller observed the shivers.

'This damned room,' he said. 'Impossible to heat. And I've always thought it looked like the women's cloakroom of a third-rate provincial casino. I should have it pulled down. Now come along, my boy.'

Squire Tøller drove his antiquated car at a very slow speed in a very high gear on the crown of the road. He used his klaxon in preference to his brakes.

Valdemar had been kitted out in a pair of plus-fours and a bulky sweater. His own shirt had been dried and ironed by Mrs Hansen: Becker's papers still lay next to his skin.

'I know you can't tell me anything,' Squire Tøller said suddenly, as they slowed down for the village with a great juddering of gears, 'but I will tell *you* something. We have a celebrated poacher here called Willem, a splendid fellow who was virtually weaned on my pheasants. Now Willem spends half his life on the other side of the border, snaring German rabbits. According to him the whole of North Schleswig's alive with troops. In my book that can mean only one thing.'

They pulled up in front of the little post office and Squire Tøller switched off the engine.

'Just tell me this, Val. Will it be soon?'

Valdemar met his gaze. For once the Squire looked grave.

'Yes, Uncle Henrik,' he said. 'Very soon.'

'I thought as much. Damn those baboons of politicos to hell.'

Olsen arranged for a military plane to pick Valdemar up at Tønder. He arrived at Kastrup airport, on the outskirts of Copenhagen, in the early afternoon. A moment after the plane had taken off exhaustion had hit him and he'd slept throughout the flight, awaking groggy but refreshed.

There was just time to telephone Rosa. Her voice sounded breathless and warm. His voice, he knew, sounded distant and curt.

'Has anything happened?'

She laughed.

'Doctor Blum says any time now. Val, where are you, when am I going to see you?'

'I'm at Kastrup. I've got to go straight to Proviantgaarden.'

'But when are you coming home?'

'I don't know. Tonight.'

'But, Val——'

'Look. I've got to go now. I'll see you tonight.'

At Proviantgaarden he sat in his little office, writing his report, while Olsen, and his chief, Colonel Købke, with other senior intelligence officers, analysed Becker's papers. At half-past six Olsen rang through on the internal telephone.

'Would you come to my office in ten minutes, Larsen?'

When Valdemar opened the door to Olsen's sharp 'In', he was surprised to find the room crowded and hazy with cigarette smoke. He recognized Colonel Købke, Colonel Eriksen, and two or three other high-ranking officers. Købke shot a look of enquiry at Olsen.

Olsen said: 'Lieutenant Larsen has risked his life, sir. I think he has a right to hear the results of his efforts.'

Købke laughed shortly and said: 'He's your man, Olsen. Very well. Sit down, Lieutenant. Sit down, gentlemen.'

Købke himself remained standing.

'For the benefit of Lieutenant Larsen and one or two others who might not be up to date on the situation,' he said, 'I will summarize briefly. About ten days ago we received a report from our naval attaché in Berlin, Captain Kjølsen, to the effect that Hitler had finalized his plans for the invasion of Denmark and Norway. Kjølsen's information came from Major General Oster,

Admiral Canaris's right-hand man, via the Dutch military attaché. It was the proof Captain Olsen and I had been waiting for. I decided to close the *Isted* network straight away but I am glad to say Captain Olsen dissuaded me. I had assumed that with Kjølsen's report in front of them the Cabinet would act. I was wrong. They did nothing. Captain Kjølsen's information was discounted. To quote a senior minister, whom I shall not name: "How can we take such a story seriously when it reaches us in such a round-about way? It is nothing but hearsay." '

Olsen stared at the blotting pad on his desk.

'Yesterday,' Købke went on, 'Kjølsen himself arrived in Copenhagen and attempted to convince the authorities. He was politely disbelieved. This afternoon, thanks to the efforts of Lieutenant Larsen,' – Valdemar shifted uneasily as he felt half a dozen pairs of eyes on him – 'we received documentary confirmation, in detail, of Kjølsen's report. We now know the code-name of the invasion operation, and we know its date. An hour ago I presented these facts to my political masters, with a recommendation that the General Staff order immediate mobilization. I will not weary you with the details of the discussion that followed. I have merely to inform you that there will be no mobilization. The Government intends to do nothing.'

There was a babble of angry comment. Everyone was talking at once. Only Olsen and Valdemar remained silent.

Valdemar's initial reaction had been physical – a great lassitude descending on him, a heaviness in every bone. Everything he had done had been pointless; everything was pointless, everything except sleep. But then, as the full implication of Colonel Købke's statement sank in, he felt a surge of energy, he felt rage revitalizing him.

He was aware that Købke and the others were filing out, still arguing loudly amongst themselves, then he and Olsen were alone.

'You have my sympathy, Larsen,' Olsen said.

'We must do something, sir.'

Olsen shrugged.

'You cannot make people believe what they do not want to believe, however many facts you give them.'

'Then give the story to the press. Let public opinion force the politicians to take action.'

Olsen smiled.

'In a democracy, Larsen, politicians *reflect* public opinion. I doubt if any responsible editor would print the truth. Even if he did nobody would accept it. In any case, for you or I, or anyone, to breathe a word of this outside the office would lead straight to a court-martial.'

'My uncle is Poul Larsen. I could speak to him.'

Olsen glanced up sharply.

'I'd forgotten that.' He reflected a moment. 'It might be a chance. Your uncle certainly has the ear of the King. He's said to wield great influence.'

He picked up the file containing copies of Becker's papers.

'You would have to return these immediately after seeing your uncle. Officially they would never have left this room.'

'I understand, sir.'

He took the file.

'Nobody but your uncle must see them. Nobody.'

'I appreciate that, sir.'

'I hope you do, Larsen.'

Poul Larsen's office in the Red House was over-heated and sparsely furnished; its functional severity, Valdemar thought, reflected his uncle's character. It contained nothing but filing cabinets and rows and rows of leather-bound legal volumes, just as Uncle Poul's mind, as far as Valdemar had ever been able to judge, contained nothing but facts and figures, tidily stored. Poul could become a little passionate about a nicety of constitutional precedent, but about little else. As for his wife, Aunt Anna, she had hardly ever been known to open her mouth at a family gathering, and according to Valdemar's mother, had never been known to do anything more energetic than embroidery. Their flat in Hauchsvej was apparently a nightmare of needlepoint. Valdemar had never seen it.

Poul Larsen removed his reading spectacles.

'You should not have shown me this, Valdemar,' he said. 'It is a clear breach of security regulations.'

'Is that all you have to say?' There was anger in his voice, and immediately he regretted it. Uncle Poul's narrow lips pursed disapprovingly.

'I don't understand why you have shown me these documents.'

'I want you to do something.'

'And what do you suppose I should do?'

'Talk to the King. Talk to the Cabinet. They'd listen to you.'

Poul closed the file, picked up his spectacles, and began to polish their lenses with a handkerchief.

'The substance of what you have shown me has already been communicated to me. I have already given my advice.'

'And what advice did you give, Uncle Poul?'

'Good advice, I hope. At least, it was accepted.'

Valdemar laughed shortly.

'I see. It was your brilliant idea to do nothing.'

'No. I merely concurred with the unanimous view of the Cabinet.'

'Uncle Poul, have you any conception of the risk involved in getting these papers out of Germany? At this very moment there's a man lying bleeding in some Gestapo torture chamber because he wanted to help our country. And you sit there and talk about good advice.'

Poul let out a barely audible sigh.

'Valdemar, you're very young, and not very logical.'

It could have been his father talking: the same smugness, the same complacency. God what a family! He stood up.

'I'm wasting my time,' he said.

'Sit down, Valdemar,' Poul said quietly. 'And listen to me.'

Valdemar sat down.

'Are you prepared to listen?' Poul asked.

'I should be fascinated to know how you have managed to add two and two together and make zero, Uncle Poul.'

Poul ignored this.

'Have you ever stopped to consider the source of all this information about an invasion?' he said. 'No. I would not have expected you to. I might, however, have expected your superiors to apply a little logic. The source is always the same: German counter-intelligence. Now I have no doubt that it would suit Hitler very well to gain some sort of control over the Scandinavian countries, just as it would suit the British. But Hitler was pledged to respect our neutrality and he cannot risk being seen to renege on his pledges. He can take no action unless he can claim that he has been provoked. If the Danish Government were to authorize a general mobilization that would be regarded in Berlin as an act of provocation. It would give Hitler the excuse he wants. It is quite clear to me that his policy is to trick us into believing that we are about to be invaded, hoping that we will mobilize, hence this positive flood of top-secret information from none other than the head of the Abwehr.'

'Canaris is known to be anti-Hitler.'

'My dear boy, if Canaris was known to be anti-Hitler he would not be head of the Abwehr. Surely that is elementary? No, no, as long as we are aware of Herr Hitler's game, and as long as we refuse to play it, we can have nothing to fear.'

'Uncle Poul, yesterday afternoon I saw with my own eyes a whole motorized brigade of the Wehrmacht moving north through Schleswig. What were they doing, do you think? Going on their holidays?'

'They were taking part in a meticulously planned deception.'

'Is that what you really believe?'

'It is.'

Valdemar began to laugh quietly. Poul stared at him. The boy looked awful − purple blotches under his eyes, skin the colour of chalk − was he ill? There was a slightly mad quality about his laughter.

'Pull yourself together, Valdemar.'

Valdemar made an attempt to control himself.

'I'm sorry, Uncle Poul − I'm rather tired.'

'What you need is a good night's sleep.'

'I'm sure − sure you're right.'

He broke down again and Poul glared at him, slightly pop-eyed.

'I'm sorry − I've − it's just that I've remembered a joke Rosa once told me.' He ignored Poul's gesture of protest and went on: 'It's about a man who gets lost in the desert. He wanders about for days and days, tortured by thirst, and fried by sun, then at last he comes to a house, a pretty white house, with a shady verandah, surrounded by palm trees. He thinks it must be a mirage − but no, there's a man walking out onto the verandah and sitting down in a deck-chair with a bottle of whisky and a glass. He crawls across the burning sand and with the last of his strength he mounts the steps onto the verandah. "Water," he croaks, "water." The man in the deck-chair looks up and raises his glass of whisky. "No thanks, old man," he says, "I prefer to drink it neat." '

Valdemar dissolved into chuckles and Poul rose from his chair.

'I think you had better go home,' he said.

Valdemar rose.

'I think you're right, Uncle Poul.'

He picked up the file and began to walk towards the door. He was so tired now that he could hardly walk. He felt he wanted to crawl, like the man in the joke. At the door he paused. Poul was still standing behind his desk, blinking through his spectacles. Valdemar raised a hand with an imaginary glass in it.

'*Skol*,' he said.

After Valdemar's clipped telephone call from the airport Rosa had given way to self-pity; it seemed to her outrageous that Valdemar should be back in Copenhagen and not see her for even five minutes; and how could she cook him a celebration dinner when she did not even know what time he'd be home?

Towards the end of the afternoon she'd pulled herself together and gone out to buy his favourite cold dishes – *gravad laks*, pickled herring, and *spegepølse*. She'd decorated the table with candles and dried flowers and elaborately folded napkins. Then she'd sat down to wait.

As the evening wore on and there was no sign of him, not even a telephone call, misery returned. At nine o'clock she was so hungry that she raided the dinner table, upsetting the careful pattern of food. Making new patterns whiled away a few minutes and she felt better after she'd eaten.

She was dozing by the stove when she heard his step outside the front door and the rattle of his key in the latch. She had rehearsed this moment three or four times. The matches were all ready and waiting. She struck one and deftly lit the candles. As she went out of the living-room, into the little hall, she switched off the light.

He was struggling out of a bulky old sweater that she had never seen before. She reached out to help him. She pulled the sweater away and his arms went round her.

'Oh, Val,' she said and began to cry a little. She sniffed and pulled away, to look at him.

99

'Hullo, darling,' he said. 'Are you all right?'

She was so shocked by the pinched, drawn look of his face that for a few seconds she did not notice the scratches and bruises, and when she did become aware of them, she instantly forgot them again because of something else she saw in his eyes; the same in-turned look she had glimpsed once before, by the buried church at Skagen.

Her impulse was to say: 'Val, what's happened? What's wrong?' but she suppressed it. She would get nothing out of him that way. Instead she said: 'Darling, you look famished. Come on.'

She opened the door into the living-room. It was warm and full of dancing shadows.

'I'm not really hungry,' he said.

'Well, I am and so is——' she patted her belly.

She sat down and began to help herself.

'Will you pour me a glass of wine, Val,' she said.

He did, and poured one for himself, then sat down as if he were a stranger in a strange place. Absently he forked some herring and *gravad laks* onto his plate and began to eat.

Rosa watched him covertly.

He looked up and said: 'Don't ask me a lot of questions, Rosa. I'm out for the count.'

'I haven't,' she said.

He smiled.

'No.'

'You might just tell me how you got those cuts on your face.'

'Ah – you should see the rest of me.'

'I can't wait.'

Their eyes met. Rosa smiled. He leaned over the table and kissed her.

Cold air on her back woke Rosa. She reached behind her to pull the blankets up round her neck and realized that Valdemar was not in bed with her. She got out of bed and hurried into a dressing-gown. It was bitterly cold.

She crept into the living-room. He was squatting by the stove, naked, staring into the embers of the fire – shivering. She went back to the bedroom and fetched a blanket. He didn't turn round as she returned to the living-room and draped the blanket round his shoulders.

'You'll get pneumonia,' she said.

'I couldn't sleep. I'm too tired to sleep.'

He pulled the blanket more tightly round him.

'Do you want to tell me about it now?' she said.

He continued to stare into the fire.

'Why not?' he said. 'I'm going away again tomorrow. No. Don't say anything. Just listen.'

He told her about Becker, about *Weseruebung*, about the station at Flensburg, the sentry at the border, Squire Tøller, Købke, Uncle Poul – everything. His voice was flat and matter-of-fact.

'After seeing Uncle Poul, I went straight back to Olsen. I asked him for a transfer to an anti-tank company in South Jutland. I leave tomorrow afternoon.'

'Valdemar – what about the baby?'

'What?'

'The baby. Hadn't you even thought about the baby?'

Now he turned and looked at her.

'You don't understand, do you Rosa?' he said.

—11—

At half-past nine in the morning of 7 April, Major Fritz Brenner strolled out of the Hotel Angleterre in Kongens Nytorv, acknowledging the doorman's polite 'Good day' with a pleasant nod.

The weather was clear and bright, with only a touch of cold, and it was a joy to be back in Copenhagen – it was without doubt his favourite city – but a joy tinged with a real feeling of guilt about the purpose of his visit.

At the briefing on the *Weseruebung* operation in Berlin Falkenhorst impressed on everybody the necessity of a swift success in Denmark. Denmark, he said, was the key to Norway, and Norway was the prize. If the Danes managed to hold up the German advance for as little as half a day, it would jeopardize the whole Norwegian campaign. Therefore they must be absolutely sure that Denmark would capitulate in a few hours.

'It is vital that we know what preparations, if any, the Danes have made to defend Copenhagen,' the battalion commander had said after the briefing.

'The simplest way of doing that would be to go to Copenhagen and have a look,' Brenner had suggested, only half seriously. But the battalion commander had raised an eyebrow and said: 'That is an excellent suggestion.'

So here he was, in a well-cut grey suit and with a camera slung round his neck to complete the picture of the leisured tourist.

He wandered up Amaliegade and into the gardens of The Citadel. A trim nursemaid was wheeling a pram along the gravelled walk, and an elderly lady was feeding scraps of bread to the ducks on one of the long, narrow ponds.

Brenner, who was something of an authority on military architecture, recognized the pattern of water and steep rises as a classic star-shaped stronghold of the seventeenth century. How delightfully typical of the Danes, he thought, that they had turned their defensive ditches into duck ponds and their ramparts into grass banks. The Danish impulse was to transform garrisons into pleasure-gardens. In Germany they tended to convert pleasure-gardens into garrisons.

To keep up the appearance of tourism – not that he had the slightest fear that anyone would suspect his true purpose – he walked down to the edge of the Sound to take a few statutory photographs of *Den lille Havefrue*, Eriksen's mawkish little bronze statue of a mermaid sitting on a rock. A silly, sentimental, but rather touching piece of work, he thought.

'Charming, is it not?' he said to a pretty young woman who was showing the celebrated sculpture to her children.

He followed the shoreline round and mounted the steps up to Langelinie pier. The two or three ships that were berthed there seemed lost in the great, straight length of the dock. He walked to the end and bought a coffee at the kiosk. There were one or two sailors idling about, but he resisted the temptation to pump them and drank his coffee quickly. Then he began to retrace his steps, walking more briskly, and with a purpose.

It took him less than ten minutes to reach the King's Gate, the main entrance to The Citadel. There was no guard at the old gate-house (built in 1663 according to the inscription over the arch, he noted), in fact there was nobody about at all. He sauntered through the tunnel-like gateway and emerged by a slender, octagonal sentry-box. It was painted a dull red, with the Royal emblem picked out in white. He thought its proportions were rather pleasing. It was empty. Ahead of him stretched two parallel blocks of barracks. The walls were red like the sentry-box and the window-shutters were white. The buildings looked spick and span.

Brenner was mildly astonished at the silence and the lack of activity. According to Intelligence this was the Headquarters of the Zealand Division of the Danish Army. It was also supposed to be the regional HQ of the 1st Infantry Regiment, Copenhagen, the General Staff HQ, and a lot of other things. But it had the air of a public monument, lovingly preserved but without a function.

It was not quite deserted though. A young private, in fatigue uniform, was coming towards him. Brenner produced a smile that was both tentative and engaging.

'Excuse me,' he said, 'is it permitted?'

His Danish was fluent, his accent almost flawless. He had been brought up on an estate near Glückstadt in Holstein. His nurse had been Danish.

'Oh yes, of course,' said the young soldier.

'May one take photographs? The buildings are so very fine.'

'Oh yes.'

Brenner, who had been a professional soldier since the age of eighteen, sensed immediately that the private was bored.

'I believe these blocks were built in 1664?' he said.

'I think so, yes.'

'And now your sergeant keeps you busy cleaning and painting them?'

The young soldier smiled.

'Sometimes,' he said.

'Ah – I know what it's like. I was in the army once.'

'Oh yes?'

'Yes. The German army. Terrible. All drill and punishment parades. One speck of dirt on your tunic button and – pah – fifty times round the parade ground, at the double, with a full pack on your back.'

'It's not so bad here.'

'No. I wish my father had been Danish and my mother German, instead of the other way round.'

103

This lie was intended to reassure the boy, in case he harboured any anti-German feelings. But he seemed to be without prejudices, and without very much guile. For all that he was intelligent. He had quite a knowledge of the history of The Citadel, and under the influence of Brenner's discreet flattery, he was only too eager to display it.

Half an hour later Brenner had completed a comprehensive tour of the place. He knew where the radio and telephone communications were housed, where the General Staff was quartered, and which gates were unguarded at night. He had also come to the conclusion that if Private Lauridsen (he had managed to extract the boy's name without giving his own) was in any way typical of the average Danish soldier, a lightning German victory was a foregone conclusion. It was not that Lauridsen was a coward, or that he lacked training or character; it was just that he was fundamentally a peaceable soul.

He reckoned that after such a satisfactory morning's work he deserved a very good luncheon and the Hotel Angleterre's chef did not let him down. So excellent was the smoked trout, in fact, that it engaged almost all his attention and he hardly noticed the very pretty girl who was sitting, alone, at the next table. But as he waited for the pressed duck to arrive he did notice her. She was tall, like so many Danish women, very blonde, and finely made. Once or twice she caught his eye and after a few moments he leaned over and said:

'I'm afraid it doesn't look as if he's going to turn up.'

The girl smiled and shrugged.

'I wouldn't mind – he's excessively boring – but it means that I'll go without lunch.'

There's a delightful openness about young Danes, Brenner thought. If a German girl had said such a thing he would have assumed that she was a whore. But this girl was no whore. The reason why she could not afford to pay for her own lunch was no doubt because she had already spent a very generous dress-allowance. She had *chic*.

'Shall we give your friend another five minutes before I very improperly invite you to join me?' he said.

She smiled.

'Impropriety should never be postponed,' she said. 'And if that isn't an old Danish proverb, it ought to be.'

He rose and bowed politely.

'Fritz Brenner,' he said.

'Karen Larsen.'

They shook hands and sat down. A waiter materialized. Karen ordered. Brenner poured her a glass of wine and lit a cigarette for her.

'What if your absent friend does eventually arrive?'

'I shall insist that he pay your bill.'

The next hour was a delight. Karen Larsen managed to talk about nothing very much with considerable wit and sophistication; she made him laugh. She was a society girl to the tips of her perfectly polished finger-nails, but there was nothing brittle or cold about her; on the contrary, she was warm and provocative. Brenner calculated that though an immediate invitation to his room might be refused (he had a train to catch in any case), after a dinner or two, and a little dancing, it would be accepted.

As they walked out of the restaurant into the foyer, she said:

'I'm sorry you're leaving this afternoon.'

'I shall be back in a few days. May I telephone you?'

'Yes. I'd like that.'

She scribbled the number on a scrap of paper. As she handed it to him she said:

'I wonder if you will.'

'You can be sure of it.'

He watched her walk away towards the glass doors. He could not help imagining, for a moment, what her body would look like stripped of that elegant silk dress. Then the feeling of guilt returned. This was such a charming place, with such charming people. It was horrible to have to deceive them. It was necessary of course – he had accepted the necessity of *Weseruebung* as he had accepted the necessity of the war itself – but, well, distasteful. He comforted himself with the thought that it would be very quick, very painless. There would be none of the excesses that, according to reports, had occurred in Poland. *Weseruebung* would shorten the war, that was the main thing. A few more victories – then peace.

12

Rosa had ringed 8 April in her diary as a possible date for the birth of her child. She had drawn a circle round the numeral in red crayon. Then she had added a smiling mouth underneath the '8' and two blue eyes on either side, so that the '8' became the chubby nose of a baby. To complete the doodle she had sketched in a frilly bonnet, framing the face. The diary lay open beside the telephone on a small table in the living-room. The telephone emitted its long, shrill, single ring.

Rosa heard the ring as she fitted her key into the lock on the front door. She made no attempt to hurry; she hadn't the energy. She had set out for her afternoon appointment at Dr Blum's clinic in Amagerbro feeling listless and tearful. Dr Blum had wanted her to stay at the clinic. 'You shouldn't be alone,' he'd said. She'd refused to stay. The journey back had been an endurance test; people had been kind, helping her on and off the tram or, as she saw it, heaving her about like a sack of flour. She'd meant to do some shopping but the thought of having to appear cheerful in front of the baker and the butcher, even for a few moments, had been too much for her. She wanted solitude and silence and sleep – God how she wanted sleep.

She opened the front door, went into the living-room, and picked up the phone; but the caller had given up. She was glad. She didn't want to talk to anybody. The face of the baby smiled up at her from the diary. She closed the book.

She slumped into a chair without bothering to take her coat off. She stared out of the window, watching the light fade. The stove was out. The room grew colder and colder. She wanted to go to bed, but the weight of the baby inside her was too much to heave out of the chair. She began to shiver. The tears which intermittently trickled from her eyes were like icicles on her cheek. She knew that the moment would come when she would have to make an effort – light the stove, cook herself some supper. She would probably telephone Dr Blum. He would send a car for her. Yes, that was what she ought to do; but what she wanted to do was to postpone the moment, postpone the decision, postpone everything.

She was shivering violently now. Vibrations from her teeth

filled her head. She knew that the cold was bad for the baby. In a minute she would light the stove. In just a minute.

There was banging in her head now – rap, rap, rap, rap – and someone was calling her name. She opened her eyes. She had been asleep. Was somebody there? No. There was silence. She had been dreaming. The room was dark. She must get up soon, she really must. A few more minutes of healing sleep and she would get up. She closed her eyes.

There was a rattle in the hall – or was it a rattle in her head? There it was again. There was somebody at the door. Valdemar. He musn't find her like this, sitting in the dark.

She levered herself out of the chair. Her legs were weak. She stumbled. She switched on the light and winced. Still those rattles from the front door. What was the matter with Valdemar? Why couldn't he open the door? She was feeling stronger now. She walked across the hall, supporting herself with a hand on the wall. She opened the door.

Mr Kristensen, the caretaker, was standing on the landing holding a big bunch of keys. He was a tiny man, Mr Kristensen. Beside him, in his thick, fur-collared coat, her father looked like a bear.

She was lying on her bed. Isak was bending over her, holding a mug from which steam was curling.

'Come on, drink it up,' he said.

He put an arm round her to help her sit up. She saw that Mr Kristensen was hovering in the doorway, looking lost and helpless.

The sweet tea scalded her tongue but she gulped at it, greedy for the heat.

'Gently now,' Isak said.

Rosa could see his breath as he spoke.

'Did I faint?' she said.

'Straight into my arms like a cinema heroine. Didn't she Mr Kristensen?'

The caretaker nodded and smiled.

'Drink up your tea,' Isak said. 'The sooner we get you out of this morgue the better.'

'Father, I don't understand. What are you doing here?'

'Taking you home.'

The tea had done much to restore Rosa. The helpless, drained feeling was going.

107

'This is my home,' she said. 'And it's not a morgue.'

'I was referring to the temperature. Now. Mr Kristensen, if you'd be so kind as to bring the case.'

Rosa had a sense that events were overtaking her. It made her cross.

'Wait a minute, Father. You can't just——'

'Doctor Blum says that on no account should you be left alone. You need warmth, rest, and good food and I'm damned well going to see that you get them.'

'Father, you have absolutely no right——'

'I have every right. Not as a father perhaps. But certainly as a grandfather to be. Now, come along. Jensine has cooked a fatted calf.'

Isak grinned at her. There were tiny points of light in his irises. Rosa suddenly realized how enormously she had missed him in the last few months. He helped her to climb off the bed. In his arms she felt totally safe, totally protected.

As a little girl she had once broken one of Isak's favourite things, a porcelain vase covered in dragons and Chinese people crossing bridges in the air. It had split into three big pieces and she had glued it together and so placed it back in its glass-fronted cabinet that you could not tell, from looking at it, that it was broken. Weeks of misery had followed. She had known that one day her father would take the vase out of the cabinet and discover the deception, and she had come to dread the sound of his key in the latch. In the end, she had screwed up all her courage and told him the truth. She had immediately felt a sense of almost physical relief; and this was exactly what she felt now, as she leaned on his arm and he helped her into the hall, across the landing and down the steep, narrow stairs.

Mr Kristensen switched off the lights in the flat, locked the front door, and followed Isak and Rosa down to the street, where Isak's car was parked. In the flat, the telephone rang again. The sound echoed briefly in the empty living-room, then died.

Valdemar replaced the receiver, then picked it up again and spoke to the girl on the switchboard.

'Could you find me a Copenhagen number? Doctor Joachim Blum. Somewhere in Amagerbro. It's urgent.'

He put the receiver back and lit what must have been his

108

sixtieth cigarette of the day. He was furious with Rosa and desperately worried. What made it worse was that there was just no time to spend tracking her down and finding out what was going on. Momentous things were happening in the world, things that demanded every bit of his concentration.

It seemed as if he had spent the whole day with his ear pressed to the warm, greasy bakelite of the telephone receiver. He had been in half-hourly contact with Olsen. In the morning Intelligence had received a report from an agent in Rendsburg that the invasion was due to start at either 4 p.m. in the afternoon, or at 4 a.m. in the morning of the ninth. Local reports had flooded into his little office. Panzers of the 11th German Motorized Rifle Brigade and the 170th Infantry Division, clearly identified by *Isted* agents operating out of Süderlüngum and Neukirchen, were massing along the border. The growl of Panzers and armoured cars had even been heard by local farmers.

And still no mobilization order had arrived from Copenhagen. 4 p.m. had come and gone, with no sign of a German advance. Olsen had rung through from Proviantgaarden. Virtually every senior intelligence officer in the army was bombarding the General Staff with requests to mobilize. The Cabinet was refusing to budge.

At seven o'clock the local commander, Colonel Holm, had summoned his officers to a briefing. Valdemar had attended, as Intelligence Liaison Officer. The Government had authorized a State of Alarm in South Jutland, but were still holding out against a general mobilization, the Colonel had announced. After the meeting Valdemar had asked Holm for a transfer to a front-line platoon. 'I'll consider it,' Holm had said.

The telephone rang. Valdemar snatched it up. It was not Dr Blum but Colonel Holm.

'Ah, Larsen. I want you to take over from Lieutenant Johansen. The adjutant will brief you.'

'Thank you, sir.'

He rang through to the switchboard.

'My call to Copenhagen.'

'Oh, yes,' the girl said, 'I'm having difficulty.'

'Don't worry. Cancel it.'

Poul Larsen very rarely attended the theatre. The dimming of the lights in the auditorium always induced a corresponding somnolence in him, which the discomfort of the average theatre seat then frustrated. He would wriggle and doze and long for the padded comfort of his own armchair. But there had been no getting out of it tonight. One could not refuse an invitation to dine at the King's table and join his party at the Royal Theatre afterwards, even after an exhausting day of invasion scares and emergency Cabinet meetings.

He had rather dreaded the dinner, fearing that the conversation would centre exclusively on the current obsession with doom; but not a bit of it. They had certainly discussed the latest sensation from Norway – the sinking, by a Polish submarine, of a German transport ship apparently full of Wehrmacht soldiers – and had speculated on the possibility that Hitler might be contemplating some military adventure in Norway; but the King had pooh-poohed any idea of a similar assault against Denmark. King Christian's cheerfulness, his solid good sense, had reassured Poul, who had been a little disturbed by his nephew's outburst and more than a little rattled by the panic prevailing in Proviantgaarden.

The King had laughed heartily throughout the opera – *The Merry Wives of Windsor*, an idiotic piece of nonsense, in Poul's view – and he had been particularly gracious to Poul.

As he walked back home after the performance – it was quite a hike, but he needed exercise – Poul still felt something of a glow, a glow of love for the good, kindly, unaffected old man he had served for twenty years. He had always felt a deep respect for King Christian, he had often felt reverence, but rarely such an intimate tenderness. This feeling of tenderness extended to his physical surroundings. It was late; there was a hush over the city; a faint breeze breathed in the plane trees that lined Frederiksberg Alle like sentinels; the breath of sleep, Poul thought – soft and regular. He stopped for a moment to listen. He felt tired; but, for once, it was not the stale tiredness of the sedentary but a healthy tiredness, such as he had known as a boy. Yes, the breath of sleep. It seemed to emanate not from the breeze but from the dark masses of the buildings themselves, as if the very bricks and stones were slumbering.

Poul smiled to himself and walked on. He was getting fanciful in his old age. But, there again, it was good to have a moment like this occasionally, a moment of silent communion with the city. It was healing, like the quiet companionableness of one's own fireside after a hectic day, with a book on one's knee, and one's pipe drawing well, and the soothing, regular clicks of one's wife's knitting needles. In a way, he thought, the city was as sure and unchanging as a wife.

There were nights when Old Johan's withered leg gave him pain. His method of combating the pain was to walk on the leg. He was convinced that if he rested it he would lose the use of it. After all, that was how he'd saved the leg in the first place, all those years ago, by telling the doctors to go to hell and walking on it. By God, yes.

He took his heavy night-glasses (a present from Mr Niels) from their leather case and hobbled out of his den onto the dock. When the pain was bad he liked to distract himself by slowly raking every inch of the outer harbour through the glasses. The lenses were powerful; sometimes he'd spot a sea-bird bobbing on the water and it would seem so close he felt he could stroke its feathers.

When he trained the glasses on Langelinie it was as if one stride could take him clean over the Sound to stand on the opposite side. It was this strange perspective that helped. It took him away from himself, away from the throb in his leg.

He leaned against the wall of No. 7, put the glasses to his eyes, and adjusted the focus. The treetops of The Citadel gardens sprang at him. He tilted his head down to explore the water for sleeping birds, but could find nothing except silky, black wavelets. Very slowly he turned his head to the right. The string of lights along Langelinie swam past him, then the cranes of the Free Port and then, as he bent his head again and stroked the focus dial, he saw the ship.

He lowered the glasses. He took out his pocket watch. It was half-past four. Old Johan was puzzled. He had an encyclopaedic knowledge of the arrivals and departures of ships, and there were few vessels putting into Copenhagen regularly that he could not recognize. But this ship was a stranger. Moreover, she was heading for Langelinie and that was out of all order. He put the glasses to his eyes again. He could read the name on her side. *Hansestadt Danzig.* He'd never heard of her.'

His arms were growing tired. He lowered the glasses again. The pain in his leg was acute. This was no good; he must walk, walk. He picked up his stick. He'd go right round the perimeter of the yards; and he must remember, in the morning, to enquire about the *Hansestadt Danzig.*

Rosa tried not to cry out. The pains in her back were awful – and they were coming more and more regularly. She switched on the bedside lamp and looked at the clock. Twenty to five. Should she wake Father? No. It was all right; the pain had gone.

The door opened. It was Isak. He was wearing his green and blue silk dressing-gown over trousers.

'I saw your light on,' he said. 'Is everything all right?'

'I think I'll last until morning,' she said, then gasped at another contraction.

'Don't get dressed,' Isak said. 'Put a coat on over your night things. I'm just going to ring the clinic.'

Rosa climbed out of bed. Her case was already packed; she closed the lid and slid the catches; she put on her coat. Jensine appeared, in her black and white uniform.

'Are they coming regular?' Jensine asked.

Rosa nodded. 'I think so. Haven't you been to bed Jensine?'

Isak came into the room. He had changed into a jacket.

'There's no need to panic,' he said. 'But we should get you to the clinic as soon as possible. Come along. Jensine, will you bring the case?'

The pains hit her again as they came out of the elevator and crossed the hall. She was frightened, suddenly, but reassured by Isak's arm round her. The car was waiting outside. Jensine helped her in and Isak started up the engine. He seemed so cool, and efficient, and in command.

'Don't worry,' he said. 'There's plenty of time.'

Isak drove out of Fridtjof Nansens Plads into Østbanegade.

'When you were on the way we had to rush your mother to hospital in a carriage and pair at three in the morning. There was no petrol because of the war.'

'Why do babies always arrive at such ungodly hours?'

'Ah, but it's good to see the dawn come up from time to time.'
Isak turned left into Grønningen.

The pains came again. Rosa clenched her teeth and shut her eyes. She felt the car slow down and stop. She opened her eyes and looked at Isak.

'Father?'

He was staring through the windscreen. She was aware of a curious noise, a rapid crunch, crunch, crunch, like soldiers marching. She looked out of the window. Ahead, Bredgade was swarming with green uniforms and glinting helmets. Troops were pouring out of The Citadel gardens. A motorbike buzzed by, then another. She heard a hollow rattle of gunfire, a completely extraordinary sound.

'Is it an exercise?' she said, knowing it couldn't be.

Two soldiers were running towards the car.

'Father – what is it? What's happening?'

One of the soldiers was peering in through the window; a square, scared face framed in steel. There was another, at the other window. He was shouting – in German. She suddenly realized that her father was replying in German. His voice sounded calm only there was a pleading note in it that seemed alien. The soldier was gesticulating, he was telling them to get away, get away.

Isak scraped the car into gear. Immediately the car leaped forward with a jolt and suddenly they were wheeling right, with a squeak of rubber, into Toldbodvej, then left. Even above the noise of the roaring engine Rosa could hear the gunfire. She knew that it must be coming from Amalienborg, from the King's palace.

Suddenly everything connected: the troops, the gunfire, the soldier shouting. It was the invasion that her grandfather had foreseen, that Valdemar had predicted, and it was happening, right now, under the very windows of the room where old Reuben had died.

Isak's face was suety and he seemed in some subtle way to have shrunk. There was another brief, distant tut-tut-tut of gunfire from the direction of the palace. Rosa turned to Isak.

'Hurry, Father, hurry.'

'Yes, yes.'

He accelerated out of Kongens Nytorv and turned left, down

towards Knippels bridge. A little colour had come back into his face.

'My God,' he said, 'what a world to bring a child into.'

Valdemar knew exactly what he had to do. It was like one of those moments of clarity one sometimes experienced in a game of chess, when not only were the next moves suddenly obvious, but the whole pattern of the game seemed inevitable. The first moment of prescience had come a few moments after dawn when the Panzers had appeared, 800 metres away across the flat fields. He'd observed them through his glasses, watched how their tracks sliced through the soft, green turf of Denmark like a butcher's circular knife through a ham. Sergeant Lund had been standing beside him, solid, dependable and sanguine.

'How do they think we're going to stop that lot?' he'd said.

Valdemar had looked at the little knots of men huddled round their 81 mm infantry mortars.

'There's not much fight in 'em,' Lund had remarked.

A minute later a despatch rider had appeared with orders to withdraw.

Valdemar had turned to Lund.

'What if I chose to ignore this?'

'Then there'd be just the two of us left here, sir.'

The second moment of prescience had come back at HQ, a few minutes after half-past six. Colonel Holm had strode into the mess as if he were announcing a victory.

'Well, gentlemen. It's official. The ceasefire was agreed a few minutes ago. An honourable surrender.'

The others had clustered round him, leaving Valdemar standing alone, looking out through a window at two privates unloading an ammunition truck on the far side of the parade-ground.

It was then that he knew exactly what he had to do. It was then that he saw that he must not take the five or six paces across the room that would bring him into the circle of his brother officers, who were firing excited questions at Holm. If he did that he would be stepping into the zone of 'honourable surrender', aiding and abetting a contradiction in terms. No. He must stand apart; he must walk away, he must act alone.

He found Sergeant Lund in his quarters and drew him outside.

There were men running from building to building, men standing about in chattering groups. Lund was willing but hesitant. Valdemar insisted.

'Now, sergeant, we must do it now, while everyone's still running round in circles. Before the Germans get here.'

Lund thought, then said:

'Very well, sir. It's worth a try.'

They walked briskly together across the parade-ground towards the armoury. The ammunition truck Valdemar had spotted from the window of the officers' mess was still being unloaded. Unsupervised, and unsure of what was going on, the two young rookies who had been assigned this task were working at a desultory pace. They were easy meat for Lund.

'All right, you two. Cut along back to barracks.'

'But sarge, Captain———'

'Sonny, we may have just lost a war, but I've still got more on my sleeve than you'll have if you live to be a hundred. Now move. At the double.'

They moved, and Valdemar thanked God for Lund's natural air of authority. The back of the truck was still half full. There were boxes of TNT, crates of grenades, Madsen light machine guns, and ammunition. Valdemar picked out a Madsen and a couple of spare clips.

'You drive,' he said to Lund.

They climbed into the cab and Lund started her up. Valdemar was aware that their movements could be observed from the mess. He didn't give a damn. They skirted the parade ground and took the dirt track between the main barrack blocks, then turned right and headed for the gate. The pole was down.

'Do we bluff it out?' Lund asked Valdemar.

'To hell with that,' Valdemar said.

Lund grinned. He gunned the engine and changed down. There were shouts and an explosive crack as the heavy truck brushed the pole aside.

The road down to the village was crowded with soldiers straggling back to base on bicycles and on foot. They stared at the truck as it ground past them and disappeared round the bend. Valdemar could see a baker's van ahead, coming towards them, blocking the way. The van had been commandeered by a group of border gendarmerie. There were men on the roof, men hanging out of the back. Lund kept his hand on the horn and Valdemar leaned out of the cab shouting at them to pull over. As they scraped past the van Valdemar heard someone shout: 'You're crazy. The Fritzies are in the village.'

Lund accelerated away and Valdemar quickly checked and loaded the Madsen.

He shouted to Lund: 'Stop just before the next bend.'

The road ran straight for a kilometre, then veered sharply right towards the village. It was empty. They pounded down it. Valdemar noticed a farm track leading off to the right. Lund brought her up just before the corner. Valdemar jumped out and ran ten paces to the right-angled bend. Using a big elm that stood on the verge for cover he peered round the corner so that his eyes could confirm what his ears had already told him. Four hundred metres ahead lay the first few houses of the village. The leading armoured car in a long column of mixed infantry and tanks was just drawing abreast of them.

'Look at those fucking bastards.'

He felt Lund's hot breath on his ear.

Two Danish Nazis, middle-aged men dressed in their best suits, with swastika armbands, were flagging down the armoured car. One of them held up a bunch of flowers. A German officer took it. The Nazis were gesticulating, pointing up the road towards Battalion HQ.

'Those fuckers are showing them the way.'

'Come on,' Valdemar said.

They raced back to the truck. Lund began to turn her round. The road was narrow; he wrestled with the wheel. The tyres whined and spun on the damp grass verge. Then they were round and blinding back the way they had come.

'Farm track, on your left, two hundred metres,' Valdemar yelled. Lund nodded. Valdemar hung out of the window, looking back down the straight: no sign of the German column yet. The lurch, as Lund swung onto the farm track, nearly flung him out of the cab. They plunged down the track, between high hedges, the wheels bouncing and juddering in the stone-filled ruts.

The track ended in a square concrete yard with open-sided barns on three sides. Lund brought the truck to a halt and turned to Valdemar.

'And now what?'

Valdemar fumbled inside his battle-dress tunic and pulled out a large-scale field map. He spread the map on the seat between them.

'We can cut across country on farm roads – look,' he traced the route with a finger, 'and come out on the back road to Rens. From there it's only three kilometres.'

'All right,' Lund said. 'But first things first.'

He climbed out of the truck, walked a few paces away and turned his back. Valdemar suddenly realized that his own bladder was bursting. He jumped out of the cab and stood by Lund. They relieved themselves in companionable silence.

As he buttoned himself up Lund said:

'We'll never do it.'

'We will. And if we get stuck we'll damned well bury the stuff in a wood.'

At first Valdemar thought he would keep a count of the number of gates he opened, but after about the twentieth he gave up. Three times the truck's wheels buried themselves in mud and he struggled with stones and brush-wood and levers improvised from fences. They did not see a soul; the fields were utterly deserted and the few farm houses they passed were silent and shuttered. After an hour they reached a road. Valdemar made Lund wait in the cover of a spinney while he carried out a quick reconnaissance on foot. There was no sign of a German patrol or road block, but even so, they proceeded slowly, stopping at every blind corner to check the way ahead.

Thus it was that they saw the Germans before the Germans saw them. Four hundred metres ahead there was a cross-roads. A motor-bicycle, with side-car, was stationary on the verge by the finger-post and two German soldiers were pacing casually, smoking. Valdemar and Lund ran back to the truck and conferred briefly; then Valdemar took the Madsen and climbed over a gate into the field that bordered the road. He moved very carefully, at the crouch, along the hedge.

He heard the murmur of the Germans' voices and dropped flat on the ground, covering the last few metres on his stomach. He peered through a gap in the hedge. The Germans were perhaps thirty paces away. He waited.

It was when he heard the noise of the truck and saw the Germans react, swinging their guns up into a firing position, that

117

he felt his throat cease to burn and calm descend on him. He saw the truck slow down and stop and Lund get out and walk towards the Germans with his hands in the air. The Germans were standing almost shoulder to shoulder – a textbook target. All their concentration was on Lund.

He opened fire when Lund was still a good twenty paces from the Germans. The Madsen jigged in his hands – it was a beautiful feeling, controlling it. A narrow arc of bullets scythed the Germans off the road as swiftly and cleanly as wind whipping foam off a wave-crest.

Fifteen minutes later they turned in at the high gates of Vidlund. There was a red graze on Lund's cheek from where he had thrown himself flat on the road a second after Valdemar had opened fire. He had been curiously uncommunicative since, and his silence had put a damper on Valdemar's exhilaration. As they drove through the park, where the deer were cropping the grass under the elms, Lund said:

'I've been in the army for twenty years but this is the first time I've ever seen men killed.'

'Well, this is the first time we've been at war.'

'It's going to be a bloody funny war with only you and me fighting it.'

Bredgade seemed to be carpeted with buff-coloured leaflets. There was no traffic, and very few people about; the street, littered and deserted, reminded Niels of an empty stadium after a football match. The leaflets had been dropped by formations of Luftwaffe planes that had swooped low over the city soon after dawn. The drone of them had woken Niels. From his bedroom window he'd watched them wheel and dive over the Sound like huge grey gulls.

The whole household had huddled round the wireless set in the morning room – Christina and Karen, in their night-clothes; the cook, the butler, and the chauffeur. Both Christina and the cook had cried.

An overwhelming need to be at the centre of events had impelled Niels to get dressed and cycle to the office. He had not known what to expect – shooting, bodies in the streets, road-blocks, German tanks? In fact there had been a sort of Christmas atmosphere: closed shops, sparse motor traffic, complete

118

strangers greeting each other, albeit only to exchange terse speculations.

He bent down and picked up one of the leaflets.

OPROP!
Til Danmarks Soldater og Danmarks Folk!
Uten Grund og imot den tyske Regjerings og det tyske Folks oprigtige Ønske, om at leve i Fred og Venskab med det engleske og det franske Folk …

His initial reaction was that this was illiterate nonsense, a linguistic hotch-potch of bad Danish, bad Norwegian, and bad German; but as he read on he felt almost like laughing out loud. If the language was stilted and juvenile, like a fifteen-year-old's school exercise, the content was preposterous. According to the leaflet, the beneficent German people had stepped in to help out their Danish neighbours, to 'protect' them from the warmongering machinations of Churchill and the English. There was much more, in the same vein, and then, at the end, an exhortation to the Danes to accept the situation, to go about their work in a normal way and to obey their Government and the German commander, Kaupisch.

Niels glanced up. A small squad of German soldiers had turned out of Frederiksgade and were marching towards him. He suddenly felt like making a protest, even if only a symbolic one. He wanted to tear up the leaflet, very slowly and deliberately, and then scatter the pieces in front of the soldiers as they passed, to give them back some of their own rotten confetti. The Germans marched past him. Not one of them cast so much as a casual glance in his direction. Only when they had passed out of sight, into Toldbodvej, did he crumple up the leaflet and throw it into the gutter.

He let himself into the office and went straight to his own room. The telephone seemed to be functioning quite normally and he dialled his brother's private number, hungry for information. Anna answered. Poul had been summoned to the Palace in the early hours and had not returned. She did not know where he was. Niels dialled the Red House but the line was engaged. After two or three minutes it was still engaged.

He went out into the street again and walked down to Kongens

Nytorv. There were more people about now, in fact there seemed to be hundreds of them, drifting in towards the centre of the capital, drawn together by the need to share their bewilderment and shock. Strøget was thronged and buzzing. Niels talked to old acquaintances and to complete strangers. He listened to the Cassandras who predicted the 'ruin of everything', to the wiseacres who had 'seen this coming months ago', and to the humorists — thank God for them. A young man kicking at a pile of *Oprop* leaflets muttered, 'Watch out, there's a lot of bird-shit about this morning.'

As he was wandering down towards the Cathedral he was approached by a short, unkempt individual whose face was faintly familiar.

'Larsen? Niels Larsen?'

The man was smiling lopsidedly.

'We don't know each other, but I am Isak Abrahamsen's brother.'

Niels found himself shaking the man's hand.

'Forgive me, but I was wondering if you had any news of your son? We have been trying to contact him.'

'No. I don't know where he is.'

'Perhaps you have not heard — about his wife, my niece?'

Again that smile — what an odd fellow.

'She gave birth to a son this morning, a few hours ago.'

'A son?'

'Yes. You are a grandfather. And I suppose that I am a great uncle.' He went on, with a rush: 'Look, my house is just here. Will you come in and have a cup of coffee? Please?'

'Well, I——'

'Please.'

Niels followed Isak's brother down four steps into one of those dark semi-subterranean bookshops with which Fioldstraede was cluttered. They passed through the shop, into a big room behind that was heaped with books, then up a narrow stair, and into another big room crammed with books and pictures. There was a young man, dressed only in a pair of pyjama trousers. Isak's brother spoke to him.

'Will you make us some coffee, dear boy?'

He turned to Niels. 'That's The Viking. He makes an excellent cup of coffee. Won't you sit down?'

Niels sat down, blinking.

'Everything seems strange and unreal this morning,' Abel said.

'Yes. Er − is your niece well? And the baby?'

'Both flourishing, according to Isak. The baby weighs—— I don't remember exactly but it sounded remarkably hefty.'

There was an awkward silence which Niels was at a loss to know how to fill.

Abel said: 'There was one drama − on the way to the clinic. Isak was driving her. They turned a corner, and came face to face with half the German army.'

'Really?'

'It's a wonder Rosa didn't give birth on the spot.'

The youth reappeared, carrying a tray. He set it down on a table, then vanished. Abel busied himself with pouring coffee. Niels refused his offer of a cake.

Abel suddenly said: 'I'm sorry − but I have to talk to someone. What's going to happen?'

'Well, I − it's surely too early——'

'I mean to people like me. To Jews.'

Niels was suddenly struck by the difference between this man and his brother: Abel was constantly running his fingers through his hair, scratching his scalp, making gestures he would never have associated with Isak.

'I went out an hour or so ago, I suppose,' Abel said, 'I don't know why. I should have stayed indoors. I went down to Raadhusplads. I saw a whole lot of them marching across the square. I felt sick, literally sick, but I wanted to run towards them and beg them to take me away, at once, I wanted to get it over with.'

He laughed and began fumbling with a tin of tobacco and cigarette papers.

'I apologize,' he said. 'I'm embarrassing you.'

'No, no.'

'Well I am certainly embarrassing myself. You see I have been waiting for this to happen for months, trying to make myself believe that it would not happen, but knowing that it was inevitable. I even thought of getting out, going away somewhere safe, and at the same time I kept making the excuse that I couldn't think of anywhere safe to go. Nobody else seemed worried. I was ashamed to voice my fears. I can't think why.'

The tin of tobacco slipped out of his hands and fell onto the carpet.

'You see what a state I'm in? My instinct tells me to pack a bag and get onto the first ship to Sweden. But of course I won't. I'll just sit here, shaking, until they come for me. I wonder why?'

Niels cleared his throat.

'We don't know what German intentions are. From everything I've heard it seems that the Government has remained intact. I have no doubt that we can reach an accommodation of some sort. I'm sure nothing will happen immediately.'

Abel appeared to be less agitated.

'Perhaps you're right. Would you like some more coffee? Or a *snaps* perhaps? The situation would seem to justify a *snaps*.'

'No. No, thank you. I really ought to be getting along.'

Niels rose and Abel rose with him.

'It was kind of you to listen,' Abel said.

'I'm a poor listener, I'm afraid.'

Abel smiled.

'Not at all.' He hesitated, then said: 'You know, you've always been something of a bogey-man to my family. I'm glad to have met you.'

'Perhaps,' Niels said, 'perhaps if you could give me the address – where your niece is. If my son should contact me——'

'Of course.'

Abel scribbled on the back of one of his headed invoice sheets and handed it to Niels.

'Well, goodbye then,' Niels said, offering his hand.

'I'll see you out.'

'No, no. I can find my own way.'

As he passed through the room behind the shop Niels recognized one of the books lying, open, on a table. It was a fat, handsomely bound volume from the complete edition of Oehlenschlaeger's plays; he had an identical set at home. He picked the book up and glanced at the page. The paper had that softened, yellowed quality that comes from reading and re-reading, and for a moment the familiar cadences of the first act of *Hagbarth og Signe* echoed in his head. It struck him as odd that Isak Abrahamsen's brother should share his own taste for Oehlenschlaeger's romantic visions of the dawn of Nordic history, for the poetry of myth and tragedy. He weighed the book in his hand. Extraordinary; it might be his own copy.

At six, the nurse brought the child to her.

'Just for half an hour,' the nurse said.

Rosa had been dozing. The voice from the wireless had been droning in and out of her dreams all through the afternoon, urging the Danish people to act 'correctly' towards the invaders, and justifying the Government's hasty and abject capitulation by claiming that it had saved the country from worse ravages and destruction. None of it had seemed to matter.

She asked the nurse to switch the wireless off and draw the curtains. She didn't want to hear or see or know what was going on outside. It didn't seem to matter either. Nothing mattered but the child sleeping in her arms. She looked down at his little, puckered Chinese face and the crop of thick dark hair on his head. 'Never seen such a head of hair on a child in my life,' Dr Blum had said. She remembered that moment of total lucidity, in the midst of the pain and fear of the birth, when she had seen this head for the first time, before the cord was cut, and had recognized it, yes recognized it as one recognizes a face in a crowd. A son! If only Grandpapa had lived to see me bear a son, she thought.

She remembered her grandfather lying in his bed, propped up on pillows just as she was propped now, telling her about his dream of the Odessa catacombs. At odd moments in the last few months she had been haunted by his image of the stones of the houses, quarried from the tunnels in which he was hiding, carrying the echoes of his footsteps, and she had seen it as expressing a particular form of dread. Now she saw it differently, as an expression of the relationship that already existed between herself and her son. Because his flesh had been hewn from her flesh, because he had lain in her belly as stone lies in the belly of the earth, she felt that his footsteps would always echo through her life.

But inevitably, as she remembered old Reuben's dream, she also remembered his warning and the prophecy he had made, the prophecy which had been fulfilled that very morning on his own doorstep. She had seen it, she had been there, yet for some reason she could feel no apprehension, neither for herself nor for her son. It was irrational, but she believed that so long as she devoted

123

every bit of her energy to nurturing her child, they would both be safe.

The door opened and Isak came in. His skin looked grey and there was no trace of lustre in his eyes. Rosa mimed for him to be quiet. He came over to the bed and kissed her.

'I know,' he said softly, 'don't wake the baby. That constituted your mother's sole topic of conversation when you were his age.' He pointed to his grandson.

'Any news, Father?'

Isak sighed. 'Well, I 'phoned his commanding officer at Proviantgaarden — Captain Olsen? — it took me ages to get through. They knew nothing, except that his name hasn't appeared on any of the casualty lists. Then I tried his father. No reply from his office. I went round there and found the place deserted. It's the same all over the city. Nobody knows whether he's coming or going.'

'It's hardly surprising. I'm not really worried.'

Isak touched the baby's cheek very lightly.

'You had a powerful pair of lungs when you were tiny. We lived in Strandboulevarden in those days, in a flat with paper-thin walls. One night our neighbour couldn't stand it any more and came round and knocked on the door. "Would you please keep that boy quiet", he said.'

Rosa smiled. There was a light knock on the door.

'I expect that's the nurse,' Rosa said.

Isak went over to the door and opened it. It was not the nurse. It was Niels Larsen. The two grandfathers stared at each other for a moment. Niels was holding a bedraggled looking plant in a pot.

'Er, I've brought this,' Niels said. 'I had to take it from the garden. I couldn't find a florist open anywhere.'

'Please come in.'

Niels advanced awkwardly into the room and Isak closed the door behind them.

'Rosa,' he said, 'this is Valdemar's father.'

Niels made a helpless gesture with the flower pot.

'It's from my garden,' he said. 'It's not very much, I'm afraid.'

'It's lovely — so much nicer, having come from your garden.'

'Shall I put it in the window? Oh, thank you.'

Isak had taken the pot from him. He placed it on the window sill.

'Have you heard anything from Valdemar?' Niels said.

'You knew he was at the front?' Rosa asked.

'No. I had no idea.'

'I think he must be all right. I think we would have heard if he'd been hurt.'

'Yes. I'm sure he'll turn up. Everything's in such a confusion.'

'We ran into the Germans as they were attacking the Palace,' Isak said.

'Your brother told me.'

'Abel?'

'Yes. We met in Strøget. He invited me in for a cup of coffee.'

'Good lord,' said Isak.

There was an edgy silence, which none of them knew quite how to break. The impasse was resolved when the baby woke and began to cry feebly. Rosa conjured up a laugh.

'Perhaps it's feeding time.'

'Yes, well, I should be going,' Niels said. 'I only looked in to see – to see that everything was all right.'

'Would you like to hold him for a moment?' Rosa said suddenly.

Niels looked a little startled, but he stepped forward and took the baby from Rosa. Rosa noticed how he held the child so that his head was supported in the crook of his arm; they looked quite natural together, she thought. The baby even stopped crying for a moment.

'You seem to have the magic touch,' she said.

Niels smiled and looked at the baby, who immediately started to cry again, more lustily this time.

'Only temporarily, I'm afraid.'

Carefully he handed the bundle back to Rosa.

'Will you tell Valdemar I came?' he said.

'Of course.'

Isak stepped up to the bed.

'I must be going too,' he said. 'I'll see you in the morning.'

He kissed Rosa and briefly rubbed the baby's cheek with the back of his index finger. Niels and Isak left the room together. As they walked down the corridor they could still hear the baby's cries.

'Valdemar was just the same,' Niels said. 'A pair of lungs like a drill sergeant.'

Isak shot him a curious, sidelong look.

They crossed the hall of the clinic and Isak said: 'I have my car. Can I drop you anywhere?'

'No, no. Thank you.'

'Well, good night.'

They shook hands. Isak turned away but stopped when Niels said:

'Um, your brother. He seemed to be in a bit of a state – about the fact that you are Jews. He's worried that the Germans may – take measures.'

'My brother Abel is rather an unstable character.'

'I just wanted to say that if there is – anything of that kind, well, I might possibly be able to help.'

'I'm sure it won't be necessary.'

'I hope not.'

'Thank you, all the same. Good night.'

'Good night.'

Fritz Brenner found himself billeted in the Hotel Angleterre where, forty-eight hours ago, he had reserved and paid for a room. He had dined with General Himer and other senior officers – an intoxicating climax to one of the most extraordinary days of his life. It had begun well before dawn when his orderly had shaken him in his bunk on the *Hansestadt Danzig*, just before they entered Danish territorial waters. They'd steamed down the Sound, unchallenged, and tied up at Langelinie as if they were mooring a rowing boat on the banks of the Wannsee. His company had entered The Citadel at five minutes to five, and by five minutes past five the entire garrison of seventy men had been taken, without a shot having been fired.

There'd been a bit of a skirmish round the Palace, where men from the crack Royal Danish Life Guards had put up a courageous and determined resistance; but of course the real battle, the psychological one, was already being lost inside the Palace, and inside the heads of King Christian and his bewildered Ministers, who, a short hour before, had been the dazed recipients of the German ultimatum, delivered in person by old Renthe-Fink, the German Minister in Denmark. The Luftwaffe's aerial demonstration had served very effectively to drive the point home to the Danes: capitulate or see your capital reduced to rubble within the

126

hour. By twenty minutes past six he had been back on the *Hanse-stadt Danzig* supervizing wireless broadcasts from the ship's big transmitter to all fighting units of the Danish army, informing them of the surrender and advising them to lay down their arms.

The atmosphere on board had been heady all through the morning as reports from other parts of Denmark had flooded in: the Danes routed in South Jutland, the airfields at Aalborg seized by the paras, and best of all – what a roar of laughter this news had provoked – the entire island of Funen captured by one motorcycle patrol! Colossal!

The laughter – so coarse – had irked him. He'd wanted to protest that the Danes were a civilized, peaceable people who had been grossly betrayed, but at the same time he hadn't been able to suppress a feeling of pride that, once again, the German army had proved itself to be the most effective fighting force in Europe. According to Himer, who had had an audience at the Palace before dinner, even King Christian had expressed his admiration for the Wehrmacht's magnificent work.

He picked up the scrap of paper that lay on the bedside table and turned it over and over in his hand. Karen Larsen. What would she be feeling tonight? Hating Germany and the Germans, no doubt. The question was: would the feeling last? Would the Danes learn to live with their new masters? He hoped so, hoped so desperately. It was the only way, after all.

He put the paper into a drawer. He would give it a week or two, then he would telephone the girl. Yes, he would definitely telephone her

14

On 9 May the beech leaves budded in Copenhagen. A swastika fluttered over The Citadel; the Royal Life Guards on sentry duty at the Amalienborg Palace had abandoned their busbies, blue-grey trousers, black tunics, and white webbing for Model 23 steel helmets and battle-dress; the shops were thronged with German soldiers, greedy for the luxuries they had not seen at home for years and buying on credit; but these were minor intrusions into the even tenor of life in the capital, small reminders of how, a month ago, everything had changed.

The only change that people outwardly acknowledged was this change in the season; the Government's advice to maintain 'an absolutely correct and dignified behaviour' towards the invaders had been widely interpreted as a licence to pretend that the Germans did not exist. After all, the policy of the blind eye and the cold shoulder had been sanctioned at the very highest level: in his regular morning rides through the streets of his capital, King Christian acknowledged the greetings of his loyal subjects with a regal wave of the hand while, with the bland aplomb of a sovereign, he contrived to remain oblivious to the deferential salutes smartly snapped at him by German soldiers, who were under strict orders to show respect for the Danish monarch at all times.

Thus people were able to bury their hatred so deep that the surface of their lives could remain level and their self-respect intact. But the hatred was there, like a reef hidden by quiet water, only waiting for some unprecedented tide to expose it. There were those – a few – who could not bury it, whose rage coloured every waking moment, who wanted to drag back the water *now*: lunatics in a word.

One such was Valdemar Larsen; and Captain Olsen was somewhat puzzled about how best to deal with him. He himself was prepared to bide his time and await events. He thought that there was a hot, lean look about Valdemar as he came into the office, almost as if he were ill.

'I have good news for you, Lieutenant,' he said, as he waved Valdemar to a chair. 'I have managed to hush up your little escapade with the ammunition truck. No action will be taken against you or Sergeant Lund, who has received a severe reprimand from his Colonel. I have been ordered to issue the same to you.' He smiled. 'Consider yourself reprimanded.'

Valdemar managed to return the smile, but there was no warmth in it.

'Thank you, sir,' he said.

'You should thank me. I had to smooth a great many ruffled quarter-masterly feathers. I even got them to believe in your absurd claim that the truck had been seized by a German patrol and that you and Lund had fled across the fields like rabbits.'

'Or like Danish soldiers in the face of the enemy.'

Olsen raised an eyebrow. 'General Prior has officially praised the attitude and conduct of the Danish army.'

'I know, sir. He's also told us that we can look everybody straight in the eye, having bravely done our duty.'

'So you can.'

'Can I sir? The first thing I did when I got home from the front was to go and see my wife and child — and in spite of General Prior's official proclamation I discovered that I could not even look my own newly born son in the eye.'

'There was absolutely nothing anyone could do to stop the Germans,' Olsen said quietly.

'As I walked away from the clinic three or four people spat at my feet. I was still in uniform, you see.'

'Fireside patriots! You'll always find them crawling out of the woodwork once the shooting's stopped.'

Olsen rose, restless as ever, and paced to the window.

'Larsen, I'm not going to ask you what you and Lund did with that truck because I don't think you'd tell me.'

'I have told you, sir. The Germans got it.'

'Of course they did. I won't embarrass you by enquiring why you do not trust me, or why you persist in insulting my intelligence with this preposterous fiction. Instead I'll tell *you* why.' He turned away from the window and looked at Valdemar: 'You think I've given up the fight, don't you?'

'Hasn't the whole army given up, sir? To say nothing of the nation.'

'No. The army has not given up. I, for one — and there are others, much higher up the scale than me — intend to do everything in my power to help the Allied cause. But I will achieve nothing if I behave like a schoolboy and start blowing up German bicycle sheds with toy bombs.'

'And how do you think you will achieve anything, sir?' Valdemar's tone was still respectful — but barely so.

'By biding my time and getting myself organized. I'm an intelligence officer, Larsen. My business is information and, in war, information is often worth more than bombs. You are an intelligence officer too, and a damned good one. I know you hate the Germans. I know you feel ashamed and betrayed and dirtied by what's happened — but use your brains, man, think — you can go around setting fire to hay-carts and shooting the odd sentry in the back, but what will be gained by it? Nothing. The Germans will take reprisals, people's lives will be made even more miserable than they are now, and you'll end up smoking your last cigarette at dawn up against a brick wall.'

'I haven't noticed that people's lives are particularly miserable, sir, but go on.'

'Effective resistance, Larsen, is resistance that directly aids your allies. I've got backing, from somewhere very near the top, to set up the most efficient news service in Occupied Europe. We're already indirectly in touch with London. In a few months we'll have organized a smooth-running courier service. We're a small group but – I like to think – an exclusive one. Join us, Larsen – you're more than eligible.'

Valdemar was silent. He wanted to say, simply, 'No.' But one could not say that to one's superior officer. After a minute, he said:

'May I have some time to think about it, sir?'

Olsen sat down at his desk.

'No, you may not. Because your answer will be no. You've already made up your mind. I want to convince you that you're wrong.'

'I don't think you'll be able to do that, sir.'

Olsen said: 'Do you ever think about your wife and family?' and instantly regretted it. Valdemar's face tautened.

'Well – I'd like to be able to look them in the eye,' he said.

All the way back to the flat, his mind raced with the fine phrases he would have liked to have flung at Olsen. It was what his mother called *l'esprit de l'escalier*. In his head, he eloquently countered Olsen's counsels of moderation by citing the example of the Norwegians. King Haakon had rallied his troops and hit back at the Wehrmacht. The Germans had beaten him but he'd chosen honourable exile rather than dishonourable surrender – and the result? The British had poured in troops to re-take Narvik, in the north. Englishmen, Frenchmen, Poles, and Norwegians were fighting side by side. *That* was 'effective resistance', *that* was 'aiding one's allies'. It would take more than platitudes to convince the British that the Danes were in fact their allies and not lap-dogs of the Third Reich.

He was developing even more powerful arguments, and

putting them with pith and passion to an imaginary Olsen, when, passing the entrance to Tivoli, he saw a party of German officers and Danish girls coming out of the pleasure gardens. He stopped to glare at them, wishing he had Olsen by his side, to show him 'absolutely correct and dignified behaviour' in action. Then all thoughts of Olsen were banished as he found himself staring at one of the girls who was being courteously handed into a car by a tall, young German Major.

It was Karen.

He could not bring himself to tell Rosa when he got back to the flat. In any case she was busy swathing little Johannes in shawls and adjusting his bonnet in preparation for his debut at his paternal grandfather's house.

'Hurry up and get changed, darling,' she said. 'Tonight's the night.'

'Are you dreading it?'

'Well,' she touched her breasts, 'I'm leaking like a rusty bucket and trembling like an aspen, but otherwise I'm fine. I just hope that Father behaves.'

As he was changing into his suit, Rosa came into the bedroom.

'Val,' she said, 'will you promise me one thing? You won't get into an argument with your father, will you? I don't think I could stand it, in and amongst everything else.'

'Why should I?'

'You know perfectly well.'

He did. On Rosa's last day at the clinic Niels had called, and there had been a brief, bitter row between him and Valdemar about the Larsen Shipping Company's continuing, indeed increasing, trade with Germany. Valdemar had condemned it as trafficking with the enemy, Niels had rather wearily pointed out that the firm had been carrying Danish exports to Germany for over one hundred and fifty years and, if only for the sake of its employees, must continue to do so.

'Things are so much better between you now,' Rosa said, 'it would be silly to spoil it.'

'I can't pretend to approve.'

'Yes you bloody well can,' she said, lightly enough. 'Just think of me and Johannes for a change.'

Niels's chauffeur arrived punctually at six o'clock to pick them

131

up in the big black Chevrolet. Valdemar was moody on the way out. As they turned off Strandvejen Rosa said:

'God I'm nervous. I'm sure your mother's going to hate me.'

'She won't,' Valdemar said.

'Well, at least Karen will be there.'

'Yes. Playing the vestal virgin as usual.'

'What do you mean?'

'Nothing.'

They turned into the drive, between the tall, iron gates, then past a line of smoking, flickering braziers. When Rosa saw the house, she said:

'You didn't tell me it was a palace.'

Christina Larsen was waiting to welcome them in the hall. Rosa saw a petite, pretty woman, with faded white-blonde hair and pale blue eyes, who stepped forward and kissed her with such naturalness and spontaneity that all her nervousness evaporated.

'My dear,' Christina said, 'I'm so very glad that our various menfolk have come to their senses at last. Aren't men a trial? Now. Let me see my grandson. I can't wait to get my hands on him.'

'Would you like to hold him?'

The baby began to cry as the transfer was effected and Christina said:

'My dear, he's utterly gorgeous. I can't wait to show him off. Come along, the ordeal's through here. Come along, Val, put a brave face on it.' She turned to Rosa. 'Val hates parties you know.'

'I know.'

'Never mind. It's only the family and a few friends.'

In fact, to Valdemar's dismay, the drawing-room was already crowded. Uncle Poul was there, with Aunt Anna, in a black sack elaborately embroidered with flowers; there were various Larsen and Tøller cousins – but not Uncle Henrik – and a score of old family friends. He saw his father consulting with the butler and went up to him. Niels shook his hand and almost beamed at him.

'Well, my boy,' he said.

'I thought you said a small family party, Father, not a tribal gathering.'

'I thought it would be easier if there was a bit of a crowd.'

'Don't you think Rosa and her father might find it all a trifle

132

overwhelming?' Out of the corner of his eye he saw Rosa and the baby being cooed and cawed over. 'Mother's passing her round like a dish of canapés.'

'Nonsense, my boy, Rosa's enjoying herself.'

Nothing could ruffle Niels's calm or upset his benignity. Having made the decision to acknowledge his son's marriage and accept Rosa and her father into his family circle, he was now anxious to enjoy the fruits of his magnanimity.

'Isak Abrahamsen is late,' he said. 'I suppose he'll come.'

'Of course he will.'

'It'll seem strange, having him in this house but——' he shrugged and suddenly gripped Valdemar's arm. 'If the invasion's done nothing else, it's at least brought us all together. I'm glad.'

'Rather a steep price to pay for family unanimity, don't you think?'

'I must go and talk to Gertrud,' Niels said, and moved away.

Uncle Poul came up – sidled up – Valdemar thought. He shook Valdemar's hand and drew him away into a quiet corner.

'You look better than when I last saw you,' he said.

'I don't feel any different.'

'You were right, Valdemar, and I was wrong. I'm glad of an opportunity to apologize. I must say, I find your wife quite delightful – and a splendid looking baby. I know her father, of course. I'm so glad that he and Niels have had this rapprochement. Times like these bring people together. I've noticed it all over the place – among politicians especially. There's a mood of tolerance and forbearance in the air.'

Valdemar laughed and took a fresh glass of champagne from a passing maid.

'You're really wonderful, you know, Uncle Poul. You talk of a national disaster as if it's something we should all be grateful for.'

'Not at all. But when you look at conditions in the rest of Europe and compare them with here – well, we do have something to be grateful for, I think. Look at your own situation. The army is intact.'

'It may be intact, but it no longer has a function – any more than the Government.'

'On the contrary, the Government still governs.'

'By gracious permission of His Majesty King Adolf. They're softening us up, Uncle Poul.'

'I think I am in a better position than you to gauge German intentions. They are as anxious as we are to establish a *modus vivendi* – but this is supposed to be a party. We're here to enjoy ourselves.'

Valdemar laughed again.

'You've just summed up the fundamental creed of the Danish nation, Uncle Poul. Well done.'

'Isn't that your father-in-law just arriving?' Poul said, anxious for a diversion.

Valdemar turned. Isak was hovering in the door and, behind him, was Abel. Something disastrous had happened to Abel's collar. One of its flaps was turned up at the end and the whole thing appeared to have become detached from his shirt. Isak, by contrast, looked magnificently sleek and thoroughly at ease, even when Niels came up to shake his hand.

'You'd better go and help your father make introductions,' Poul said.

Valdemar moved away, collecting another glass of champagne as he went. The room was crammed now – it was all jostle and jabber and smoke. He looked for Rosa. She was at the far end, hemmed into a corner by a press of aunts. His father was busy introducing Isak to a circle of friends and neighbours and Abel was standing a little apart, a quizzical look on his face. He caught sight of Valdemar and they pushed their way towards each other, finally meeting in the lee of Aunt Anna's ample black skirts.

'My dear boy,' Abel said.

'Hello, Uncle Abel. Isn't it ghastly?'

'Oh, I wouldn't say that. It's a very beautiful house. Lots of intriguing things. I shall have a good explore later on.'

'Don't you find the spectacle of forty or fifty solid citizens knocking back champagne and flapping their tongues rather a grotesque spectacle, considering the present state of the nation?'

Abel smiled.

'Grotesque perhaps,' he said, 'but not surprising. You would have us all wearing sackcloth and ashes, Valdemar, but that isn't the mood.'

'What is the mood? I don't understand it.'

'Shock, shame, hate – but mostly relief, my dear. Relief is what people feel – I feel it myself I can tell you. We all have something to celebrate: the businessman, that his factories and warehouses haven't been blown to pieces; the parent, that his sons haven't been massacred; the worker, that there is no forced labour; and above all the Jew, that there are no pogroms. Even you have something to celebrate.'

'And what is that?'

Abel made a sweeping gesture. 'Harmony,' he said. 'Look at Isak – fascinating your mother. Look at your father, drooling over Rosa and the baby.'

'Uncle Abel if you produce one single platitude about how war brings people together, I'll be sick on the spot.'

Abel laughed.

'You're too vehement, Valdemar. And you never stop to consider that in anathematizing one cliché you reproduce another. Sick on the spot, indeed.' He glanced away. 'Good lord – I do believe I see a familiar face – Professor Gregersen. I must go and astonish his frail wits.'

He moved away; and Valdemar felt more than a little nettled. He had envisaged his role as steering Rosa's unusual uncle through the shoals of the party, and here he was striking out on a course of his own. Nobody else came up to talk to him. He took another glass of champagne and looked for Rosa. She was deep in conversation with his father, making him laugh; for some reason the sight irritated him. He saw that Aunt Anna was standing alone and felt he should go and talk to her, but the idea bored him. He wandered into the hall and through the morning-room. He opened one of the French windows and stepped into the garden.

Rosa had gone upstairs with Hildegaard, Valdemar and Karen's old nurse, to feed the baby and settle him down to sleep, and Niels found himself, for a moment, at a loose end. On the other side of the room Christina and Isak Abrahamsen were still deep in conversation. Christina was animated; he could hear her laugh piercing the general hum; she kept unconsciously touching Isak, a sure sign that she found him fascinating. Niels remembered something that he had deliberately put out of his mind: old Reuben Abrahamsen, and the hold he had once had over his own father and mother. They had entertained him in this very room, forty-seven years ago, on the night of his engagement. Even after all ties with him had been severed, his mother had

135

continued, at odd moments, to talk wistfully about his charm and panache. Yes, there was something magnetic about the Abrahamsens − even that curious brother − but Niels suddenly felt that it was a dangerous magnetism. He had half a mind to go over and intervene between Isak and his wife; but he saw Anna standing alone in a corner and took pity on her.

Karen was suddenly exhausted. The strain of playing the immaculate daughter was always magnified at her parents' dreary parties − an audience of two was easier to handle − and, besides, it had been a trying, if exciting, day: first of all wheedling a fresh supply of contraceptives out of that sleazy little doctor, then lunching with Fritz and his amusing brother officers, the fun of it all being slightly blighted by the necessity of looking over her shoulder all the time to make sure she wasn't being observed by a friend or acquaintance; then his room at the Angleterre − tricky that, most of the hotel staff knew her pretty well − making love with him with one eye on the clock and finally having to deny him a second bout − always the best − for fear she should not be back in time to appear demurely in the hall to welcome the guests with her mother. All very wearing. She managed to escape from Aunt Gertrud and decided to go into the dining-room to check the dinner arrangements and enjoy a brief respite. In the hall she met Valdemar. He was holding a glass in one hand and a bottle of champagne in the other.

'Hello brother,' she said. 'You've been avoiding me.'

Valdemar eyed her coldly. 'Unlike you, apparently,' he said, 'I don't enjoy trafficking with the enemy.'

'What are you talking about, Val? Are you tight?'

'I saw you this afternoon − outside Tivoli.'

'Oh.' She paused, then: 'Don't be boring, Val.'

'Well what the hell do you think you're playing at?'

'It's none of your business.'

'A month after they walk in I find my own sister walking out with one of the bastards.'

'He happens to be highly civilized and rather attractive.'

'Christ!'

'Val, we have a pact, remember? Live and let live.'

'Are you sleeping with him?'

Karen flushed. 'That's my business.'

'Christ, I can't believe it − even of you.'

136

'I don't give a damn what you can believe or what you can't believe. Just don't tell father. I mean that, Val. If you breathe a word——'

'Oh don't worry. The mood father's in he'd probably invite the bastard to the party.'

Karen stalked away towards the drawing-room, and as she disappeared Rosa came down the stairs.

'Your old nurse is wonderful. She seemed to hypnotize Johannes to sleep,' she said. 'What's the matter, Val?'

'Nothing.'

She took his arm.

'Aren't you enjoying it? I think your parents are being wonderful.'

'Wonderful, wonderful – can't you think of any other word?'

There was a sudden surge of people from the drawing-room. Dinner had been announced. Rosa was claimed by Christina and carried away into the dining-room. A sumptuous buffet was laid out on the long table and there were several gasps and shrills of appreciation. Valdemar said, rather loudly: 'The horrors of war!' Rosa heard, and wanted to go over to him but Niels was pressing food on her and it was impossible. She ate, she drank, she talked, and sparkled, but only half her concentration was on social chit-chat, the other half was on Valdemar, at the far end of the room, eating little, talking little, and drinking a great deal of wine.

At the height of the uproar – extraordinary, she thought at one moment, how much noise a group of well-bred people could generate – she saw Niels pick up a glass and a teaspoon. As he tapped the spoon on the glass, and the high-pitched dinging spread quiet through the room, she felt apprehensive.

Niels cleared his throat.

'Ladies and gentlemen,' he said, 'I do not propose to keep you from your champagne and scandal for very long.' Laughter and a few cheers. 'But while there is still something left in your glasses I would like you to drink a toast to three very special people. One of them has been known to most of you all his life – my son, Valdemar. The other two you may have met for the first time tonight – my delightful new daughter-in-law Rosa and my equally delightful grandson Johannes.' Cheers and applause. 'I don't think that any father could hope for two more charming additions to his family.' A smattering of applause. 'And so I ask

137

you to raise your glasses and drink to Valdemar, Rosa, and Johannes.'

The names were repeated in a murmur that ran round the room and the toast was drunk. Rosa saw Valdemar step forward and imitate his father by ringing a glass with a spoon. It cracked. One or two people, standing near, cheered ironically, then there was an expectant silence.

'I would also like to propose a toast,' Valdemar said and Rosa detected a slur in his speech. 'I would like you to drink to another very special person. I don't think any of you have ever met him, but you've all known about him for a long time. In a way it is he whom we have to thank for all the good food and wine we have enjoyed tonight because it is through him that the Larsen Shipping Company is able to make such fat profits, thus enabling my father to be such a generous host.' There was a tentative clap from the back of the room, but most of the guests just stared at Valdemar, their smiles turning rapidly into gapes. 'One day, perhaps,' Valdemar went on, 'he will do us the great honour of visiting our country, where his – ambassadors have received such a warm welcome, and I'm sure that, if he does, you will greet him with the greatest enthusiasm. For the moment though you can only raise your glasses and drink his health. Ladies and gentlemen, the toast is—— Adolf Hitler.'

In the middle of the night Valdemar began laughing. It was a quiet, self-contained laughter, but it shook the bed. Rosa, who had hours ago resigned herself to a sleepless night, said: 'For God's sake.'

'Father's face – it was a study. And Aunt Anna actually raising her glass. She must be feeble-minded.'

'It was cruel. It was the cruellest thing I've ever seen anybody do.'

'It was kind. It'll give them all something to natter about.'
Rosa got out of bed.
'Where are you going?'
'To feed the baby.'
'You fed him an hour ago.'

She huddled into her dressing-gown and left the room without replying. Valdemar lay on his back, his hands clasped behind his head. There was a sour after-taste of drink in his mouth and he felt at once elated and frightened, elated by the bomb he had exploded in the self-satisfied faces of his father's guests, frightened by the way his mother had cried and the way Rosa had sat silent in the car on the way home, holding Johannes as if she were protecting their baby from his father. Still, he had struck a blow, even if only a verbal blow. He was committed.

He swung out of bed and padded into the next room. Rosa was sitting, hunched, by the cot. The baby was asleep.

'Rosa,' he said. He put his hand on her shoulder. She drew away from him.

'Try to understand,' he said.

She looked up at him.

'I thought I did understand,' she said. 'I thought I knew you when I married you.'

'Oh, for God's sake——'

'It's true, Val. Tonight, when I heard you saying all those horrible things, I thought – that isn't my husband.'

'Rosa, my father's got warehouses packed to the rafters with butter and margarine and fish and bacon – all of it about to be shipped off to Germany to feed Hitler's army. How do you expect me to feel?'

'Your father talked to me about that. Do you realize that half his ships were on the high seas when the Germans invaded? All except one of the captains steamed straight off to British ports and handed over their vessels to the Allies.'

'Good for them.'

'I agree. And so does your father, as you'd know if you bothered to talk to him. The point is that he's got to try to keep the business going somehow. He has to work with the Germans. There's no alternative. My father does – and he's a Jew, for God's sake.'

'Of course there's an alternative. They could both refuse to do business with Germans.'

'But that's about the only business there is to do.'

'So what? Neither of them needs money. Can you imagine what the effect would be if they took a stand?'

'Go back to bed, Val.'

'You can't sit in here all night.'

'Just go away. Please.'

He went. He climbed back into bed and lay still. He stared up at

139

the dark ceiling, and as he watched it turn gradually grey with the approach of dawn, he thought about the crates and boxes that lay hidden in the cellars of Vidlund. 'It's a start,' Uncle Henrik had said, smearing his forehead with dirt as he wiped the sweat away, 'by God it's a start. I can construct an army on this.' He wondered how recruiting was going down in South Jutland. He wished the Squire could have been at the party, could have seen the blast and watched the people running for cover.

He remembered something he'd overheard at Abel's a few days before. There'd been the usual crowd of students, refugees from The Cannibal, the university refectory, who liked to cluster round Abel's *samovar* and exercise their wits in his intellectual gymnasium. They had been chuckling about a so-called act of sabotage. Someone had set fire to a hay-cart carrying fodder for German horses – a great joke. One of the boys had rattled a match box and said: 'That to you, Adolf.' Everybody had laughed. But was it such a joke? That was all you needed, after all, to resist the Germans: a box of matches.

In the morning Rosa deposited Johannes with a friend for a couple of hours and took a tram up to Raadhusplandsen to do some shopping. In Strøget she ran into her Uncle Abel.

'Come back to the shop and have a coffee and a post-mortem,' he said.

The Viking was out. Abel floundered round the tiny kitchen until Rosa rescued him and took over the grinding of the beans herself.

'Well,' Abel said, 'that was one of the most remarkable speeches I have ever heard. Valdemar should try politics.'

'He was drunk.'

'*In vino veritas*, I'm tempted to say – except that it's so hackneyed.'

'And inappropriate in this case.'

'Oh, I don't know.'

'What happened after we left?'

'A genteel stampede for the door. Christina Larsen bravely tried to stem the tide – you know, the gracious hostess rising above a disaster – but I'm afraid it was no good. Valdemar had popped the balloon most definitively. Your father and I murmured a polite platitude or two and stumbled out into the night, aghast.'

'Will his parents ever forgive him?'

'Will *you* ever forgive him? The look on your face as you swept out seemed to spell doom for the marriage bed.'

'It isn't a joke, Uncle Abel.'

'No, I suppose not.'

'How could he do a thing like that? I feel I don't know him any more.'

'Perhaps you know him better?'

'I know he's got a streak of cruelty.'

'Do you call it cruelty – to break up a party? My dear girl, from that point of view, he's made a positive contribution. People will be talking about "that night at the Larsens'" for years to come.'

'That's what Valdemar says.'

Abel chuckled. Then, more seriously, he said: 'I thought it was a great act of courage.'

'Courage?'

'Yes. Could you have done it? I certainly couldn't.'

When she left her uncle's shop she found herself wandering towards Kongens Nytorv and Bredgade. She decided to obey her instinct and walk up to The Citadel gardens; it was such a relief to be out of the flat and away from Johannes for a little. She sat on a bench by the pond; there was some warmth in the sun and she unbuttoned her coat. What a luxury it was to feel, even for half an hour, that no demands would be made. God, she was tired. Every night the clock in her head, its alarm set by the needs of her baby, dragged her out of deep sleep; she had almost forgotten what it was like to feel energetic; but, as always, it was peaceful here, healing. What was it Grandpapa used to say? There's nothing more restful than green grass – especially when you don't have to mow it.

She was suddenly aware of gulls croaking and crying nearby, and men shouting and laughing. She turned her head. A few yards away a group of three or four German soldiers were tossing pieces of bread to the gulls. The gulls were wheeling, diving, jockeying for position, squabbling over the scraps, and the Germans were shouting excitedly, and laughing as if the gulls were performing ridiculous antics for their amusement.

She stood up and began to walk off. For the first time since the

141

Germans had come she felt the enormity of their presence. She hadn't been able to take it in before, but now she saw what a desecration it had been, the desecration of her own precious sanctuary – sand heaping up on an altar.

She had been too bound up in her baby to grasp what had happened. Now, as the tram clattered down towards Kongens Nytorv, she saw the city in a new light, as a place violated. The evidence of the alien presence seemed to be everywhere. The British Embassy empty and shuttered; Mercedes and Opels outside the Angleterre; every other figure in the streets wearing that loathsome blue-green uniform; every other face, the face of a stranger.

I've been asleep, she thought.

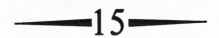

15

Old Johan could interpret the random, varied sounds of the night and locate an alien presence as if by instinct. In spite of his age, and his withered leg, he could move with stealth; and he knew every loose cobble and patch of gravel in the yards and could avoid them in the dark.

The intruder was by the fuel store at the back of the refrigerated sheds. He was trying to force the door with a short crowbar. In his effort to create as little noise as possible, he was making slow progress. It would be two or three minutes, Old Johan calculated, before he'd succeed in ripping the hasp from the wood.

Old Johan crept away, a slight pounding in his ears. He reached his little den, at the side of No. 7, and closed the door carefully behind him. He dialled the number of the harbour police and spoke briefly. When he got back to his vantage point near the fuel store he saw that the door was open. So the man was inside – but what the hell was he after?

The man emerged, a tall, broad shape in the darkness – a big fellow – carrying two jerry-cans. He took the cans over to the back wall of the shed, deposited them, then returned to the fuel store. He kept collecting cans from the store and setting them in a line by the wall of the shed. Old Johan crept nearer. He found cover in the shadow of a chain bunker, a few feet from the cans.

The intruder came back, carrying two more cans. Old Johan could hear him panting. He set the cans down and then began to move along the line, unscrewing the tops. He moved back towards Old Johan and picked up the first can. He began carefully slopping the contents – what was it? petrol? kerosene? – onto the wooden wall of the shed.

Where the hell were the police? They should be here by now. The timber of the wall was glistening with fluid and there were rivulets and pools at the base. The man was pulling something from his pocket – ah, a newspaper. He was rolling it into a tube. He dipped the paper into one of the cans, completely absorbed in what he was doing.

Old Johan moved out of cover. As the man fumbled, with his free hand, in his jacket pocket and brought out a cigarette-lighter, Old Johan raised his stick; then, as the man was about to flick the lighter under the roll of paper, he brought the stick down, with all his force, on his wrist. The man cried out. The lighter bounced off a can with a tinny clang. Old Johan stepped back. The man was doubled up. He was nursing his wrist and whimpering. Had he broken the bone? Suddenly there were torches and the scrunching of feet – Sergeant Thomsen and three of his lads. They bunched round the man and shone a torch in his face.

There were tears of pain on Valdemar's face. He was clutching his right wrist to his chest, feeling it with his left hand. Old Johan found his voice.

'It's all right, sergeant. I know this fellow.'

Thomsen was examining the cans. He dabbed his finger into one and sniffed.

'Kerosene,' he said. He picked up the lighter and the rolled up newspaper. 'Doesn't look all right to me. Looks more like attempted arson.'

'I prefer to call it sabotage,' Valdemar said.

'You admit it then?'

'I'm proud of it.'

Sergeant Thomsen suddenly let out a guffaw.

'Proud, eh?' he said. 'I wouldn't be. Caught in the act by an old man of eighty-five? A fine saboteur you are.'

He jerked his head towards Old Johan.

'You say you know him. Who is he?'

Old Johan hesitated.

143

'My name is Valdemar Larsen,' Valdemar said.

Thomsen whistled and peered curiously at Valdemar.

'What's all this about then?' he said.

Old Johan intervened.

'Look, there's been no harm done. I've got a bottle of *snaps* in my locker. Let's all have a nip and forget about it.'

'Can't do that, grandad,' Thomsen said. 'This is a serious matter. It'll have to be reported.' He turned to Valdemar. 'You'd better come along.'

Valdemar looked at the sergeant. The pain in his wrist was easing.

'Do you call yourself a patriotic Dane, sergeant?' he said.

'Come on, now. We'll talk about it at the station.'

'Do you?'

'Of course I do.'

'Then give me back my lighter, and let me set fire to this place.'

Thomsen turned to Old Johan. 'Is he cracked, or what?'

Old Johan didn't reply. He couldn't.

'Do you know what's inside?' Valdemar persisted. 'Food. Food for the Germans, food for the enemy. Mountains of it.'

'Yes, well, I wouldn't know anything about that. You just come along now.' Valdemar stood his ground. He turned to the policeman standing beside him.

'Do you want to feed the enemy?'

The young man goggled at him and Thomsen's voice cracked out sharply:

'That's enough of that. Are you going to come along or aren't you?'

'No.'

'Right then. Petersen. Hansen.'

Valdemar attempted to break free but the policemen were too strong for him. He yelped as the cuffs snapped onto his damaged wrist.

Thomsen shook his head. 'You know,' he said, 'what you want to do is grow up, my son.'

'It's lucky for you that Inspector Knudsen is a friend of mine,' Olsen said. 'Otherwise you'd have more than a bruised wrist to worry about.'

Valdemar said nothing. Olsen found his sullenness thoroughly aggravating; Knudsen's call had got him out of bed at seven o'clock.

'Well, what have you got to say?'

'Nothing, sir.'

'I see. Well you can just listen then. Your performance with that ammunition truck was idiotic but at least it was competent – I can hardly say the same for your latest effort. What the bloody hell did you think you were playing at? Farting about in the middle of the night with cans of kerosene in your own father's shipyard. What baffles me is how any officer of mine, having made up his mind to set fire to a building, should end up with his wrist in a bandage and his arse in a police cell.'

'I thought it would be easy, sir. I didn't plan it properly, and I was acting alone. It will be different next time.'

'You're quite right. It will be different next time. Next time, your resistance activities will consist of obeying my orders and concentrating on useful intelligence work against the Germans. In the meantime if you want to develop your talents as an arsonist you can practise on fishermen's huts.'

Valdemar stared at him.

'You're going on leave, Larsen. That's an order, by the way. Two months in Skagen – to cool off in the sunshine.'

'But, sir——'

'There's no argument, Larsen. A lot of people know about what happened last night and my friend Knudsen can't stop their tongues from wagging. If the German authorities got wind of it they might demand a prosecution. But in a couple of months it'll have all blown over.'

'I could resign my commission.'

'Larsen, I have been very patient with you and extremely forbearing, but don't try me too far. I've stuck out my neck for you for one reason and one reason alone – because I think you'll be prepared to sweat blood to fight the Germans in the only way we can fight them. Is that understood?'

'Yes, sir.'

'Good. Now get the hell out of here.'

Valdemar snapped to attention and turned. As he was about to leave the office, Olsen said:

'This is the second time I've bailed you out, young man. I won't do it a third time. Remember that.'

As June came in the sun rose and it seemed that for day after day it never set, but that at night a veil of gauze was drawn over it, so that the sky and its great reflector the sea were infused with indigo, while an afterburn of blue and gold pervaded midnight with noon.

Their world had three boundaries: the brown and russet marsh; the white dunes, baked and crusted like bread; the sea. In the shallows it was warm, warm enough to dip Johannes's pink bottom in, and set him gurgling, but further out the brilliant water was still seamed with the glacial threads of the Arctic, six hundred miles to the north.

The Germans were in Skagen, and in Frederikshavn down the coast; gunboats patrolled the Kattegat. Twice a week Valdemar and Rosa walked into Skagen to buy supplies. There were few holiday people about and Brøndums' dining-room was dismantled. Valdemar spent much of his time in the ramshackle boat-house, below the cottage, working on the dinghy and the rowing boat, scraping off the old varnish and applying glistening new coats, patching soft, weathered sails, and buffing and greasing running tackle; yet he never took the boats out. Sometimes he would set out on a solitary walk and twice Rosa found him sitting by the buried church. Once, after a storm had raged all night, filling the old cottage with random creaks and mischievous draughts, he woke Rosa at dawn and they walked up to Grenen Point, Valdemar carrying Johannes.

There, at the northernmost tip of Denmark, the two seas, the Skagerrak and the Kattegat, met head on. Boiled up by the storm, they clashed and warred; the phalanxes of the Skagerrak, long, arch-backed, white-crested rollers, confronted the legions of the Kattegat, steeper and thicker, and they exploded together in a straight line of battle, a wall of green water and grey spume, that stretched away from the land towards a point where sky and sea were fused by the retreating storm.

But such excursions were rare. By tacit consent they did not stray far from the cottage, nor, in their talk, did they stray far from the trivial and the mundane. If there were invisible barriers that physically hemmed them round, and kept them as voluntary exiles from the world beyond the dunes, there were other barriers that made them exiles from each other.

The greatest of these, Rosa thought, was the one that divided their bed. Johannes had turned her body into a machine. As a result of her pregnancy, the place of Valdemar's entry had become a public thoroughfare, prodded and probed and inspected by doctors and nurses. Then it had been stretched and torn to provide a route to life for her son, and finally it had been treated like a wound, with more inspections, and applications of ointment. And her breasts – they were glands, swollen with milk, Johannes's private larder, untouchable by Valdemar.

They made love, of course, and she enjoyed it in the same way that she enjoyed being stroked or cuddled: it was comforting; but she knew that Valdemar was not satisfied. There was no true intimacy, and it was intimacy he craved. She thought that if only she could break down this barrier, and give her body exclusively to him as before, then the other barrier, his inability to talk, would fall.

In the event, it was the other way round, and it happened quite easily and naturally one evening when Johannes was asleep in his cot and they were sitting outside, drinking wine, and watching sky and sea turn from coral to crimson.

Rosa said: 'You would have been proud of your son this afternoon when we went into Skagen. I left him in the pram outside Mr Stenbroen's and when I came out there were a couple of women admiring him, you know, making baby noises. Johannes was grinning at them and going ba-ba-ba-ba and generally playing up. Then one of the Germans from the wireless station came along, rather a sweet-looking man. He stopped to look at Johannes and told us that he had a baby boy back home in Hanover. But the minute he leaned over the pram Johannes screwed up his eyes, opened his mouth, and let out a yell they could have heard in Oslo. He cried so lustily I swear he frightened the seagulls off the church tower. The German mumbled an apology and fled in confusion.'

Valdemar laughed. 'Out of the mouths of babes and sucklings,' he said.

'Exactly. I think you've sired a natural resistance leader.'

'It'd be nice to think that there was a resistance to lead.'

'There will be, Val.'

'You've changed your tune a bit, haven't you? I thought you were all for "absolutely correct and dignified behaviour".'

She told him about the morning in The Citadel gardens, about how she had walked away from the German soldiers.

'I felt ashamed,' she said.

'I know the feeling only too well.'

'Do you?'

'Why d'you think I've never told you about that night down at the docks? Because whenever I think about it I'm so ashamed I want to crawl away and hide.'

'What did happen, Val?'

He paused to sip his wine, then said:

'I tried to sabotage one of my father's warehouses.'

Rosa was silent.

'And I made a total mess of it.'

He lit a cigarette and offered one to Rosa.

'It was an impulse,' he said. 'I suddenly couldn't stand the idea of all that stuff being shipped off to Germany. I thought I'd break into the fuel store, pour petrol or something over the walls and set light to the place. I didn't think there'd be any difficulty; there's only Old Johan on night-watch and he's over eighty and half a cripple. I thought he'd be snoozing in his lair.'

'But he wasn't?'

'No. He was prowling around like a cat, the old bugger, and he caught me in the act. I tell you I felt like a naughty little boy being nabbed scrumping apples. When the police arrived they could hardly stand up for laughing. And the awful thing was that not only did it make me look ridiculous, it made the whole idea of resistance look ridiculous too.'

'I don't think it's ridiculous, Val.'

'But it *is* Rosa. There's no organization, no leadership, nothing. Just a lot of fools like me acting on impulse and going off at half-cock. Captain Olsen wants me to join up with some group of armchair officers and send "information" – whatever that means – to the Allies. But what's the point of it? What would it achieve? Sometimes I feel like saying to hell with the whole thing and spending the rest of the war sitting up here with you and Johannes and going fishing every day.'

Rosa threw away her cigarette. She stood up and went over to him. She sat on his lap, straddling his legs, facing him. She put

148

her arms round his bare back and as he drew her to him, she kissed the nape of his neck. His skin tasted briny from the sea.

'I'm glad you've told me. You don't have to feel ashamed. At least you tried. It may have been a bit of a fizzle——'

'It was literally a fizzle——'

'But you did something. That's the important thing.'

She was running her hands over the hard muscles of his back. He slipped his hands inside her loose cotton dress and stroked her. They kissed – a gentle mingling of their tongues. She reached down, fumbled with the buttons of his shorts and released him; then, with her hands clasped at the back of his neck, she lowered herself onto him and they rested like that, with their faces so close together that his breathing out became her breathing in. After a time he put one hand between her shoulder blades and the other at the base of her spine and rose, lifting her with him, then lowered her onto the coarse grass so that they lay together, his body covering hers, her legs twined round his, in love's most antique attitude.

All his movements were tender and lingering; he wanted to flow into her strongly and gently; and she knew that the barrier between them must be washed away, not broken down, and that only tenderness could do it.

They lay in the sand, side by side, her head pillowed on his chest, her fingers playing in the arrow of hair below his navel. She laughed suddenly.

'That day we first met – at Uncle Abel's – did you wonder what my body would be like?'

'Yes, I did.'

'Was it all sex then, to start with?'

'Of course not.'

'I can feel your tummy tighten when you tell a lie.'

He laughed.

'All right then – ninety per cent.'

'I thought so.'

'Well, did you wonder about *my* body?'

'Not really.'

'Oh.' He sounded disappointed.

149

'Why is it that men always assume that women are as fascinated by their penises as they are?'

'I'm not particularly fascinated by mine.'

'No. But then you're different.'

'Still, I'm sorry you're not a little bit fascinated by it.'

'Ah, but I am − now.'

She touched it lightly, then rested her hand on his thigh.

'Was it because I was different that you were attracted to me?' he said.

'I suppose it was, yes.'

'In what way was I different?'

'Well, you were nothing like most of the boys I'd met at Uncle Abel's.'

'I should hope not.'

'I don't mean in that way. I mean that they were always talking a lot of hot air and arguing, but you were quiet and thoughtful and rather mysterious. I felt there was something wild about you. You didn't seem to belong to city life at all. And you don't, you know.'

'Am I still mysterious?'

'Yes, you are.'

'Rosa——'

'I don't mind. I respect it − even though it frightens me at times.'

'Frightens you?'

'Yes. I sometimes feel that there are two parts of you and that you haven't reconciled them.'

'You sound like an amateur psychologist.'

She laughed.

'My grandfather despised psychology. He used to say that the whole thing was based on a misconception. Freud had analysed a lot of enervated, middle-class Viennese Jews and then claimed that their terrors and traumas were relevant to Norwegian lumberjacks, Chinese war lords, and Zulus.'

'I wish I'd known him.'

'So do I. He was so wise in many ways, and although he would have nothing to do with Jews, so very Jewish.'

There was a long silence. Rosa sensed what Valdemar would say before he said it.

'Rosa, do you really believe in resistance?'

There was another silence, then she said:

150

'I know why you've been spending so much time on your boat.'

Valdemar sat up. He got to his feet and began brushing the sand from his skin. Rosa sat up too, and looked up at him.

'Do you think you can do it?' she said.

'I know I can. I suppose it's pride. After what happened at the docks I was – I don't know – confused and full of self pity. Then I realized that if I really wanted to achieve something I would have to be ruthless, and completely dedicated.'

He picked up his shorts and was about to step into them when Rosa put out a hand and touched his leg.

'No,' she said. 'Lie down with me again.'

He lay down beside her. There were tears on her face.

'Oh, Rosa,' he said. 'I don't have to. I can stay with you and Johannes. To hell with it.'

'No,' she said, fierceness in her voice. 'Listen. We'll plan it together. I'll help you. But when you go, Val, just go. Don't tell me. Just go.'

'Don't you want to say goodbye'

'Yes – but I want to say it now. I want you to make love to me, just as you did before – here.'

The next few days were dazzling, not just for the incandescent quality of the sunlight, but for the light in Rosa's eyes which seemed to reflect the glint and sparkle of the sea. They worked on the dinghy and the rowing boat together, never once referring to the purpose of their labour; they played with Johannes on the beach and at night they slept wrapped round each other.

One afternoon Rosa wheeled Johannes's pram along the sands to the buried church. While the baby slept in the shade, Rosa sat in the sun, staring up at the old brick gables, listening to the incessant chatter and thrum of the birds and insects in the forest. When Johannes woke she put him to her breast and fed him, then, as the light was fading, she pushed the pram back along the beach. It was almost dark when she reached the cottage. There was no light showing in the window. She lifted the baby out of his pram and walked down to the boat-house.

The boats were gone.

She looked out to sea. There was no wind. The Kattegat was

quiet and calm and empty. She held her baby a little more tightly, turned her face from the sea, and walked slowly away, back to the cottage.

Part Three
1943

17

When he jumped, and the blast of the Halifax's engines blared briefly in his ears before dying away into a drone, he wanted to scream for joy. It was like diving into the sea in mid-summer after a day in the city, when you left the heat and dust behind and drove to the beach, flung off your sticky clothes, and plunged into the water. The salt held you buoyant, your arms and legs could move with absolute freedom, all the accumulated stalenesses of your body and mind were washed away; you were cleansed. He felt the wrench and tug of the parachute harness, the sensation of lift – and then he was floating. It was the air that buoyed him now, and the air that was washing away two and a half years of sweat, confinement, and frustration. The hum of the Halifax was faint; the plane was disappearing into the night, and, with it, was going his last physical contact with the world of England, with Hatherop Castle, and S.T.S. 17 Hatfield, S.T.S. 51 Ringway, and that final, hermetically sealed institution, S.T.S. 61 Huntingdonshire.

The endless, baffling exercise in patience was over. The enigmas and the secrets that his laconic British masters wreathed round their activities like a London fog were being blown away in the crisp February air of Denmark. He caught a whiff of the land, a delicious fragrance of damp earth and leaf mould, and he played with the toggles as the dark mass rushed faster up at him.

He landed neatly on his feet (there, Sergeant MacBride, what do you think of that?) and ran a few paces forward in the soft, clogging plough before turning back to pull in the lines and damp down the billowing silk. A few feet away he saw Mogens land. His legs folded under him and he rolled, out of control. Hope the silly sod hasn't cracked his ankle, he thought. There were men running towards him. He struggled out of his harness and walked forward to meet them. One of them, a short, lean figure in a bulky poacher's jacket, held out his hand.

'I am Willem,' he said.

'I am Table Mountain – Lynx.'

'Welcome home, Lynx.'

They shook hands.

'Come with me, please. My men will deal with all this,' he

indicated the six or seven collapsed 'chutes ballooning in the breeze. 'We will have to hurry. There's a panic on.'

'I must say goodbye to my friend.'

'Hurry, please.'

He went over to Mogens — or Table Cloth or Marten — the British had a schoolboy passion for code-names — and held out his hand. Mogens was limping slightly.

'Are you all right?'

'I turned my ankle — bloody silly.'

'Well, good luck.'

'And you.'

They shook hands. Willem seemed agitated.

'Please hurry,' he said.

Lynx walked away with him, Willem moving very fast, with the countryman's effortless lope. They entered a wood and crossed a meadow.

'We've had trouble. We've had to make different arrangements,' Willem said.

'I must see The Rhino. I have instructions to contact him.'

'Don't worry, you will. Very soon. Just don't be surprised by anything you see. Follow me and keep quiet.'

They walked for half an hour, Willem maintaining a tremendous pace which Lynx, who was as fit as a Buffs P.T. instructor could render any man, found no difficulty in keeping up. The night was black and misty and Lynx could not see any natural features as he had hoped; it would have been nice to have scored a point over Captain Baynes, that master of mystification, who had talked vaguely about 'a kettle somewhere in South Jutland'. They took a path through a spinney, and at the edge of the trees Willem paused.

'From now on, not a word — and not a sound. You may see Germans. Don't be alarmed. It's all right. We're going to move slowly. Watch where you put your feet.'

They crossed a field of cropped, springy turf. Ahead Lynx could see the outlines of buildings, stables perhaps — it was too dark to make them out clearly. They halted in the shadow of a low brick building — yes, definitely stables, Lynx could hear horses kicking and blowing — and looked across a cobbled yard towards the back of a great house. There were lights in one or two of the windows and at the side of the house, perhaps sixty paces away, four or five German staff cars were parked. There was more light here: Lynx could make out the insignia on the paintwork of the cars; there were figures moving about, a mutter of talk, glows of cigarettes waxing and waning.

Willem led him along the back of the stables and through a gate in a high wall. Then, coolly, as if it were his business to be there, he sauntered across a corner of the yard, well out of sight of the Germans, and into the house by a back door. Lynx followed, utterly bewildered. He had recognized the place. Willem led him down a familiar stone-flagged passage into a room full of fishing tackle, harness, old shot guns.

'You must wait here,' Willem said. 'I will have to lock the door behind you. Please do not smoke. I will come for you in an hour or two.'

Lynx nodded, and when Willem had gone he smiled. Strange, to be locked in a room in Vidlund.

The candles, over fifty of them, lit in honour of his birthday, did much, Squire Tøller thought, to soften the garishness of his grandmother's pretentious dining-room; they gave it the sort of dignity required for a banquet of this importance, and created a suitably impressive setting in which to entertain his distinguished guests. The most eminent of these was General Kurt Possel, who was perhaps second only to General Hanneken in the German forces of occupation. Possel was a bluff, agreeable fellow and something of a *bon viveur*. He was flanked by a gaggle of colonels and majors, some of whom seemed to be in distinct awe of their surroundings, and the rest of the company consisted of the more prominent local Danish collaborators – swamp Aryans as someone had aptly termed them – part of whose reward for licking the Fritzies' arses was the social cachet of being entertained, occasionally, at Vidlund.

The Squire rose from his seat at the head of the table and announced:

'Gentlemen, there will now be a slight lull in the proceedings. If you will excuse me.'

There was a smattering of applause from those who had attended this particular function before, and the Squire bowed and left the room.

He returned after three or four minutes, dressed in a chef's hat and starched apron, wheeling a trolley on which reposed a silver tureen of heroic proportions. Amid much cheering and clapping he lifted the lid of the tureen to reveal a whole roast goose decorated with sprigs of parsley, segments of orange, and curls of bacon. He picked up a carving knife and fork and held them aloft for silence.

'Gentlemen,' he said, 'I would beg only one favour. Do not enquire too closely how I obtained the oranges!'

There was an explosion of laughter and the Squire overheard Possel say to his aide: 'Wonderful. A unique character, our Squire.'

At the end of the feast the toasts began – to the King, to German-Danish friendship, to the Führer, to Squire Tøller, to anybody or anything that provided a suitable pretext for downing yet another glass of *snaps*. The Squire noticed that Possel was a trifle unsteady on his pins as he escorted him to his car; he was also inclined to be maudlin.

'A wonderful evening, my dear Henrik. Unforgettable——' and so on.

When the last of the guests had gone, the Squire, still in evening dress and smoking a cigar, crossed the hall and went through the green baize door into the servants' quarters. Willem was sitting at the scrubbed table in the kitchen, drinking beer, and Mrs Hansen was struggling with piles of dirty plates and glasses.

'Magnificent, Mrs Hansen,' the Squire said. 'A triumph as always.'

Mrs Hansen grinned.

'I thought the soup was a little bland, sir,' she said, 'a touch of arsenic would have improved it.'

'The day will come, Mrs Hansen, the day will come.'

He looked interrogatively at Willem. The poacher nodded and stood up. Together they walked down the dank passage to the tack room. Willem unlocked the door and stood back to let the Squire enter.

A man rose from the collapsed horsehair sofa in the corner and the Squire examined him with interest. He was tall and very thin, almost gaunt. His pale yellow hair was receding and his nose was a curious shape, like a boxer's. Although his face was still daubed with black camouflage paint the Squire could see that his cheeks were flat. Above them his eyes were a faded blue. It was difficult

157

to put an age on him. Thirty? Forty? So this was one of the new breed – rum looking chap.

The Squire extended his hand.

'You are Table Mountain, I assume,' he said. 'I believe I am known as The Rhino.'

They shook hands.

'This is a great honour,' Lynx said.

'Is it? I was under the impression that my friends in London and Stockholm rather disapproved of my methods – altogether too bizarre. Haven't you come to administer a ripe raspberry?'

Lynx smiled. 'Not exactly,' he said.

'Well, let's talk somewhere more comfortable. Oh, don't fret, my honoured guests have departed.'

He turned to Willem.

'I'll see you in the morning, Willem.'

Willem nodded. Lynx was fishing in his pocket; he brought out two packets of Players and offered them to the poacher. Willem's eyes gleamed.

'Thanks,' he said, taking the coveted cigarettes.

'It's I who have to thank you.'

The Squire showed Lynx to the smoking-room and waved him to a chair by the fire.

'I know you chaps are sticklers for code names and security and all that,' he said, 'but do you have a name other than Table Mountain?'

Lynx smiled. 'My operational code name is Lynx.'

'Good God. Well, I suppose it's fractionally less silly than Table Mountain. People call me Squire – even General Possel, bless his innocent, black heart.'

The Squire poured two glasses of brandy and handed one to Lynx.

'French,' he said, 'the fruits of collaboration.'

He sat down, raised his glass, and they toasted each other.

'Now,' he said, 'let's have the raspberry.'

'There's no raspberry, sir. On the contrary, I have been asked to convey Hollingworth's warmest personal regards and congratulations on your work.'

'Really?'

'Yes, sir.'

'I wouldn't have thought that from the tone of some of the

158

cables I have been receiving recently. I imagined that London regarded me as a maverick.'

'I think London feels that you do not quite appreciate the new order of things, sir. That's why they wanted me to meet you and explain personally.'

'I see. Well, explain away.'

'It's a question of coordination and cooperation. London is committed, at long last, to a massive build-up of active resistance in Denmark. They're prepared to send all the arms, ammunition, and explosives we need for effective sabotage. Scores of highly trained operatives will be parachuted in to organize a concerted campaign − and that is the key: organization. The Danish resistance must operate within the framework of the whole Allied war effort. We must leave it to London to select our targets and to London to control the overall strategy. At the moment there are isolated groups operating all over the country and there's very little contact between them. The result is a state of anarchy.'

'Quite so,' the Squire said. 'And are you the man who is going to bring order out of chaos?'

Lynx smiled. 'Oh no, sir. My training has been in sabotage. My job is recruitment and action. I am merely acting as a messenger tonight.'

'Well, you put your case very eloquently.'

'Thank you. Take your own position, sir. Only a handful of people know that you are The Rhino——'

'Ridiculous name!'

'I know about your work, and so do a few others, but the world regards you as a collaborator of the worst kind. The time will come when the Resistance will want to take reprisals against traitors. It would be tragic if you became the victim of your own cover through lack of a central organization.'

The Squire laughed.

'Don't imagine I haven't thought of it. I take your point. I am no longer to be a lone wolf, is that it?'

The Squire stood up and replenished his brandy glass. 'You must understand certain things,' he said. 'Three years ago, when all this started, I thought that I could build an army, a great host of patriotic Danes willing to harass the Germans on every side and drive them out of our country. I had the means − weapons, ammunition, explosives − stolen from the Danish army and hidden here in my cellars. But what did I find? I found that almost everyone I spoke to had an excuse for doing nothing. Oh, they hated the Germans all right, and were full of admiration for the British, but as for direct action – it wasn't "sensible", it wasn't "prudent". After three months my forces consisted of my housekeeper, a notorious poacher, the local doctor, and the innkeeper and his sons. Hardly a platoon, let alone an army.' He sipped his brandy. 'However', he went on, 'I didn't lose faith. I persisted. Gradually more people were recruited – a lot of them women, I'd have you know – and then another problem arose – informers, and I don't mean just Nazis either, but ordinary people who saw that betraying their country was a quick way to riches. I realized that it was only a matter of time before the Germans found out about me, so I decided on a gigantic bluff. Overnight I turned into the greatest lover of the Herrenvolk since Erik Scavenius. And it worked. How could I be suspected of Resistance activities when General Possel dined at my table? I was also careful. All my business is done through Willem. I have never met a fraction of the people who work for me. You talk to me of security – I invented it!'

'I appreciate that, sir.'

'I hope you do. And I hope you appreciate that from the beginning I have been forced to act alone, to devise my own methods and systems, to decide for myself what railway lines to blow, what convoys to sabotage. I have invented my own bombs and timing devices, I have recruited blacksmiths and clockmakers to construct guns for me. Do you wonder that I resent the arrival of so-called experts, who know nothing of what it is like to operate in the field?'

'No, sir. It's natural enough.'

The Squire poured three fingers of brandy into Lynx's glass and said, more gently:

'But London is right of course. We must have organization. The only thing that matters is to smash the Fritzies. Personalities don't count.'

He sat down and looked quizzically at Lynx.

'Are you a military man, Lynx?'

'Well——'

'I thought so. And your superiors are also military men, is that not so? That's fine as far as it goes, but the military mind has

160

limitations. You have brought me a message from London; well I have a message for you to convey to your bosses and it's this: it isn't simply a military battle we're fighting here, it's a political one as well. Resistance is growing, but it is still desperately weak. Why? First, because the Danes are a very cautious race: when it rains they put up lifebuoys by the puddles. They are also a very law-abiding people and they have a constitutionally elected government which urges them to behave like good little citizens and keep their loathing of the Germans to themselves. Our job is to destroy that government, force it out of office, go on hitting Best and Hanneken again and again until they have no choice but to resort to martial rule. Then you'll get the Danes out onto the streets, then you'll get the people to fight. Do they understand *that* in London?'

'Some of them do.'

'I'm glad to hear it. I want you to tell them again and keep on telling them. The Germans know they're sitting on a time bomb, but they think they've disconnected the battery. Restore power and tick, tick, tick, boom – we'll blow them all the way to Berchtesgaden. End of sermon.'

Lynx grinned. 'That's what I'm here for,' he said.

'Good. Now – it's late. Willem will be coming to collect you soon after dawn.'

He yawned mightily. 'I'm exhausted,' he said. 'You can't imagine the strain of entertaining high-up Germans. They have the conversation of pimps and the manners of stevedores.'

The Squire ushered Lynx into the hall and up the broad staircase.

'How do you do it?' Lynx asked. 'How do you keep up the bluff? After all, you were a notorious German-hater before the war.'

'How do you know that?' the Squire asked sharply.

'Oh, there's quite a file on you in London.'

'How flattering.'

He opened the door of a bedroom. Lynx glimpsed an enormous four poster and a heavy seventeenth-century armoire.

'How do I do it? – I think you'll be comfortable in here – I'll tell you. Most Germans have simple minds, they're easy to bamboozle. But the clever ones look for base motives and I have supplied them with one. My family has been conducting a legal action in Schleswig for over seventy years – it's become quite a legend and made rich men out of half a dozen lawyers, damn them. It's for the recovery of certain estates we used to own. Well, the Nazis have intimated – subtly, you understand – that the courts might be persuaded to give a favourable verdict, in exchange for cooperation on my part.'

'I see. It would be ironic if you did win your case.'

'My dear fellow, with a bit of luck there won't be a Nazi alive, or a square metre of land worth owning in the Third Reich by the time the Allies have finished with it. Good night. Sleep well. Mrs Hansen will wake you – that's the house-keeper. I don't rise till noon. I have a reputation for eccentricity to maintain. I don't suppose we'll meet again.'

Valdemar smiled and said: 'I'm sure we shall.'

18

Wake up. Come on – stir yourself.'

Karen had not been asleep, merely dozing, but she resented the intrusion of Gunther's harsh, curiously high-pitched voice. She kept her eyes shut.

'Leave me alone,' she said, then added what she knew would please him: 'You've worn me out.'

'Tonight I will wear you out some more,' he said, with a chuckle, 'but now we have to go to the reception – at the parrot house, remember?'

The 'parrot house' was what Gunther called the German Cultural Centre. The Danes called it, contemptuously, *Deutsches Eck*, German Corner.

She opened her eyes. Gunther had climbed out of bed and was standing over her.

'I don't want to come. I'd rather stay here,' she said.

'Because you don't like to be seen in public with me? You are ashamed, yes?'

'No – of course not.'

'Most girls would be proud.'

'I prefer our meetings to be discreet. Surely you can understand that?'

'Nevertheless you will come.'

It was an instruction. He moved away, bent down, and picked up his trousers from where, earlier in the afternoon, he had kicked them. Their clothes littered the room; she remembered how he had torn her dress, and laughed. Karen stared at his body. Everything about him was abnormal – his height, his white hair, and dark blue eyes, his long, gangling limbs, like an old man's yet at the same time like a boy's. He was revolting, yet he fascinated her; and he was right, she did feel ashamed, she felt ashamed to be in the same room with him, she felt soiled by sharing his bed. Whenever she thought about the things he did to her, and the things she did for him, she was disgusted with herself – but excited all the same. Even after all these months she lusted for him as intensely as on that first night at the party at the German-Danish Association when he had loomed over her in his black and silver uniform and introduced himself. And he had known, the bastard, he had sensed what she felt; he was clever that way, he could read people. It was the only area in which he was sensitive, probing people's weaknesses; in every other way he was a barbarian, without education, culture, or taste. He had been bred in the gutter and had used the Nazi Party to climb out of it. He boasted about how he had got into the Gestapo by informing on his brothers, who had been Communists; his greatest pride was his honorary rank in the SS: this son of a Düsseldorf factory worker saw himself as a member of a new aristocracy, a new race of gentlemen, and she, as a representative of the *ancien régime*, was privileged to be his consort.

He went into the bathroom and she heard him splashing about, and gargling with that sickly mouth-wash that made his breath smell like a hospital dispensary. Thank God she only saw him two or three times a month – or was that the trouble? Perhaps if she saw more of him her disgust would grow to a degree at which she could finish with him for good? That was the way it had been before, that other time when she had fallen helplessly for a man's body while despising his mind. She had been only eighteen and had been able to write it off as 'experience'; she had convinced herself that it could never happen again. He too had been gross, but horizontally rather than vertically, a great fat purser on one of her father's ships, with teeth like a row of fossils. The trouble was that if she did contrive to see more of Gunther it would be that much more difficult to keep the affair secret. As it was, her constant lies and evasions were making her father suspicious. If he found out — well, that would be that. No home, no allowance ...

Gunther came back into the bedroom, drying his neck.

'Hey — not up yet?'

He sat down on the edge of the bed and then, with a deft flick, whipped the covers away.

'Gunther, you know I hate that.'

He stared down at her, put his hand out and touched the bruises on her breasts.

'Shock tactics,' he said with a grunt of a laugh.

'All right, all right, I'll get up.' She pushed his hand away. 'Leave me alone.'

Again that laugh, coarse and full of contempt.

Alone in the bathroom she tried to do something with her hair and face, though she could hardly bear to look at her own reflection in the glass. Yes, she decided, she must see more of him. She must satiate herself with him to the point of nausea, in the way that farmers tied a chicken carcase round a dog's neck to cure it of killing fowl. The trouble was that Gunther was such a busy man — she did not like to think about the nature of his work — and so evasive. It was always he who summoned her. Perhaps she should simply refuse to see him again after tonight? But she knew that the temptation would be too great, that if he came into the bathroom now, even while she was in this mood, she would want to submit to him. It was a sickness — she knew it — but where was a cure?

It was a warm June evening and the streets were crowded. She sat well back in the car; she felt that people were staring at it as it went by, and she didn't want to be seen.

Like all German jollifications, the reception at *Deutsches Eck* was an assault on the ear-drums. She contrived to become separated from Gunther as soon as possible, not that, even in this crowd, she could ever escape his notice: he towered over the other men and she felt that his eyes were following her wherever she went.

When a familiar voice said: 'Careful, we are being watched,' she started and turned.

'Fritz!'

Fritz Brenner bowed and kissed her hand.

164

'Is it safe to talk to you?' he said. 'I have heard that an angry giraffe is a dangerous animal.'

'Come over here,' she said, pulling his sleeve. They found a haven of comparative quiet by the buffet.

'Haven't you noticed the difference in me?' he said, with his lazy smile.

'You look just the same to me – and it's so good to see you.'

'Ah, but I've changed – dramatically.' He touched the lapel of his uniform.

'Fritz, you're a colonel!'

'Yes.'

'Congratulations. When did it happen?'

'Oh a month or two back. How are your father and mother?'

In the heyday of their affair she had taken Fritz home, correctly calculating that he would impress her father and charm her mother without arousing any suspicion that they could be sleeping together.

'Oh they're well,' she said.

'And you? How are you?'

She looked away.

'Don't ask,' she said, then, rallying, 'I want to hear about you.'

But Fritz, who had always been so adept at the light touch, would not be diverted.

'Do you? he said.

'Don't be tedious, Fritz. Amuse me. God knows, I need it.'

'Doesn't Gunther Kleist amuse you?'

'What do you think?'

'This is hardly the time or the place to voice my opinion of Herr Kleist.'

'Well then, let's talk about something else.'

'On one condition.'

She looked at him enquiringly and he drew her further apart from the crowd.

'Just listen to me,' he said, 'and don't interrupt. I don't understand what it is between you and Kleist, I never did. I can't see how any girl could fall for a creature like that. But I don't think you know what kind of man he is. You can't. He's poison, Karen, he'll bring you nothing but suffering. I'm not saying that because I want you back, I'm saying it for your own sake.'

He was looking directly at her; there was an unfamiliar

165

earnestness about his expression. Then the smile returned.

'That's enough of that,' he said. 'Now I'll keep my side of the bargain and amuse you.'

He did. For ten minutes Karen was able to step back into her own world: urbane, not very profound, but relaxed and civilized. Then she saw Gunther making his way towards them, and Fritz said goodbye quickly.

But that brief taste of the easy companionship that she and Fritz had once shared, and the memory of the light-hearted lust they had once enjoyed, gave her the will to refuse Gunther's suggestion that they leave early and return to his flat. She would find no companionship there, no wit, no fun, only the emptiest and most degraded kind of lust – and suddenly she had no taste for that. Was she cured?

'What's the matter with you?' Gunther said, puzzled and angry. 'Are you sick?'

'On the contrary, my dear,' she said.

She took the tram back to Hellerup, chatting gaily with complete strangers, flirting with the conductor, and making him laugh.

Three years of war and occupation had in some respects aged Niels and in others they had given him a more youthful look. His hair was greyer, and scantier, and there were fine, deep lines under his eyes: Valdemar's disappearance, incessant business problems, and perhaps a touch of conscience that he was making money, if only indirectly, out of the razing of Europe, had done that to him; but he was also thinner and leaner, and there was a lithe look about him: and that, so Christina declared, was due to the rationing of oats and the impossibility of having porridge for breakfast every morning. Niels could, of course, have continued to enjoy his morning porridge if he had been prepared to buy on the black market, but he was not. He attributed his new fitness to the daily bicycle rides in and out of town. Petrol was virtually unobtainable and he had given his Chevrolet to the Bispebjaerg Hospital for use as an ambulance. Starved of decent cigars, he had taken to smoking cigarettes made of substitute tobacco, and uniquely among his circle of friends and acquaintances, he actually enjoyed them. *Pokal* was his brand; he liked the red and brown packet. He was smoking a *Pokal*, standing in the hall, and looking at his favourite picture, while waiting for Karen to come home.

The picture was a Krøyer, a study of a young girl sitting on the beach at Skagen, her hair down and cascading over her shoulders, and her parasol lying beside her on the sand. He saw the picture as an evocation of purity both in what it expressed – the girl was fresh and young and virginal in her flowing white dress, yet eager and vibrant, with no hint of prudery or artificial innocence – and in the manner of its execution, with the paint as luminous as the light it sought to capture, and every brush stroke as natural and right as the inflorescence of a wild plant or the lobes of a leaf. The picture also evoked peace, of course, the utter peace of a flat sea at sunset; but there were other associations. This sea, shown by Krøyer as a pale blue plane, studded with fishing boats, was the same sea which had taken the life of his son. The coastguard at Frederikshavn had found the wreck of Valdemar's dinghy floating, half-submerged, off the shores of Læsø. Niels had mobilized every influential contact in North Jutland in the search for the body; Swedish associates in Göteborg had moved heaven and earth to trace him, in case, by some miracle, he had survived. But after months without any positive news, Niels had been forced to face the fact that his son's brief and inexplicable life had ended in a futile attempt to do – what? He had never been able to understand Valdemar's purpose, still less had he been able to understand Rosa's attitude. 'I want you to believe that he's alive,' she had said. 'I know he's alive. I can't prove it, but I know it.' Women! Incurable mystics. Christina was just the same.

The front door opened and Karen came in. She looked washed out but oddly exhilarated.

'Hello, Father,' she said. 'You look as if you're lurking.'

'I want to talk to you.'

'Does it have to be now? I'm exhausted.'

'Yes, it does have to be now. Come into the study.'

Karen sighed and followed him. He took a plain white envelope off his desk and handed it to her.

'This arrived today. Nobody saw who delivered it.'

Karen noticed that the envelope had already been opened. She drew out a sheet of paper and stared at her own photograph which had been pasted onto it. She recognized the picture; it was taken from the society column of a magazine which had recently

167

featured a full length portrait of her at some function or other. Several copies of the picture must have been used: her arms and legs and trunk had been snipped away and arranged in the form of a swastika, with her face in the middle. Underneath the swastika, in type cut from newspaper headlines, was pasted: 'Today, paper – tomorrow, flesh.' Karen tried to laugh, but she was on the edge of tears.

'Well?' Niels said.

He took the paper from her, crushed it in his hand, and threw it into the fire-place.

'What have you got to say?'

'I don't understand what it's about.'

'Don't you? This is the sort of filth so-called patriots send to girls who are—— carrying on with Germans. Are you having an affair with a German?'

'Of course not, Father.'

'What about that fellow you brought here once?'

'Fritz Brenner? I haven't seen him for ages. Anyway he was just an acquaintance. You've got several German acquaintances yourself.'

Niels stared at her. He was almost sure she was lying – for years he'd suspected that she was nothing but a clever little actress – but the trouble was that he did not want his suspicions to be confirmed.

'Are you suggesting that somebody's made a mistake?' he said.

'Obviously, Father. You don't really think I'm a field mattress, do you?'

'I don't know what you get up to when you're out of this house, Karen.'

'Do you really care, Father? Isn't this sudden interest in my welfare just because Valdemar's not here any more?'

She had made him angry, she could see, but she had also succeeded in diverting his attention. Niels controlled himself and said coldly:

'I think it would be wise if you went away for a while.'

'Are you throwing me out? Because of a filthy bit of paper shoved under the door?'

'Of course I'm not throwing you out. I just think it would be wise if you spent some time in the country. You could go to Aunt Gertrud's.'

168

'Very well, Father, if that's what you think best. But not Aunt Gertrud's. Couldn't I go to Vidlund?'

'Certainly not. That man's nothing but a Quisling. He's gone mad.'

'Whatever you say, Father.'

'I'll write to Gertrud tomorrow. You'd better go to bed. Where have you been all day?'

'At my Red Cross committee.'

'Hmm. Well, good night.'

'Good night, Father.'

She kissed him submissively.

Alone in her room she collapsed onto her bed. She felt at once apprehensive – terrified – and relieved. That letter and her father's barely concealed suspicion put the seal on it. No more Gunther. No more men, in fact, for quite a long time. Patience, she thought, patience. Only two years to go before she came into great-Aunt Sylvie's money: then she could do what she liked. In the meantime – no more Gunther.

19

'Mummy, there's a funny man,' Johannes said in that serious, emphatic way of his.

It was a Saturday and Rosa was taking him to Abel's where Isak was to meet them, after the service in the synagogue round the corner, so he could take his grandson to Tivoli for the afternoon. In the last year Isak had taken to visiting the synagogue occasionally, where, according to Abel, he would sit at the back, bemused by the ritual, and looking as if he had indigestion. Isak never referred to these visits and would not set foot inside his Uncle Simeon's Reformed synagogue.

'Nonsense, darling,' Rosa said.

'But there is,' Johannes insisted. 'A funny man with a nose. He's been watching us.'

They were walking down Nørre Voldgade, and Johannes was tugging at his mother's hand. She stopped and looked back.

'Well where is he, the funny man?' she said. 'I don't see him.'

Johannes peered.

'He's hiding,' he said. 'He's a Fritzie bogey-man.'

'You're always seeing bogey-men. Come along.'

'He had a nose,' Johannes said. He kept looking back over his shoulder.

'Of course he had a nose. Everybody has a nose.'

'But it was a funny nose.'

When they got to Fioldstraede Johannes rushed into the shop and flung himself at Abel.

'Uncle Abel I saw a bogey-man!'

'Did you now?' said Abel.

'Yes. I want to shoot him.'

Abel and Rosa exchanged smiles.

'You've got a furious demon on your hands,' Abel said.

'I bet he's watching us now,' said Johannes, looking out of the window. 'Grandpa!'

Isak came down into the shop, scooped up Johannes, and kissed Rosa.

'Why are you wearing a hat, Grandpa?' Johannes demanded.

'To keep my hair on.'

'Do you think you can manage him this afternoon, Father?'

'Two rides on the helter skelter and he'll be putty in my hands.' He put Johannes down. 'Come on, young man. I'll deliver him to the flat at about five, Rosa.'

When Isak and Johannes had gone, Rosa followed her uncle out to the back and up the stairs to the top floor. Abel unlocked a door and they went into the attic room that housed the mimeograph machine and what Abel liked to call the 'editorial offices' of *Truth*, the illegal news-sheet which, with the help of his student friends, he had been producing since the summer of 1942.

In the fight against German censorship of the official press *Truth* played a minor part. Its main purpose was to counter directly, by means of elegant satire, the Danish Nazi Party newspaper *Faedrelandet* and the anti-Semitic rag *Kamptegnet*. Its circulation was nothing compared with *De Frie Danske* or *Frit Danmark*, the big underground papers, but its production gave Abel the feeling that he was contributing something towards the Resistance, and it amused him, though he lived in a perpetual terror of discovery. For Rosa, who organized the distribution, it gave a purpose to life, apart from Johannes.

She picked up a thick wad of freshly mimeoed sheets and put them in her big shopping bag.

170

'Rosa,' Abel said, 'you don't think Johannes really did see someone – following you, I mean?'

'Of course not, Uncle Abel. He's got bogey-men on the brain. He sees one behind every bush.'

'All the same, I'm worried. Why not let The Viking do the deliveries this week? He knows the system.'

'Certainly not.'

Abel stroked his hair.

'Things are changing,' he said. 'Every day there's another sabotage, every day the Germans are tightening their grip. It isn't a lark any more, it's getting damned dangerous.'

'I never thought it was a lark. Obviously it's dangerous. Denmark's becoming a dangerous place – and not a day too soon.'

'Well be careful.'

'I'm always careful.' She smiled. 'Don't worry.'

'Don't worry? You might as well tell me don't breathe.'

She took a No. 7 along Frederiksborggade, over the Queen Louise Bridge and into Nørrebrogade, getting off by the Assistens cemetery. There were V signs for Victory daubed on the high wall of the churchyard. The white paint had run, giving them a melting look.

It was when she entered the leafy maze of winding paths and overgrown burial plots that she had the first faint feeling that she was being shadowed. She decided to linger for a moment by a marble monument – a florid affair of grinning angels and cherubs – and watch and wait.

After a moment she heard footsteps, cautious and shuffling. She feigned fascination with the monument, then glanced round. The knot in her stomach relaxed: an old woman in a black dress was coming down the path. She carried a posy of fresh flowers. She smiled at Rosa.

'It's a beautiful afternoon.'

Rosa smiled back.

When the old woman was out of sight, she walked off in the opposite direction. She came to the big litter bin in the centre of the graveyard, looked round carefully, then took out a sheaf of *Truth*, and dropped it into the bin. She walked briskly away.

She made two more drops: in an alley off Nylandsvej; and in

171

the saddle-bag of a bicycle chained to the railings behind the Slotsgaarden Restaurant; then she went on to the final distribution point, Møller's vegetable shop in Istedgade.

'Good afternoon, Mrs Larsen,' Mr Møller said. 'I have your order all ready.'

He took her shopping bag and disappeared into the back of the shop. After a moment he returned and heaved the bag onto the counter. It was now full of potatoes and carrots; and empty of *Truth*.

The sense of relief she felt as she made her way back to the flat, a few streets away, was short-lived. Again she had the feeling that someone was following her. She stopped at a corner and turned her head quickly round; she could have sworn she saw a tall figure disappearing into a doorway.

She rounded the corner and put on a spurt. Half-way down the street she halted again, transferring the heavy shopping bag from one hand to another, and taking the opportunity of looking back down the street. Yes, surely it was the man again, a thin, lanky shape among the passers-by. He was pretending to look into a shop window.

She hurried now, panicky thoughts flashing through her mind. She must warn Abel. They must move the machine again, to a safer place; they must find new drop-off points. They probably wouldn't arrest her; they were only monitoring the system; they'd choose their moment to strike; mop up in one operation; that was the way they worked. Christ, what a mess.

She got to the flats. She didn't look round, but went straight in and up the communal stairs. She put down her shopping bag and fumbled for her key. Then she thought, no, wait. She picked up the bag again and mounted the next flight of stairs. She crouched on the half-landing. Through an angle of the metal banisters she could see her own front door. She decided to wait five minutes by her watch.

After two minutes she heard the footsteps. It could be Mr Kristensen or one of the other tenants, but somehow she knew that it wasn't. Whoever it was was coming up slowly – up to the first floor, the second. The click-click of heel on stone was louder now. She saw a shadow and a shape.

It was the man. He stopped by her door. He was wearing a grey, striped suit. He pressed the bell and she heard its faint ring.

172

She had a terror that old Miss Schumacher from upstairs would suddenly emerge from her flat and give her away by saying something. The man pressed the bell again, then turned, facing her.

In the first instant she thought: he's the man with the funny nose. In the next, as he began to move away from the door, she whispered:

'*Val.*'

She rose and stumbled against the shopping bag. Potatoes bounced and rolled down the stairs.

'*Val.*'

Her heel jarred on one of the potatoes, she clutched at the banister, missed; she was falling; then two strong arms were round her, holding her up, and her face was pressed against a hard, warm chest and her eyes were awash.

Slowly, with the tip of her index finger, she traced the outlines of his features. The high cheekbones were gone, so was the straight nose; his hairline had retreated giving him a dome-like forehead.

'It's incredible, Val,' she said.

They were lying in their bed, Valdemar on his back, Rosa leaning over him, her head propped up on one hand while the other explored his body minutely, inch by inch, as if she were blind and reading braille.

They had stood in the hall, wrapped round each other, sobbing and laughing – the first time she had ever seen him cry – and then there had been a kind of paralysis. Her mind had swarmed with so many questions that it had almost seized up. She'd asked him ridiculous things: 'How long have you been back?' 'Where are you living?' – a babble. And his replies had been stilted. She'd fussed about the kitchen, making him a cup of ersatz coffee which he didn't want, and it had been as if they were strangers spending their first evening together. 'Come on,' she'd said, 'you must be longing to make the grand tour. Nothing's changed.' In the bedroom he'd said: 'Rosa, you haven't made the bed.' She'd laughed. 'I told you nothing had changed.' He'd taken her in his arms then and she'd whispered: 'Oh, Val, I've longed for you so desperately,' and then it had been all right. The shyness, the embarrassment had evaporated, all the old tenderness had returned, and the familiar passion, and when it was over he'd

173

said: 'I didn't know if it would be – I thought –' and she'd closed his mouth with hers.

'Incredible,' she said again.

'But you knew me.'

'Oh yes.'

'Uncle Henrik didn't. I saw him on my first night back and he didn't begin to recognize me.'

'But why, Val? Why did you have to have it done?'

'So that I could operate here. You know what it's like – everybody knows everybody. Someone would have been bound to recognize me and blow my cover. Is it horrible for you, Rosa? Can you bear to look at me?'

He sat up. His face was haggard – she put her arms round him.

'It's only your face they've changed. They haven't changed you.'

'Maybe they have.'

'Val, I've got so many questions. Let's start again.'

'Rosa – can you really accept me, as I am now?'

'Of course I can.'

'I thought I might repel you. Deep down I thought that. I was glad I'd been instructed not to contact you. My bosses thought they were being cruel, but I was grateful. Then I saw you this afternoon, by the park, getting off the tram with Johannes and, I don't know, I just had to follow you. I thought I'd just follow you, then go away. Then I saw Johannes go off with Isak, then you came out, alone, and when you came back here I knew it would be safe to see you. When I rang the bell and you didn't answer I was relieved. I couldn't wait to get away.'

Rosa began laughing. 'You gave me a terrible fright,' she said. 'I thought you were the Gestapo.'

Valdemar began laughing with her. They held each other and laughed helplessly. Then, when the tension in them had been eased, Rosa said:

'Right, start from the very beginning, from the moment you set off that night. I want every detail.'

He reached out and fumbled for cigarettes and matches.

'Well, it went like clockwork,' he said. 'Not a sign of a patrol boat, no moon, a fresh breeze. I stove in the dinghy when I was well past Læsø and took to the rowing boat, just as we'd planned. The rest was just elbow grease – and luck. I saw a few lights

174

during the night but once the sun was up, not a sign of a ship. I heard they found the dinghy.'

'Found it? Your father organized the biggest man-hunt in history.'

He grinned.

'Go on.' Rosa said.

'Well, I landed. There was nobody about. I walked into Göteborg and took the train to Stockholm. That's when the trouble started. I thought there'd be an organization of some kind, but there was nothing. I couldn't even get a flight to England. There just weren't any. I got a job in a hotel kitchen – well it was a brothel actually – you know, no questions asked – and kicked my heels for months. Then at last I managed to make contact with the British and the next thing I knew I was on a train to Moscow.'

'*Moscow*?'

'Yes. Then to Turkey, and then a plane to Egypt, and South Africa, and then a ship to England.'

'Wasn't that rather a long way round?'

'It was the only possible route.'

'And then what?'

'Oh – training, endless training.'

He paused; she waited for him to continue and when he didn't she said:

'Val you're as wretched a raconteur as your father. *Tell* me.'

'It's not that I don't want to, Rosa, but I can't, I really can't. You shouldn't even know I'm in the country. Now you tell *me*. Tell me about Johannes.'

'He'll be back any minute – with Father.'

'They mustn't see me. It's vitally important.'

They jumped out of bed and began collecting their clothes and struggling into them.

Rosa said 'But I can see you again, Val?'

'I don't know. It's dangerous. I'll try. I must go now.'

In the hall they kissed, then he broke away.

'I must go.'

'Try to keep in touch.'

'I'll try.' He paused. 'Rosa, I'm so glad you don't mind about—' he touched his face.

175

'Don't be silly, Val. If you'd smashed yourself up in a car or something would you expect me to shun you?'

He opened the door.

'I wonder how you recognized me so easily?'

She didn't answer, and he kissed her again, briefly, then he was gone.

She closed the door. She went back into the bedroom to tidy up any traces of their love-making; she put their cigarette butts in the kitchen waste. Why *had* she recognized him so quickly, where his own uncle had failed to (and what had he been doing at his uncle's? Oh, the questions she hadn't asked him!)? Why had she recognized him? An answer suggested itself to her, a strange answer. There had been something intensely familiar about his face, his new face; not so much the individual features, but the whole cast of them. It was Valdemar, but at the same time it was not Valdemar, or rather it was another Valdemar. It was a Valdemar she had met before, once by the buried church in that first summer, a lifetime ago, then again in this very room, just before the invasion, when he'd squatted by the stove and she had put a blanket round his shoulders.

When Isak and Johannes erupted into the flat a few minutes later, Johannes clutching a huge fur rabbit, she said:

'Well, did you see any more bogey-men?'

'Lots and lots.'

'And he wanted to shoot them all,' Isak said.

20

It was a sweltering July afternoon and the temperature in the flat was almost unbearable. For once all the members of L Group were together: Lynx, the leader; Sven Carlsen; Christian, the cut-out; and little Birdie, the W/T operator. Lynx was reading the latest cables from London, Sven and Christian were playing piquet, and Birdie was fussing with his pet canary, pushing a piece of cuttle-fish through the bars of its cage.

Lynx smiled to himself. The trouble that bird caused! Once, when a German detector van had been only two streets away and they'd had to evacuate their house in a hurry, they'd left the cage behind. Birdie had been frantic for a day and in the end Lynx had been forced to prevail on *Holger Danske* to detail a couple of men to rescue the creature. Two lives risked for a scrap of yellow feathers: the Germans could easily have been watching the house. Then the damned thing had got caught up in the whole mesh of security, being passed from anonymous hand to anonymous hand as if it were a case of bazookas or a critical despatch from London. And when it had reached base at last Birdie had cooed and drooled over it. Still, he was the best W/T man in Copenhagen, an odd little fellow who'd been a librarian or an archivist or something. He never showed any fear, never displayed any signs of fatigue or boredom or frustration like the others; he seemed to reserve all emotions for his canary.

He looked across at Sven. Sven – his old friend – had no idea that Lynx was Valdemar Larsen, and Lynx had never, not by even the vaguest reference to the past they had shared, given him cause to suspect the truth. Sometimes Lynx marvelled at the ease with which he maintained the deception, without conscious effort or thought. It was as if Valdemar Larsen had really drowned in the Kattegat, and another being – Table Mountain, Lynx – had stepped onto the Swedish shore, with his own personality, his own past, his own mission.

But Valdemar Larsen was about to enjoy a brief resurrection; London had sanctioned it. The cable was in his hands:

Personal for Lynx. In view of potential tips from the horse's mouth it has been agreed that Lynx should take his hat off. But put it back on again quickly, in case you catch a cold in the head.

The other cables referred to Operation Pineapple, scheduled for tonight, the biggest thing so far organized by L Group. There was a characteristic postscript, in which Lynx detected the graveyard humour of Baynes: 'If necessary the baby must go with the bathwater.'

So be it. He stood up.

'I'm going out for a couple of hours. I'll be back before six.'

The others looked at him, Sven apprehensively.

'It's all right,' he said. 'A little side-show. I can't tell you about it.'

When Lynx had gone Sven said: 'He's so damned mysterious.'

'He's a fanatic,' Birdie said.

Karen was walking through the Citadel gardens on the way to catching a tram back to Hellerup. She had endured exactly a week

177

of Aunt Gertrud's querulous domestic complaints and interminable reminiscences, then she had gone home. Feeling that it would be prudent to conciliate her father she had feigned an interest in working and Niels had given her a job as a filing clerk at the offices in Bredgade. She had cut Kleist right out of her life and even resisted the temptation to contact Fritz. There had been no more anonymous threats and not a peep out of Gunther, who no doubt reckoned he was playing a clever game by biding his time. She thought of him now with nothing but revulsion, and only occasionally did she worry that the consequences of their association might yet have to be faced.

She was not aware that a man was following her until she heard a voice behind her say:

'Excuse me.'

She slowed down and turned to see a somewhat unprepossessing individual standing a few paces away and smiling very oddly.

'Yes?'

'I wonder if I could have a word with you?'

What was this – a pick-up? An emissary from Gunther?

As witheringly as she could she said: 'Well you can stop wondering. The answer is no.'

She turned and began walking away. He followed. She stopped again.

'Look – just leave me alone will you?'

He laughed.

'What are you so nervous about – Karen?'

She stared at him. He was a complete stranger; there was nothing familiar about him, except that he rather reminded her of Gunther – tall and gaunt, neither young nor old. She was suddenly apprehensive.

'I don't know you,' she said.

He didn't reply, but took an envelope out of his pocket. From the envelope he took a clipping from a magazine – her photograph, just like before, only not cut up this time but smeared with something.

'I wouldn't touch it if I were you,' he said. 'It's not very clean.'

Karen was suddenly terrified.

'Why don't we sit on this bench?' he said.

'If you touch me——'

'I'm not going to hurt you. Please sit down.'

She found that her legs were trembling and she obeyed him. He put the clipping back in its envelope, and the envelope back in his pocket, then sat down beside her.

'It was to have been delivered tonight,' he said, 'but I managed to forestall it. You've been a good girl recently.'

'Who the hell are you?'

There *was* something familiar about him. It wasn't the voice — it was—— She didn't know.

'This is difficult,' he said. 'Haven't you any idea who I am?'

She shook her head. She was even more frightened. Gunther's behind this, somehow, she thought.

'Oh well,' he said, 'prepare to swoon. I'm Valdemar.'

She didn't swoon, of course, she thought, my God it *could* be Valdemar, but——?

'Do you remember my wedding day,' he said, 'when you pissed behind a snowdrift?'

Old Johan had been put out to grass at last. Mr Niels had been very decent about it, talked about the war, the need for security, pressure from the Germans — he hadn't really understood. There were sabotage guards at the yards now, five of them; they called themselves 'harbour guards', and other people called them Quislings, whatever that meant. They were decent enough lads in their way, though; didn't mind him wandering about at night — thought he was cracked. 'The Old Man Of The Sea' they called him, and laughed at him behind his back. But he couldn't keep away. He couldn't be expected to change the habits of a lifetime, sleep at night and get up in the morning, it wasn't natural to him.

Mind you, he wasn't the man he had been, he had to admit that. He'd sit himself down in an odd corner of the yard and nod off — age, he supposed, though he didn't feel any older, except that it was harder to drag his leg around and nothing seemed to matter any more.

He'd tried talking to the Quislings but they weren't interested in his stories; didn't seem to have much stomach for the job either. Very keen they'd been at first, upholders of law and order, but they weren't so full of that kind of lip these days. He didn't really know what they were there for, he didn't know what all the fuss was about. There were a lot of Germans coming and going, of

179

course, at least he supposed they were Germans, but he didn't know.

He liked to play little games with the Quislings, creep up on them and eavesdrop. They were a dozy lot, they never heard him or saw him. A fine bunch of guards! Still, they let him wander about, and that was good; you could think in the dark, remember things. Lately he'd been remembering things far, far back, like watching his old father sitting under his boat on the beach at Skagen, sewing his nets, or like walking along the dunes after a storm looking for treasures. He'd forgotten a lot of the other things, the things that had come later; he liked to remember the early things: his first pair of boots that came up to his thighs and the nights when the wind rattled the tiles and he snuggled in with his brothers, warm and safe, with sleep washing over him like a wave. Then morning, seemingly only a second later – no dreams, no wakings in between – not like now. What was there now? Nothing much: a smoke, a *snaps*, his little games with the Quislings, memories.

He picked up his stick and began to shuffle along towards the main gate. He'd have a listen-in, that would keep him awake. They were always bragging about the women they'd screwed, boy's talk, a lot of lies – it made him chuckle sometimes.

He paused in the shadows and looked towards the gates. There was a truck approaching, and the Quislings were stirring themselves. Comings and goings! At this time of night! The truck halted. There was some talk – he couldn't hear it clearly – and the two lads were raising their hands in the air, as if someone was pointing a gun at them. Guns! It was all guns now. The Quislings had them, he'd seen them fingering them like children with toys. He'd never had a gun, never needed one.

The truck spurted forward and men jumped out of the back – one, two, three, four, five of them. They were running off, scattering. One of them ran right past him. Comings and goings! Here was a game! He'd move about and spy on them. They wouldn't see him or hear him – oh no.

As he moved away, placing his feet with infinite care – no stiffness, no pain now – he thought he heard shots, gun-shots. Here was a game! He'd find out what was going on; but they wouldn't see him, they wouldn't hear him, oh no. Ah, there was one of them, by No. 7, going at the door with a crow-bar. 'Phone old Thomsen – that was the thing – like he'd done before. Those Quislings were useless. They didn't know what to do.

Hah – the fellow had got the doors open – big chap, like Mr Valdemar. He had a pack on his back. He was going into No. 7. Bide your time, bide your time, old Thomsen's on the way. He'll settle their hash all right.

The big fellow was running out of No. 7 now. Run as hard as you like – you won't get away. He heard the roar of the truck, distantly, and thought – here's Thomsen.

He limped slowly out of cover, turning his head to left and to right. Now we'll see what Mr Valdemar's been up to. It was dark inside the warehouse. He pulled his torch out of his pocket and flicked it on. He played the beam around. The place was full of engines – they looked like engines – stacks and stacks of glinting metal things.

Now what would Mr Valdemar be wanting with a lot of engines?

Sven and Christian were waltzing round and round the room and Birdie was blinking and smiling. Lynx was drafting a cable to London.

Sven lurched past, holding out the bottle; he was drunk. Lynx took the bottle and tipped some *snaps* into his mouth. When the plastic had blown, with a great crump and buffet, one of the *Holger Danske* men had hugged and kissed him in the back of the truck.

He'd felt no particular sense of triumph, no more than a forester might feel when, having felled a pine, he looked ahead along the ride and saw the hundreds and hundreds of trees he had yet to bring down.

He wrote: 'Operation Pineapple was a complete success. Our observers report that the Larsen yards have been completely destroyed, including all the machine parts and weaponry delivered from the Globus factory in the last month. Several vessels were damaged. One of the sabotage guards, who resisted, was slightly wounded, but otherwise there were no casualties on either side.'

Then he added: 'All bathwater gone, all babies alive and kicking.'

The explosion had woken Gunther. He'd rolled out of bed and gone to the window. He'd pulled back the blackout and a faint orange glow had lit up the room. Then he'd gone into the next room and Karen had heard him telephoning. She'd got out of bed and gone to the window. Beyond the roof-tops she'd seen a smudge of light, like a loom at sea. It was coming from somewhere on the other side of the Sound. She'd got back into bed and lain on her back, waiting for Gunther to return, dreading the thought that, now he was awake, he would want to make use of her again. She could hear him talking in the other room, his voice high and hoarse with excitement.

He came back into the room and flopped into the bed, his weight tilting the mattress so that she slid towards him.

'What was it, Gunther?' she said.

He laughed – jeeringly she thought.

'What's so funny?'

'You'll find out in the morning.'

He lay on his back, making no move to touch her. She was relieved; but after a moment she thought, no, I've been a whore all my life, and now there's a purpose to it I should act like a whore. She snuggled up to him; then, without any preliminary strokes or caresses, she sought for the object of whose size he was so inordinately proud. She knew he loved that – it made him feel that she worshipped it, like a totem.

He grunted and said:

'Haven't you had enough?'

'I thought I had,' she said, 'but all those weeks – I couldn't get you out of my mind. I've got a lot of you to catch up on.'

Her fingers were busy – he gasped, and laughed again. For the first time since they'd met she felt a sense of power over him. What a fool the man was, what a vain, ugly fool. She knew all his nasty, perverted little secrets, she knew how to make herself indispensable to him – and she would, by God, she would. She wanted to murmur endearments – he liked that – but she was not sure that she could keep the mockery out of her voice; and in any case, there were more practical uses for her tongue.

182

21

As his car passed through the Amalienborg, Brenner told the driver to slow down. He peered out of the window. Yes, there were his own men, standing guard outside the palace. He sat back and told the driver to speed up. He wondered if Hanneken would relent and allow the Life Guards to resume their duties; after all, they were interning every officer and man in the Danish armed forces; surely a few privates could be spared as a sop to Danish pride? Yes, he would press for that.

The twenty-ninth of August was the day on which he was to have begun his leave. On the 27th, two days ago, all leave had been abruptly cancelled. It had hardly come as a surprise, not after what had happened in Ribbentrop's office in Berlin. He had flown to the capital as a member of General Hanneken's suite, to be a witness to the triumph of the Wehrmacht and the humiliation of the rival civilian administration in the person of Plenipotentiary Best. He had almost felt sorry for little, bureaucratic Best, standing there, blinking down his long nose, looking like a country lawyer – which he had been, of course – being verbally dismembered by a judge. And the Foreign Minister, with his silken voice and his aura of power, had made a formidable judge.

Best had tried to defend his record, had tried to persuade Ribbentrop that Denmark would settle down, that the policy of moderation could still work, but of course the facts were against him: the Larsen yards destroyed, the Forum Exhibition Hall blown sky high in broad daylight, over a hundred acts of sabotage in the first half of August alone; dockers' strikes in Odense and Esbjerg, riots and street fighting, German officers attacked by mobs – no, it was a sorry picture and Ribbentrop had made a meal of it. Hanneken had barely been able to conceal his delight when the Foreign Minister played his ace of spades: the Führer's patience was exhausted; the Führer's view was that the time had come for the iron hand. Best had paled. The judgement of God! Ah well, at least the poor fellow had been spared a personal tirade from his hero.

And so the long struggle for power in Denmark between Hanneken the military man and Best the civilian had ended there, on a thick Turkey carpet, with Generals and Under-Secretaries watching grimly from the ringside, and Hanneken clasping and unclasping his hands behind his back.

Brenner wished he could feel more elated by the victory. It had been a total rout for Best: Hanneken had come back with an ultimatum to the Danish Government in his pocket whose terms he knew they would refuse. And they had: at 3.45 this morning. Hanneken had laughed: 'Very well, gentlemen,' he'd said, 'let's get down to it.'

It had been 1940 all over again: lightning action, swift success; Danish army units surrendering all over the country, telephones cut, all strategic buildings seized, a complete takeover, all in three hours – and he'd felt the same ambivalence: shame that a decent, defenceless people should be so treated; pride in German efficiency. He had been secretly delighted by the Danish navy's unexpected show of spirit: they'd scuttled their ships rather than surrender them.

The car was passing through Hellerup, and he glanced out of the window. There was the turning to Karen's place; he wondered how her father had taken the sabotage of his precious shipyards. A fine man, Niels Larsen, if a little dour and humourless. Thinking of Karen made him think of Kleist. Well, that bastard would have to sing small now. He was one of Best's stars and, like his master, he would be eclipsed – not before time.

All things considered, he thought things had turned out for the best – yet he was uneasy – seriously uneasy. This arrest – what was it about? Why arrest a banker? Because he was a Jew? Was that it? Was that madness going to start here of all places? Surely not. After all there was still a chance that things would cool down. With strikes outlawed, a proper curfew, and German military courts to deal with Resistants, the country would soon be under control. But once let the Nazis' obsession with Jews run riot and – no. Hanneken would never permit it. But still he was uneasy.

The car passed through Rungsted and turned left, running through some pleasant country, wooded and undulating. As they turned in by a pretty, thatched lodge, he glanced back to make sure the motorbikes were still following. They drove up a long, curling avenue, past a lake, and pulled up on a gravel sweep in front of an imposing mansion.

Brenner deployed his men in a semi-circle on the gravel, and sent two off round the back of the house, then he marched up to the front door and rapped on it with the heavy brass knocker. The door was opened by an elderly maid. She looked terrified. She must have been spying out of the window, he thought. He walked past her into a large, overfurnished hall.

'I wish to see Baron Mendez,' he said gently.

The old woman goggled at him.

'Baron Mendez – where is he?'

'The – the Baron is at his breakfast,' she said.

'Show me, please.'

He followed her down a passage to the back of the house. She opened a door, then shrank away. He walked into a square, sunny room. There was an old couple sitting at a table in the window. The man was raising a cup to his lips and the woman was reading a book propped up on a silver coffee pot. Brenner bowed courteously.

'Baron Mendez?'

The old man lowered his cup.

'I am Mendez.'

'Colonel Brenner, Staff Headquarters. I'm afraid I have to ask you to accompany me.'

The Baron set his cup down carefully. 'Are you arresting me?' he said.

'Hans, what is it?' The woman turned to Brenner. 'What are you doing? He's having his breakfast.'

'Hush, Ruth.'

The Baron rose.

'Do you want me to come now?'

'If you would, please.'

'Should I pack some things?'

'I'm sure that will not be necessary.'

The woman – the Baroness, Brenner presumed – stood up.

'Where are you taking him? What has he done?'

'Be quiet, Ruth,' the Baron said, 'I shall be back shortly. There's nothing to worry about.'

He kissed her quickly. Brenner stood back to let him precede him through the door. The sight of the soldiers standing in his drive seemed to shake the Baron. Brenner gestured towards the car.

185

'Have you any idea what this is about, Colonel?'

'None at all. Truly. Please.'

The Baron got into the car. As they started off down the drive the Baron said:

'Surely you must have some idea what it is about, Colonel?'

'I really have none, sir, believe me. But I'm sure that it's nothing serious.'

The Baron was silent for a moment, then he said:

'Well, you have been most courteous. I'm grateful.'

Brenner hated himself at that moment, hated the duty he had to do. Was the Baron being arrested because he was a Jew? He couldn't get the idea out of his mind. He turned, to find that the Baron was staring at him. He was paler and his former assurance seemed partly to have deserted him. He's a shrewd old man, Brenner thought, he can read my mind.

'It's most probably routine. Bureaucracy, you know.' He tried to smile. The Baron nodded and stared out of the window.

22

'My dear sir,' Poul Larsen said, 'I can positively assure you that these fears are groundless.'

Simeon Mendez shifted in his chair and leaned forward.

'I have no doubt you're right; but there are certain things that puzzle my Committee — and worry them. Why, for instance, was my brother arrested? Why was Rabbi Friediger arrested, and Henriques?'

'My dear sir, why was the entire Danish army arrested? Our Government had resigned, the Germans were filling the vacuum. There was an extraordinary atmosphere — these things happen. After all your brother was released within five or six hours and received a personal apology from an officer on General Hanneken's staff.'

'But Henriques was held until only a few days ago and the Chief Rabbi is still in custody. And there are other matters, Larsen. Did you know that my synagogue was raided last week by German police? They took away files and lists, with the names of the members. Does that not strike you as ominous?'

'Not at all.' He leaned forward, placing his finger tips together.

'That particular action has been explained to me by Dr Best personally. It was purely a matter of police routine, information gathering.'

'Larsen, I think perhaps it is difficult for you, as a Gentile, to understand what we Jews felt on 29 August.' Simeon paused and then continued. 'A friend of mine had a summer cottage in Hornbaek and drove up there one night. There was a storm raging, and he was thankful to reach the shelter of his house. He lit the fire and warmed the room and looked out of the window at the lightning and rain, enjoying the spectacle, now that he was securely indoors. Then he went up to bed. He opened his bedroom door – and stepped straight into the storm. The roof of his house had been blown off. The rain was pounding into the room, the wind was blowing the furniture about. He was, he said, quite paralysed with the shock. All the assumptions he had made, by the fire, about how safe and protected he was, had been destroyed in an instant.' He leaned forward, his hands on his knees. 'Our Government was the roof which protected us Jews; suddenly it is gone. We have martial law, direct rule by the Germans. We can no longer make any assumptions. Do you understand that?'

Poul was silent for a moment, then he said:

'There are certain assumptions, however, which remain valid. The most important of these is the overriding policy which governs all the Germans' dealings in Denmark; that policy is for an ordered, stable society. It was to maintain order that they resorted to martial rule. Any action against Danish Jews would seriously jeopardize the social stability they rely on. It would simply be playing into the hands of the Resistance movement. I know for a fact that General Hanneken is totally opposed to any such measures——'

'They have been considered then?'

'Naturally there are some hard-line National Socialists who would like nothing better than to move against Jews, but these people have no influence. Hanneken is the power here. With every day that passes he consolidates his position and he would never countenance anti-Jewish measures. Never.'

'And all the rumours?'

'Obviously the work of extremists and anti-Semites. That surely is clear?'

187

'Yes, I suppose—— you are absolutely sure that there is nothing to fear?'

'My dear Rabbi, just look at it from the German point of view and ask yourself; what on earth would be the point?'

Riposte! Swift, subtle, and sure — a knife through Hanneken's guts. What a master Werner Best was, what a tactician — and what a fighter!

Kleist paced the tarmac; a chilly wind was blowing over Kastrup airfield, a foretaste, perhaps, of the blizzards about to blow round Hanneken's stiff neck. Major Günther's plane was late. The other members of the reception committee looked bored and cold. Kleist was not bored, nor was he cold: the prospect before him was sunny, thanks to the ingenious mind of Dr Best. Best needed to restore himself in the Führer's favour — he had done it! Best needed men — SS, Gestapo — to counterbalance Hanneken's little army — they were on their way! Best needed a weapon with which to destroy Hanneken's prestige — he had found it; the solution to all his problems, the 'final solution' perhaps (he smiled to himself): the Jews.

They would be rounded up and shipped off — no problem there; they'd had it easy for too long, they thought they were untouchable; but of course large forces would be required, forces that would act under Best's personal orders, not Hanneken's. Yet who would get the blame — there would no doubt be some bleating from the pious Danes? Hanneken would get the blame! Wonderful! But in Berlin, ah, in Berlin, the credit would go to Best and to Best's friends. There would be promotions; perhaps even, for him, a transfer to somewhere more interesting, Poland maybe, or France, somewhere where there was a real job of work to do.

He wondered if it would be possible to take Karen with him. Difficult — he couldn't marry her of course — but not out of the question. He hungered for her; the more she satisfied his appetites the more he hungered. She was perfect for him; she understood him.

A plane was dipping out of the grey sky. Kleist watched it land, turn, and taxi towards them. Surreptitiously he wiped his palms on the trousers of his uniform, then he stepped forward, with the others, to welcome SS Major Rolf Günther — an important man, a personal friend of Eichmann, a breath of the great world to liven up this dim little backwater.

23

Where the hell was she? What a time to choose to be late! But Karen was always late. She said that the only solution to her unpunctuality was for every clock in the world to be put back by half an hour.

Brenner rose from the bench and paced up and down by the duck pond for a minute or two; then he sat down again. Must have been mad to have arranged to meet her here, he thought; too bloody conspicuous – The Citadel only half a minute away, place crawling with his own men.

He looked round. He couldn't see any uniforms about, in fact there was only a girl playing with her little son on the grass, whirling him round and round by his arms. The little chap was screaming with delight. It reminded Brenner of that afternoon at Karen's house and her sister-in-law gambolling with her boy on the lawn. Dark-eyed creature: she'd subtly refused to talk to him, and then gone away quickly, the little boy protesting and whining. He'd asked Karen why. 'She's a Jewess,' Karen had told him, and he'd understood the hostility.

Where the hell was Karen?

He looked at his watch. Twenty minutes late already. He laughed to himself. Here he was, ready to rip up his oath of allegiance, keyed to the most fundamental betrayal – court martial and a firing squad, no doubt, if he were caught – and Karen hadn't even turned up. She had no sense of occasion, none at all.

Hanneken had done his best to stop the madness – bombarded Berlin with cables, to Jodl, Ribbentrop, everybody, but no, the Führer was adamant. Madness! Ah – there she was at last. She was running, she was breathless.

'Fritz, I'm sorry,' she panted, 'there's a bit of a panic on at the office. I can't stop long.'

'Sit down and for Christ's sake make it look as if we're here for a kiss and a cuddle,' he said.

They sat down on the bench and he put his arm round her.

'What is it, Fritz? What's it about?'

'It's about your sister-in-law.'

'Rosa?'

'Whatever her name is. You once told me that she's a Jew———'

'Yes.'

'Well you've got to warn her, and tell her to warn all her friends and family. The Jews are going to be arrested.'

'I know.'

Fritz blinked at her.

'What do you mean you know?'

'That's what all the panic's about at the office.'

'But how could you know?'

Karen was instinctively cautious. She trusted Fritz – but after all he was a German. 'It's all over town,' she said.

Fritz laughed shortly.

'My God,' he said, 'I've been agonizing all day about whether I should———'

'Fritz you must tell me everything you know.'

'It seems to be stale news.'

'No, go on, please.'

'Well – the arrests will start in two days' time, on October the First – at night. It's the Jewish New Year or something. The whole thing's been highly organized. They've drafted in special SS commando units, and ships will be coming to – take them away. Look, I'd better go.' He stood up.

He felt a strong sense of bathos and it made him want to be cruel.

'If you require any more detail, I should ask Gunther Kleist,' he said, and walked away.

Niels's brisk stride was the physical expression of a condition of mind, a condition he had hardly known since April 1940: purpose, clear purpose. Poul's telephone call had acted like the touch of cold water in the morning, or the report of a gun at the start of a race. All the doubts, and wavering, and questionings of the last few months had crystallized in an instant. It was not the work of an instant, of course – he realized that – it was the culmination of a whole series of nudges and shocks, some great, some small, that had been pushing him further and further towards a point he had never thought in all his life to reach: the point where the scales could be balanced no longer, but would

190

have to tip. And Poul's call had tipped them.

He could trace the process so precisely; from the very beginning, when he had seen those German soldiers marching up Bredgade, to the moment, only two months ago, when he had stood surveying the ruins of his yards − craters and metal skeletons − and had felt relief, yes relief, that he would no longer have to go on cooperating, go on compromising, go on making himself believe that his duty was to do business with the devil if need be. And when they had shown him the fragments of Old Johan's body, a severed arm, a section of trunk like butcher's meat − horrible − he had thought: this is what it means, this is war; for millions of people these are familiar sights, yet I have never seen a corpse before, not even the bodies of my mother and father. And just as at the beginning he had waited until the soldiers were out of sight before screwing up that leaflet, so then, as he had walked away from the lumps and splinters that were all that remained of his old friend, he had planned to retrieve it all, rebuild. Yet he found he had no zest for the complex wranglings over insurance and compensation; he was almost stand-offish with the fellow owners who offered him facilities and help; he had a feeling that the saboteurs had blasted away more than just the foundations of his stores and warehouses.

Now, his ideas were as firm as the crisp, energetic paces that were taking him down Bredgade, through the Amalienborg, into Tolbodgade, and up the broad stairs to Isak Abrahamsen's offices.

He brushed aside clerks and secretaries and marched straight into Isak's sanctum. Isak was alone; he looked up, startled, from some bills of lading. Niels closed the door, and dispensing with polite preliminaries, said:

'Abrahamsen, I have very grave news, terrible news. The Germans are going to move against Jews. They are going to arrest every Jew in the country.'

He had not thought about what Abrahamsen's reaction might be, but if he had, he might have expected shock, alarm, disbelief even; but not anger, certainly not anger. Yet Isak was rising.

'How dare you come bursting in here with this monstrous lie?' he said.

Niels gaped at him.

'*How dare you?*'

191

'I – I apologize if I've shocked you, perhaps I should have——
but it is true, I assure you, it is quite true. You are in very great
danger.'

Now Isak laughed – shortly – and sat down again.

'You of all people,' he said. 'I would never have thought that
you were capable of believing these hysterical rumours, still less
of repeating them. I had always given you the credit of being, at
least, a responsible man.'

Niels realized that he had acted too precipitately.

'Please listen to me,' he said. 'This is not a rumour, it is a solid
fact. The Germans intend to arrest the Jewish community on the
night of October the First. That is Rosh Hashanah, is it not, your
Jewish New Year, an important festival when Jews are supposed
to remain in their homes? You see how easy it would be for
them?'

Isak glared balefully at him.

'I don't understand your motives in telling me all this, I can
only assume that they are sincere, but I happen to know that you
are mistaken.'

'Is it because *I* am telling you that you don't believe it? Is it
because of the – differences we have had in the past?
Abrahamsen, I beg you to believe me, I implore you. You and
Rosa and your brother must come to my house immediately. We
will hide you. And you must warn all your friends.'

Isak laughed again.

'Have you any idea how ridiculous you look? You look like a
ham actor in a third-rate melodrama.'

Niels had attended enough business meetings in his life to
recognize an impasse.

'I see that I cannot convince you,' he said. 'Very well, I will
leave. But please remember that my house is your house, and that
I will do everything in my power to help you.'

When Niels had gone Isak sat for a moment, playing with a
pencil. What the hell was happening in the country, he
wondered, that could turn such a pillar of propriety as Niels
Larsen into a panic-monger? What was behind it? Should he
contact the chairman of the Committee? No. Why spread the
poison?

He picked up the bills of lading again. What on earth had got
into Larsen? He leafed through the documents – really, what

192

next? – he began to concentrate on more important things.

'Andersen, Andersen, Aaronsen,' Christina Larsen stopped and made a mark in the margin of her address book.

'Are the Aaronsens Jewish?' she asked.

'I don't know,' Niels said. 'I don't think so.'

'It's a Jewish sounding name.'

'I suppose it is.'

'Well, good heavens, Niels, you've known Flemming Aaronsen for twenty years; surely you know if he's Jewish or not?'

'I've never thought about it.'

'Well we'd better put them on the list. Now, the Bardfelds, surely they're Jewish?'

'You were at school with Lotte Bardfeld, you should know. Didn't you go to her wedding?'

'Yes I did.'

'Well, was it in a synagogue?'

'I can't remember. I rather think it was at her home.'

'Well, put her on the list anyway.'

After half an hour Niels and Christina had a list of twenty families, friends of theirs, who they thought might be Jewish. The only family of whose religion they were sure was the Abrahamsens.

Christina said: 'It's extraordinary. I lunch with Lotte Bardfeld at least twice a month and we discuss everything under the sun, I mean I regard her as an intimate friend – yet I have no idea what her religion is.'

'Well never mind that now,' Niels said, 'is there anybody locally we should warn? What about that little man at the clothes shop in Hellerupvej? And Golinsky at the garage?' He stood up. 'I'm going out. You'd better get on with telephoning. If Isak Abrahamsen's reaction is anything to go by, half of them won't believe you. If they don't we must just go round and persuade them personally.'

Niels walked as quickly as possible to the little garage in Strandvejen where, for over fifteen years, his cars had been serviced and repaired. It was getting on for dusk and the curfew, and he had no pass. He found Golinsky in his workshop, struggling with a large, synthetic rubber tyre.

'Good day, Mr Larsen,' Golinsky said cheerfully. He gave the tyre a kick.

'Golinsky,' Niels said, 'forgive me – but are you by any chance Jewish?'

Golinsky stared at him. Niels thought, damn it, I've done it again – but how the hell *do* you ask such a question?

'I'm sorry,' he said. 'But it's extremely important. Are you?'

Golinsky scratched his head. 'Well,' he said, 'I don't really know – I think I was at one time – yes, I suppose I am, if you put it like that. My old papa didn't go in for that sort of thing much.'

'Would your name be on any list? Do you attend a synagogue?'

'Well, my wife goes, I think. Not very often, you know. She's always at me to take a bit of interest, but what I say is work first, then play – I like to get out into the countryside, get a bit of fresh air into my lungs and——'

'Golinsky, I think you might be in very great danger.'

He explained. Golinsky seemed puzzled at first, but he was perfectly willing to accept Niels's story – he had a genuine respect and liking for this rich shipowner, who'd never put on airs; what he failed to grasp was that this business of rounding up Jews had anything to do with him.

'You don't have to worry about me, Mr Larsen,' he said. 'I haven't done anything wrong. I keep myself to myself, always have.'

'You don't understand. It isn't a question of what you have or haven't done. If your name is on a list you will be arrested – and your whole family. You must go into hiding.'

Golinsky laughed, but he looked nervous suddenly.

'Go into hiding? How can I do that? I have my business.'

God, this was hopeless, Niels thought. He said:

'Listen, Golinsky. Contact your friends. Get your wife to contact her rabbi. He will confirm that what I say is true. I will come back tomorrow. Have you any friends, non-Jewish friends, who could hide you?'

Golinsky looked bemused.

Niels said: 'If you can't find anywhere, you must come to my house and bring your family. I will come back tomorrow.'

Isak was startled by the ring of the doorbell. With the curfew, it was rare to have visitors after dark.

194

'All right, Jensine,' he called out, 'I'll see who it is.'

He opened the door and blinked. It was Poul Larsen.

'I suppose your brother sent you,' he said – rudely, as he instantly realized.

'He asked me to come.'

'You'd better come in.'

Isak ushered him into the drawing room and Poul refused the offer of a drink.

'Abrahamsen,' Poul said, 'I have come to tell you that everything my brother said is true. The Germans will move against the Jewish community on October the First. It is certain. You are in great danger.'

Isak eyed him coldly.

'I am astonished to hear such a statement from a man in your position,' he said. 'For months the Jewish community has had to put up with rumour and counter-rumour, gossip and speculation. The Germans will do this, the Germans will do that, the Jews are doomed, the Jews have nothing to fear. Can you imagine the effect this has on people?'

Poul attempted to say something but Isak went on:

'Only a week ago you personally assured my uncle, Simeon Mendez, that an action against the Jews was an impossibility. My uncle reported your views back to the Committee and to the members of his synagogue. Now you stand here and tell me that an action is imminent.'

Poul rubbed his hands together in a nervous gesture and said: 'What I told the Rabbi – I sincerely believed to be true. But there have been developments. I don't fully understand as yet, it is a question of the rivalry that exists between Doctor Best and General Hanneken, but there is no doubt about the source of my information, no doubt at all.'

Isak stared at Poul, conscious of a growing feeling of apprehension – there could be no doubting the Extra Secretary's sincerity. Yet he was still sceptical.

'What information?' he said.

'This afternoon I had a call from – well, from a prominent member of the Social Democratic Party, a man I have known for many years. He told me about the proposed action. He had received his information directly from a member of Doctor Best's staff.'

'A stool-pigeon at German Headquarters? Really Larsen, how can I believe that?'

Poul looked at him keenly. 'I have been asked not to reveal his name, but I will tell you. I think you know the man. It is Duckwitz.'

Now Isak stared. He did know Duckwitz, the German naval attaché, he knew him and liked him. Isak was suddenly a very frightened man.

'You see, you must make arrangements immediately,' Poul said. 'My brother will help you. You must warn your family and friends. Are you in contact with your daughter? She must be told.'

But Isak was hardly listening. He had sat down in his armchair. He couldn't remember having taken his handkerchief from his pocket but there it was, in his hand, and he was twisting and pressing it.

——24——

Simeon's voice was clear and strong and the cadences of the petitional prayer for a good year filled the Synagogue. Isak sat in the gallery, alone, looking down on the rows of black Homburgs and skull-caps. There were perhaps a hundred people at the special pre-Rosh Hashanah service. In his white vestments Simeon looked broader and taller than usual and when he moved his head there were glints of reflected light from his spectacles.

Already Isak felt drained. There had been an emergency meeting of the Committee at half-past nine, a lot of badly scared men struggling to be businesslike, to make sensible arrangements. Below the surface of the debate Isak had sensed a mounting atmosphere of every man for himself. He had detected the attitude in his own actions as he made efforts to contact Meyer, so that he could make arrangements.

The prayer came to an end. Isak saw Simeon's assistant move forward, carrying the *shophar*. His knowledge of ritual was sketchy; it was the muted reactions of the congregation below that alerted him to the fact that this was somehow out of order.

The long, plaintive note of the ram's horn sang out and died away. Then Simeon, without preamble, announced that there

196

would be no New Year service tomorrow, and no Tashlikh ceremony. Isak felt the shock waves rise from below, almost like a wind; but he hardly listened as Simeon explained to a silent, staring congregation that they had only a day to go into hiding: his mind was full of another scene – Valdemar Larsen standing with a glass in his hand, his pale cheeks a little flushed, inviting a room full of shocked, bemused people to drink a toast to Adolf Hitler.

On the way to Abel's complete strangers accosted him, singled him out – how, why, because of his appearance? – and offered him help. It was extraordinary and rather horrible. In Strøget a woman came up to him and said: 'I have heard. I know all about it.' She dangled a key at him. 'You can go to my cottage at Ejby. It's completely isolated. They won't find you there.' She began to scribble the address on the back of an envelope.

By the time he reached Abel's he was in a state of mild panic, his confidence eroded, his emotional bearings adrift. Abel's attitude was the final incomprehensibility.

'No,' he said, 'no, no. I won't go.'

'For the love of God, Abel, you must come with me.'

'There's no point, Isak, none.'

'But you can't possibly stay here, Abel.'

'Why not? My name is not on any list. I'm not a Jew. I've never been a Jew.'

Isak gaped at him. Then he said:

'If you don't want to go to the Larsens', you can find somewhere else. You have hundreds of friends.'

'Of what conceivable use would it be for me to run off and hide in somebody's cellar? I might just as well stroll down to Dagmarhus and say here I am, I am a Jew, I think you might have missed me out. And say I do go scuttling off – what then? Do I spend the rest of my life sitting in an attic somewhere, shivering with fear at every knock on the door? I can see there's some sense in your lying low, Isak, you're a well-known man; but who am I? And anyway,' he made a stage gesture and thickened his voice, 'who'd mind the shop?'

Isak was completely flummoxed.

'I don't understand you, Abel. I simply don't understand you. What can I say to make you see reason?'

'My dear fellow, nothing you could say would induce me to do anything but remain quietly where I am. You really mustn't worry about me. I shall be perfectly all right. Look to yourself – and Rosa.'

'I can't just leave you here.'

'Listen, if anything does happen, I'll do a vanishing trick. Does that make you feel easier?'

'But how?'

'As you said yourself I have hundreds of friends, I really am quite capable of looking after myself, you know.'

'Why not just come to the Larsens' with me now?'

'No, no – it wouldn't be congenial. Look, you'd better be on your way. Have a cup of coffee before you go. I'm sure we could persuade The Viking to do us a cup.'

'Abel, you really are quite extraordinary.'

He was baffled. Abel seemed positively cheerful. Was it an act? Could it be? Or was it simply his stubbornness, that maddening stubbornness of the weak?

'Well, I've done my best,' he said, feebly enough.

'Indeed you have, Isak. Believe me I'm very touched. Now what about that coffee?'

'No – no, thank you. I'd better go.'

Abel ushered him through the shop, and opened the street door for him.

'I think you're mad, Abel, completely mad.'

'Ah, Isak, you've never credited me with any sense, have you? You've always felt you should play the elder brother and guide my faltering footsteps. But you really must allow me to do what I think is right, you really must.'

Abel held out his hand. Isak took it and as he shook it he felt an extra pressure from his brother's fingers.

'Goodbye, my dear fellow,' Abel said. 'I'm sure you'll be all right. Don't worry about me.'

Abel returned to the back room and sat down. He felt exhausted. What a performance! Idiotic of him not to have pretended from the start that he'd made arrangements to go into hiding. Isak would only fret now, poor, dear chap. Still, as long as he didn't worry Rosa. Wouldn't do to have Rosa worried. But Isak would have more sense, surely?

'I think you'll be comfortable in here,' Christina Larsen said.

'Rosa and Johannes are next door. I hope you won't mind sharing a bathroom with the Golinskys. Not that there's much hot water, I'm afraid.'

Isak put his case down on a chair. He'd felt horribly conspicuous carrying it through the streets. Once or twice he'd almost dumped the thing – there was nothing much in it, anyway – a few clothes, shaving kit, money, various business papers. He'd wandered round his flat trying to think what he should take – like in that game one used to play as a child: the house is on fire, you can choose three things, what would they be? – and had found his mind was a complete blank. Silver? Photographs? Books? Jewelry? Well, he'd taken Miriam's diamond necklace, the one he'd given her on their first wedding anniversary. It was worth a lot of money – he'd need money, he supposed. Or would he? What was going to happen? He didn't know. It was all so completely unreal. Even Christina Larsen was unreal, chatting gaily as if he were an ordinary visitor just staying for a weekend.

'I'll leave you to unpack,' she said. 'Niels is in his study. I think he'd like a word with you. Dinner's at seven – rather a crowd.'

'How many people have you, I mean——'

'Well, with the family and the Golinskys and the Bardfelds it's – let me see – it'll be ten, not counting children.' She laughed gaily. 'Quite a party. I'll see you at dinner.'

A few minutes later Johannes burst into the room, followed by Rosa.

'Grandpa, Grandpa – are you staying too?'

Isak wrestled briefly with the boy, then kissed Rosa.

Rosa looked at the open case. 'What did you pack?' she said. 'I couldn't think of anything. Johannes made all the decisions. I've come away with half a toy shop.'

Isak laughed and picked Johannes up.

'Have you got your rabbit?'

'He's going to sleep in my bed all night,' Johannes said firmly.

'Father, where's Uncle Abel? I thought he was coming.'

'He's made his own arrangements,' he said quickly – better not to worry her. 'You know what an independent so-and-so he is.'

'He's all right?'

'Oh yes.'

'What about Jensine?'

'She's staying on at the flat. She absolutely refused to budge. I pity the German that tries to——'

He faltered. Rosa said:

'I'd better get Johannes to bed. Come along, darling.'

'Why are you looking so sad, Grandpa?' Johannes asked.

Isak attempted a smile.

'Grandpa, you can have Rabbit to sleep in your bed if you like.'

Niels looked up from the typewritten sheets.

'Are you sure this is what you want?'

'It's a question of whether you're prepared to take it on,' Isak said.

'But is there nobody else?'

'I don't know. I haven't had time to think. I don't know what's going to happen. I may have to leave the country. I must make provision.'

'I am rather a curious choice.'

'I don't think so. Even if I had had time to consider I think I would have asked you. We have never been friends, Larsen, but I have never had any doubts about your probity – or your business abilities.'

'Are you sure this document is valid?'

'My lawyer drafted it this afternoon. It's perfectly legal.' He smiled briefly. 'I'm surprised you're so reluctant. I thought you might feel that you were only getting back what was rightfully yours in the first place.'

'I might feel just that – doesn't the idea worry you?'

'Not in the least. You are not the man to take advantage of an abnormal situation. In a way the special circumstances that exist between us are a guarantee.'

'But we have been competitors – enemies, if you like – all our working lives.'

'Exactly – and as a result I have been able to judge your qualities and weigh you up. Put yourself in my position, Larsen – suddenly uprooted from everything, probably facing months of hiding, even capture. I must be sure that my affairs are in safe hands.'

Niels laid the papers down on his desk.

'Very well,' he said.

'Thank you.'

Isak took out his pen and signed the papers quickly, then he pushed them towards Niels.

'If you would sign there — and there.'

He offered him the pen. Niels took it; he bent forward; his neat, trim signature glistened black beneath Isak's flamboyant scrawl.

Niels felt curiously awed; it was an extraordinary moment, difficult to take in. By this irrevocable deed of transfer, he stood owner, absolutely and in his own right, of Isak Abrahamsen's entire wealth: his bank accounts — there were the balances efficiently noted — his freeholds and leases, all listed — his shares in various companies, over thirty of them — his income from the Mendez family trust — everything; everything including the largest asset of all: his controlling interest in R. Abrahamsen & Son Shipping. How many millions of kroner — four, five?

'It's traditional, at the conclusion of a business arrangement,' he heard Isak say. He looked up; Isak was offering his hand. He took it. Isak was smiling somewhat tautly.

'Don't spend it all at once,' he said.

'You and Isak were closeted for hours,' Christina said. 'What were you talking about?' She was already in bed, and Niels climbed in beside her.

'Business.'

'Niels, you're incorrigible. Business — at a time like this!'

'Abrahamsen has made over all his assets to me. Naturally there was a lot of detail to thrash out.'

'I don't understand — what do you mean, all his assets?'

'Everything he owns. What else can he do? There's a lot of money involved. He has to make some sort of arrangement.'

'Niels, how perfectly priceless!'

'It's a great responsibility.'

'But you of all people! Still, I think he's wise. He'd never find a more honest man. Do you want to read?'

'No — no I'm tired.'

She switched out the light and they shifted about until they were lying comfortably side by side.

'Niels,' Christina said, 'I've been trying to think ahead. The Abrahamsens, and the others, they can't stay here indefinitely. They'll have to get out of the country.'

201

'I know. I have been thinking about that too. They must go to Sweden.'

'Yes – but how? There must be thousands of Jews in hiding tonight, all over Denmark. They're safe for the moment, but the Germans won't just give up, they'll go on hunting for them. Somehow we've got to smuggle them out – all of them. Well, that'll need organization.'

'It will. I wish to God I knew someone in the Resistance. I shall make enquiries tomorrow. It shouldn't be too difficult to make a contact.'

Christina was quiet for a moment, then she said: 'I can give you some contacts.'

'I mean with Resistance people.'

'So do I. I – well, I have been doing some work for them.'

Niels sat up and switched on the bedside light. He stared at his wife.

'You?'

'I don't do much – just carry messages, pick things up and deliver them. Don't look so cross.'

Niels wasn't cross, he was astonished.

'But why have you never told me?'

'We're not allowed to.'

'How long have you been involved in this?'

'Oh – quite a time. Lie down, Niels, I'm getting cold.' She tugged at the blankets.

'How long? When did you start?'

'You'll laugh.'

'No. Tell me.'

'Well, it was after the fall of France. When they marched into Paris.'

Niels did laugh.

'You see. I knew you'd think it was funny.'

'Why the fall of France? What about the fall of Denmark?'

'I don't know. It just seemed as if they were destroying everything, everything beautiful and precious.'

Niels lay back on the pillows. What a night of revelations! Christina a Resistant! How had she managed to get away with it without his finding out? How had she kept the secret?

'Well, you're the sly one,' he said. 'Have you got a lover as well?'

202

She chuckled. 'I certainly wouldn't tell you if I had. Do you want me to give you a name – of someone you can contact?'

'Yes. We must do everything in our power.'

'I'm so glad, Niels. I've hated having to keep secrets from you. But you were always so anti.'

'I'm not now.'

They lay in silence for a while. I shan't sleep, Niels thought. Christina suddenly said:

'There's something else, Niels, another reason why I joined, in a way. When Val disappeared, I knew at once what he was trying to do and I was sure he'd succeeded. I'm certain he's alive. He's here somewhere, fighting. I think Rosa knows it, I think she's seen him – but of course she can't say anything.'

'My God – this war – it's turned everything upside down. Surely Valdemar would have given us some sign?'

'He couldn't. I know the way they work. He wouldn't be allowed to.'

Niels was silent for a long while, then:

'I didn't realize – that people were so dedicated.'

'Some of them are. Totally.'

'I feel like a fool.'

'Don't.'

'I do. I feel ashamed.'

'Well, don't. Go to sleep.'

'I shan't sleep.'

She smiled to herself. Sure enough, in a very few minutes he began to snore, but very softly and inoffensively – how else, bless him?

25

Abel stood in the passage by the door of The Viking's room. It was quiet, uncannily quiet; he could hear the boy's deep, regular breaths through the thin wooden panel; each intake of air was as if he were sniffing a sea breeze, each exhalation was like a sigh – beautiful sounds.

Thursday had been a strange day, today even stranger: there had been this same quality of quietness, with hardly any customers in the shop, only the odd friend, breathless and conspiratorial, offering him shelter. Rather mean, really, to dash the cup of noble self-sacrifice from their lips with the lie, tripping more and more lightly off his tongue with every visit and every telephone call, that he had already made arrangements. Well, the telephone was dead now – an ominous sign. In a telephone-crazed country like Denmark, cutting the lines was like severing the collective vocal chords of the nation.

He was fascinated by his own state of mind. What had he been thinking about in these last two days? Practical matters? Yes, but not to any great extent. His father? Yes, obviously his father. Food? Yes, he had thought quite a lot about food. His appetite had remained good. He'd made rather a pig of himself, in fact. Books? Yes, to a degree; one could hardly rid oneself of the habit. But mostly he'd thought about – well, nothing; just nothing. Very odd. A defence mechanism? Or was it simply that, in the circumstances, there was really nothing to think about?

He opened the door, letting a shaft of light into The Viking's room; but the boy did not stir. He walked very softly over to the bed and stood looking down at the sleeper, sprawled on the bed, his limbs barely covered by the sheet. Ah, this was the very essence of beauty; every dip and curve spelt perfection, purity even, yes purity; there was true purity, after all, in an unconscious form; its display was utterly natural, there could be no posing, no coquetry, no falseness in it.

The boy stirred and turned over; he was awakening. Damn.

'What is it?' – a groggy mumble.

'Go back to sleep. I didn't mean to wake you.'

The Viking rubbed his eyes.

'Why are you dressed? What time is it?'

'I don't know. It's late. Go back to sleep.'

But The Viking was fully awake now. He grinned.

'I don't mind,' he said. 'If you want to.'

'I don't want to.'

'I bet you do.'

'I don't.'

'Well, I wouldn't mind.'

'I – don't – want – to.'

'Oh, all right. Why did you come in then?'

'No reason.'

'Go on, you must have had a reason.'

204

'I just wanted to look at you, that's all.'

'Look at me? You're cracked.'

'There's no doubt about that, I'm afraid.'

'Why would you want to just look at me?'

'I can't explain.'

'Well, I think it's cracked.'

'And I think the rest of the world would agree with you. Go back to sleep now. Good night.'

He closed the door gently. The Viking would soon drop off again – he was a very sound sleeper; in fact he was hardly ever truly awake.

He went downstairs to the big sitting-room at the back of the shop. The clock on the mantelpiece said half-past two. He had somehow decided that they'd come at three. It seemed to be a suitably macabre hour; he was sure the midnight knock never actually fell at midnight.

He thought about his father again. Such instinct, and such a command of language – he should have been a poet. Perhaps I should have been a poet, he thought, I can see, I can imagine, I *know*. But this was not the time to revive those nightmares, he'd done enough imagining when Isak had first brought the news to him. Poor Isak, he hadn't a gram of poetry in him; he'd go blundering bravely on, through all the pain and horror and degradation – for what? For life, he'd no doubt say. The most sacred thing in the world, life. Was it?

He took the case of duelling pistols from the shelf and put it on the table. He sat down and ran his fingers over the dark walnut. Ivory inlay, and tastefully executed to boot. He opened the lid and took out one of the slender long-barrelled pistols. There was ivory in the butt too – a touch of rococo in the asymmetrical swages and curlicues. Craftsmanship! They understood that in the eighteenth century, and they understood beauty. The sacredness of life – a nineteenth-century idea. None of that nonsense when this barrel had been turned, when gentlemen strolled out into a meadow at dawn and did their best to kill each other defending some nice point of honour, concerned only that they should die with elegance, if they had to die, or kill with grace, if they should be so fortunate or skilled as to prevail. Life given up for a trifle, life taken for a bagatelle.

He put the barrel of the pistol to his lips; the metal had an electrical taste, with a touch of oil to it. It would work; it was primed and loaded; he'd tested it. Of course it would work; it had been fashioned by craftsmen. Better hold it like this, to his mouth, while he waited. He had taken the first step, why bother to take it again? Was time moving, or was time standing still?

Ah – there – surely? Yes. A truck pulling up in the street – a squeak of brakes – boots on the cobbles, rifle butts battering on the door. Yes, time had stopped, it had definitely and distinctly stopped.

It was the shot that woke The Viking, not the rattle of the truck's engine, or the tramp of feet, or the shouts. He stumbled down the stairs, wrapping a towel round his waist, and half fell into the sitting-room. There were five or six soldiers in the room, and Abel had slipped off his chair, and there was a splash of red and grey on the wall behind him.

His mind said: 'Run.' But his body wouldn't move.

'Grab him.'

Then his body obeyed. But it was too late; there was agony in his groin, vomit in his throat.

He screamed again and again: 'I'm not a Jew, I'm not a Jew, I'm not a Jew.'

Rosa watched the dawn very gradually infuse the pattern of flowers in the curtains with colour. Johannes had fallen asleep clutching his rabbit; he held the furry toy in a tight embrace and there was an intent look on his face, as if sleeping demanded all his concentration. She herself had slept fitfully, too excited to let her mind close down. Fleeting dreams had been interwoven with scenes vividly conjured from her imagination: meeting Valdemar in the flat, and lying with him in their bed, while anonymous men guarded the street outside; following a trail of cryptic instructions to a lonely farm and finding him there; a theatre ticket in an envelope pushed under the door, groping for the right seat in the dark and finding him waiting. She was sure that he would make contact; she knew that he was thinking of her, worrying about her safety; she had proof. The young man who had come to the flat to warn her about the German action – 'Christian' he called himself – was obviously an emissary from Valdemar, though equally obviously he had no idea that she was the wife of the man he served, whom he doubtless knew by another name.

206

Christian would come again – she was certain of it. He would bring a message; there would be a time and a place and Valdemar would be there. He would have a plan to get her and Johannes – and Father too – out of the country. It was no dream; she knew it. Dreams! She had dreamed about Grandpapa and she had thought about him; both her conscious and her unconscious mind had turned over, again and again, the memories of that last day of his life, those visions and intuitions of his, now reality: Jews being driven out of the city, ordinary Danes transformed into Jew-baiters. But that part of it was wrong, surely it was wrong. Niels Larsen was not behaving like a Jew-baiter, nor was anyone else. All the rumours and reports spoke of a great rising up of the Danes in defence of their fellow countrymen, a great stretching and blinking and waking through the nation, thousands of individual acts of compassion and courage adding up to a rebirth of faith, a rediscovery of principle. What did it all mean? Grandpapa had glimpsed the future, no doubt about that, but his view had been blurred and distorted – by what? Illness? A degeneration in the tissue of his brain? She remembered death crackling in his throat and her father's grip on her shoulder, Uncle Abel's blind flight, and Grandmamma shooing them away.

Grandmamma!

She sat up in bed. Grandmamma! Nobody had warned Grandmamma! She felt a surge of guilt – but no, surely Father would have rung her or Rosenhus. Of course he would have.

She hadn't thought about Grandmamma for months, and she hadn't seen her for three years. Grandmamma had never accepted the marriage and had been profoundly shocked by Johannes's chronologically embarrassing arrival. She had written a letter, cold, accusing, and bitter. Father had tried to patch things up, with the sole result that he had quarrelled with his mother and stopped going to her tea parties. But they had not fallen out to the extent that he could have forgotten to warn her, surely? Yet he had not mentioned her – not a word. She got out of bed, slipped into a dressing-gown, and went into the room next door.

His voice came out of the half-light, thick and nasal.

'What is it? Can't you sleep either?'

'Father, what about Grandmamma? You have warned her? Somebody's looking after her?'

Isak sat up. *Mother!* He'd never checked with Salomon that he'd rung Rosenhus. Salomon had volunteered to contact all the institutions – old people's homes, schools. Twice he'd remembered to check with Salomon, but there had always been another problem. Three or four times he'd reminded himself that he must find out what arrangements had been made for the old ladies at Rosenhus, make sure that Mother was safely in hiding; and each time something had happened to put it out of his mind. He'd hardly seen his mother or thought about her for months. She had made her own world, living in the lap of luxury, waited on hand and foot, and playing the grand old lady to all her Mendez relations.

'Of course she will have been warned,' he said.

'You don't sound certain. Didn't you ring yourself?'

'No – I didn't have time. But all the institutions have been warned – they must have been. Anyway, Hans or Simeon will have rung her – bound to have. That's where she'll be – with Hans.'

'But haven't *you* spoken to her?'

'No, no, I – my God, I should have done. I'll do it now.'

'The telephones are dead – they went dead last night.'

'Of course they did. Look, I'm sure she's all right. There can't be a single Jew in Denmark who hasn't heard the news.'

'I'm going to go up there.'

'Rosa, you can't.'

'It's only a fifteen-minute walk.'

'But the curfew.'

'It's getting light.'

'You can't be seen on the streets – it's madness.'

Isak climbed out of bed.

'I'll go,' he said. 'It's my responsibility. I'm certain she won't be there, but——'

'You can't possibly go, Father. That really would be madness. But the name on my passport is Larsen. I doubt if they'd arrest me – and anyway I'll make sure nobody sees me.'

'You can't possibly risk it, Rosa. Think of your son. I'll ask Larsen to go.'

'No. One of us should go. It's our responsibility. I feel terrible. How could I have forgotten about her?'

'*You* feel terrible? No, I must go.'

208

'No, Father. If they picked you up, you wouldn't have a chance. But if I take my passport with me——'

'I'll wake Larsen.'

'No. We can't ask any more of him. Anyway – I'd rather he didn't know.'

They avoided each other's eyes.

'I'll get dressed,' she said.

Charlottenlund was always quiet but at that hour it was deserted; the big villas, half-hidden behind their walls and gardens, had a curtained, shut-in look about them. Rosa walked as quickly as she could, almost running; it was cold and her breath plumed in front of her, and her mind raced and whirled. She was not frightened of being stopped and questioned – she had a well-rehearsed story – no, she felt too guilty to be frightened. She felt as guilty as when she had broken that vase of her father's. No rationalization could remove the feeling. Of course Grandmamma had been moved to safety; of course, when Rosa got to Rosenhus, she would find the non-Jewish staff rattling around in an evacuated building; they would give her a cup of coffee and breathlessly relate the tale – 'Your grandmother made such a fuss! Insisted on taking all those old photographs of hers!' – of course that was the way it would be; yet she and Father should not have forgotten about the old lady all the same. But Grandmamma had always been so remote and unapproachable. While Reuben was alive his warmth and generosity of spirit had made their home an inviting place; after his death Hannah had deliberately sought seclusion in the enclosed world of an institution, and after a period of rather irritating nostalgia – 'If only Reuben were alive', 'It's what Reuben would have wanted' – she had expunged virtually all references to her husband from her conversation. It had seemed that, having buried him, she wanted to bury all memory of their forty-six-year marriage, write it off as a regrettable interlude. She had turned her face away from her own children and had looked to her Mendez relations, especially after the row over Valdemar. All the narrowness of her nature, for so many years softened and tempered by Reuben's tolerance, had emerged – a cold, rigid puritanism that had hurt Rosa, repelled Isak, and amused Abel – 'Mother froze solid in approximately 1882 and there's absolutely no prospect of a thaw. For the social historian she's a perfectly preserved specimen of an extinct type, but for her family I'm afraid she's a burden.' She had impinged less and less on their lives; communication had virtually ceased. Yet to have forgotten her ...

Rosa came to the high wall that surrounded the grounds of Rosenhus. She knew that there was a little door in it somewhere – on the few occasions when she had visited the place Hannah had never failed to complain that nobody ever locked it properly – and she felt it would be wiser to approach the house cautiously, through the gardens, than to march up the drive.

She found the door – sure enough it was unlocked – and it creaked when she pushed it open. Ahead there was a belt of well-grown trees, then a thick shrubbery, and beyond, out of sight, the lawn and the gravel sweep in front of the house.

She heard a sound, like dogs barking on some distant farm, and a terrible foreboding brought out a sweat on her scalp. It was not dogs she had heard but men's voices, curt and harsh. She moved through the shrubbery, cold, clammy leaves brushing her face, until suddenly there was the façade of Rosenhus looming through a tracery of bare branches and thick evergreen.

Four armoured cars were drawn up in front of the house, and beyond them, two open trucks. There was a ring of soldiers, standing motionless, their guns at their hips, and within the circle there were more soldiers – SS – and it was they who were shouting – 'Move! Move! Come on move you Jewish bitches!' – an almost hysterical series of barks; yes, like dogs – as if they had something to fear from the stumbling, limping, weeping old women they were herding towards the trucks. One of the women, in a pink, quilted dressing-gown, was blind. She was leaning on the arm of a nurse and dabbing about with a stick. Suddenly she struck out at one of the SS. Rosa could hear her shouting:

'Can't you see I'm blind? Can't you see I'm blind?' They pushed the nurse away and dragged the blind woman by her arms towards the truck. There was another commotion by the front door. A thin voice was wailing:

'I cannot walk. I am unable to walk, I tell you. Please, please, I cannot walk.' Rosa recognized her – old Miss Glicksten. She'd been bed-ridden for years – she was over ninety. They were strapping her to a stretcher – the others, some in their night-dresses, some in shawls, were staring, and the SS were screaming at them to move, butting them with their guns. And there, there, coming out of the door, dressed in her fur coat, her silvery hair blowing wispy in the breeze, was Hannah. She was talking to the others, gesturing them towards the trucks. One of the old ladies stumbled and Hannah took her arm and walked with her to the truck. Two nurses – one of them crying, Rosa could hear her sobs – were helping the old ladies to climb into the truck, pulling them up by their white, scrawny arms. Rosa saw Hannah shake her head, saw her clamber, unaided, into the truck. She saw her take off her coat and wrap it round the shoulders of the blind woman, who was moaning rhythmically. And all the time the shouts, the shouts, pointless, meaningless sounds, dogs barking at shadows.

You shouldn't have cut yourself off. You shouldn't have driven us out of your life.

Hannah was sitting upright, with an arm round each of her neighbours, giving them comfort. Her silver head was high above the bowed mops of grey and white.

You shouldn't have been so cold. You shouldn't have been so proud.

They were slamming the tail-gates of the trucks, still shouting, shouting.

You shut yourself out of our hearts. You shut yourself out of our minds.

Billows of black smoke, the clatter and blare of engines, dogs baying the moon.

You shouldn't have let yourself die.

26

He's grey, Lynx thought, and he's thin. Look at the gap between his collar and his throat, look at the way that damned old blue suit hangs on him – he must have lost ten kilos. Was it an illness? No. Look at those eyes – bright, alert. Look at his skin – it almost glowed. There was something vibrant about his father; his voice was crisp and direct and he seemed to have shed his circumlocutions along with his excess weight. Extraordinary.

Extraordinary too to sit almost opposite one's own father at a table and not be recognized by him; extraordinary to be able to observe him, and observe how the others reacted to him, in a completely detached fashion. They were showing great deference to him, even the Controller, Dragonfly – but then Dragonfly was a crashing snob – and in a curious way his father seemed to be able to command them; he had authority. This exclusive group, six of the hardest men in the Resistance movement, appeared to respect him. Damn it all, they were hanging on his lips!

'To summarize,' Niels was saying, 'my house would seem to be perfectly placed as a gathering point. It's out of the city, but an easy tram ride from the centre. It's big enough to house up to fifty or sixty refugees at a time. Above all it's in a part of town where I don't think the Fritzies will be looking.' There were smiles. Niels went on: 'That's all fine and good; you pass the word, you get your men to direct the Jews to my house and I'll hide them all right. The problem arises at the next stage – getting them up the coast and onto fishing boats. I've already lined up a dozen or so captains willing to operate a ferry service – but we need more, many more, and we need couriers, to escort people to their departure points and see them safely onto the boats. I know all the harbourmasters and most of the customs men – but I don't know who's reliable and who isn't. You do. There's also the problem of transport. I've had a thought on that. There's a man called Jens Sandager. He's a wholesale chandler. He's got four vans that do a regular delivery run from the Freeport up to Helsingør and Frederiksvaerk. Now Sandager owes me a favour – in fact he owes me several thousand kroner.' Smiles and chuckles. 'And I think I can persuade him to let us use the vans. Whether he can be trusted or not is up to you to decide.'

Niels put a cigarette into his mouth and lit it. Nobody spoke; they waited for him to continue.

'Now,' he said, 'finance. The captains will have to be paid. They're not only risking their lives, they're risking the confiscation of their vessels, and we all know that a fisherman values his boat a great deal more highly than his life.' There was laughter, in which Lynx found himself joining, somewhat wonderingly. Was this his *father*? 'Many of the escapers can well afford to pay their own fares, of course, but there are hundreds who have come away with nothing. The trustees of the Jewish Community are trying to raise a loan, I know, but we still need cash, urgently. I have made a modest personal contribution' ('modest' Lynx thought, really Father, we all know that it's

100,000 kroner) 'and I've persuaded several friends in the business community to match it. But we need a central fund, with a properly appointed treasurer, to distribute the money where it's needed. And we need information. That is vital. We must know the movements of German harbour patrols, gunboats, all that sort of thing.'

He stopped and looked round.

'There must be many factors I haven't thought of – I look to you to guide me.'

'Apart from accurate meteorological reports – which will be essential – and copies of Hitler's breakfast menus for the next three months, I can't think of anything you've left out,' Dragonfly said dryly.

Niels joined in the laughter, then said: 'Very well. I've got forty-two Jews under my roof at this moment, so perhaps we could get down to details.'

For the next hour the meeting concentrated on practicalities, and Lynx, whose own contributions were infrequent, terse, but very much to the point, marvelled at his father's grasp of the problems of secret work. He seemed to be able to accept the complexities, made inevitable by the need for a vacuum of security round each link in the chain, and had no illusions about his own position.

'I must operate in the open,' he said, 'and the less I know about your business the better.'

Lynx began to see the qualities in his father that had enabled him to build up the Larsen Shipping Co., make it prosper and grow through the slumps and disasters of the Thirties. He saw how shrewdly he handled Dragonfly's vanity and power-hunger, how unobtrusively he steered the debate away from irrelevancies, how quietly authoritative he was on matters in which his knowledge was superior, and how delicately and unerringly he picked the brains of anybody who could tell him something he didn't know. He could not help comparing the qualities of leadership in Dragonfly and his father, who were the only two natural leaders in the room. Dragonfly charmed and inspired and blatantly exploited his position as one of London's senior Danish representatives. Niels, who was after all a total newcomer in Resistance circles, with an unsavoury record of cooperation with the Germans, and whose personality was colourless, dominated

through the quality of his mind: he exuded competence --
unspectacular, rock-solid competence.

For the first time in his life Lynx felt proud of his father, felt
respect, even affection for him; he saw the goodness of the man,
the moral balance that he had always written off as ossified
conformity, the practical intelligence he had always regarded as
mere mercantile opportunism.

When Niels had gone Dragonfly said: 'Well, my friends, we
have made a valuable recruit today. I hate to say it but that man,
in his quiet way, is worth a hundred zealots.'

It was true, and when the others had gone, leaving Lynx alone
except for Birdie's canary, picking at its plumage in its cage, he
felt a passionate elation which he longed to communicate to
somebody. But there was nobody there, and in any case the secret
of his identity, and his relationship to Niels, had to be guarded.
But he could not bottle it up. He went over to the canary's cage
and squatted by it.

'Tick, tick, tick – boom!' he said. 'We wiped out the
Government and waited for the lid to blow off, and nothing
happened. But now, *now* we've won, we've really won. When
my father throws away his hat and stick and picks up a gun, then
we've won, you stupid, bloody bird, we've won.'

Kleist was in a rage. He was also in a sweat, a mental sweat that
made every day a debilitating ordeal. The heat was coming from
the sun itself, from the Führer's private office, and it was radiating
down via Eichmann and Günther to the men in the field in
Denmark. The disaster had, according to rumour, sent the Führer
into one of his frenzies, and his voice, the most terrible voice in
the world, reverberated down through the hierarchy, and seemed
to echo even in the corridors of Dagmarhus.

For perhaps the hundredth time Kleist studied the returns for
the operation of the 1st and 2nd October. Two hundred and two
arrests in the Copenhagen area, eighty-two in the rest of the
country. A handful! Hardly enough to fill a cattle truck, and
mostly old women, cripples, and children. He picked up the
report on the previous day's pickings. Three! Three! And they'd
been turned in by an informer. He'd had to pay the man 5000
kroner.

And out there were over seven thousand of the creatures,

214

hiding away like rats in a cellar, and laughing, laughing up their filthy sleeves. And they were slipping away, too, hundreds of them, scurrying off through the sewers. Berlin was screaming for action – double the coastal patrols, house-to-house searches, ferret them out – but how could he? He hadn't the men. And the army weren't playing – so-called gentlemen like Brenner – they were turning a blind eye, actually releasing what they called 'half-Jews' – what the hell was a half-Jew? And the Danes themselves – not just the politicians and the bishops with their contemptible babblings about justice and humanity – the ordinary people, millions of them, harbouring the infection in their own homes. He couldn't understand it.

But by God he wouldn't let them get away with it. He'd teach them the meaning of terror. In a way he was glad. There could be no restraints now.

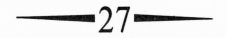

27

Rosa had expected an angry protest from her father, followed by passionate arguments, with the full weight of his persuasive personality behind them; but instead there was merely dazed incomprehension.

'I don't understand why you want me to go alone,' he said. 'Why don't you want to come with me?'

She had not realized what the double blow of Abel's suicide and his mother's arrest had done to him; having steeled herself to resist parental pressure, she found herself in the disconcerting position of having to treat him like a child.

'It's not that I want you to go alone, Father, it's just that I have work to do here – important work. I'll follow on as soon as I can, I promise, but you must go now.'

'It isn't safe for you.'

'It's perfectly safe.'

Was it? She didn't know. Some said that as the official widow of a non-Jew she would be released, if arrested; others said that if the SS or the Gestapo got their hands on her, they'd ship her off to Germany with the rest. It didn't matter anyway; there was a job of work to be done and she meant to do it whatever the risk.

'If anything happened to you it would kill me,' Isak said.

Rosa squeezed his arm and rallied him rather in the way she rallied Johannes when he fell over and grazed his knee or awoke crying from a nightmare.

'No it wouldn't, Father. And anyway nothing will happen to me. Now come along. It's time.'

Isak took up his case obediently and they picked their way through the mattresses, piled-up cushions, and other improvised beds in what had been Niels and Christina's room and was now a dormitory for fifteen refugees. They met Christina bustling along the passage with an armful of sheets. Christina seemed to thrive on the domestic turmoil into which her well-ordered house had been thrown.

'Isak — there you are. The van's arrived. You'd better go down.'

She dumped the sheets on the floor and quickly kissed Isak, blushing, and then laughing to cover her confusion.

'There — don't tell Niels! Good luck and God bless you. I won't come down. I hate goodbyes.'

Niels was in the hall, with the Golinskys and their three children.

'Ah, there you are, Abrahamsen,' he said.

The driver of the van appeared in the door.

'Hurry it up,' he said, 'I'm behind schedule.'

The Golinskys were clustering round Niels, Golinsky pumping his arm, Mrs Golinsky crying. Niels was urging them towards the door. Rosa took the opportunity to put her arms round Isak and hug him. He put his arms round her and squeezed her fiercely.

'Say goodbye to Johannes for me,' he said — Johannes had been sent to play with a neighbour.

'I will.'

There was a ghastly brightness in his eyes, they seemed to bulge with the strain of holding back tears. Niels came up. He shook Isak's hand.

'I can trust you to look after the Golinskys, I know,' he said. 'You'll be met in Humlebaek and you'll have to lie low until tonight. You've got money — and everything?'

Isak nodded.

'I can't thank you——' he began.

Niels stopped him with a gesture and a smile.

'Now, now, none of that,' he said. (*Niels* is treating him like a

216

child, Rosa thought.) 'I can just about take it from Golinsky but you and I have no need to——' he stopped, then added. 'I'm only sorry about your brother and—— Well, come along, you'd better be on your way.'

Rosa watched her father climb into the back of the van. It was ancient and covered in rust patches; the two big gas bottles on its roof gave it a squat, top-heavy look. It was bizarre and rather horrible to see her elegantly dressed father sitting on a crate in the back of this old tin can, squashed between Golinsky and one of his sons. Isak didn't say anything, he just stared at her. It was a relief when Niels slammed the doors of the van.

As the van pulled away Niels said: 'I should really have slipped something into your coffee and sent you off with him.'

Rosa smiled. 'You keep forgetting that I'm a Larsen. Nobody would dare arrest a Larsen — surely?'

'I wouldn't put money on it — and I certainly wouldn't wager my life on it.'

'Well anyway — I've got to go now. I'll be back in a few hours.'

'You've got your pass?'

'Oh yes.'

'Well, good luck.'

It was almost dark by the time Rosa found the house in Virum. It was a modern shoe-box villa in a long street of almost identical houses. She knocked on the door and waited. Presently she heard bolts being drawn back and keys being turned in locks and the door opened an inch. She saw a pair of frightened eyes and said:

'It's all right. I come from the house by the sea.'

The door opened wider and she stepped into a small, sparsely furnished hall. A syrupy picture of a peasant girl milking a cow hung over a chrome and glass table. The owner of the peasant girl, a large, faded woman in her late fifties, said: 'They're in the back room. I'm at my wits' end and so is my husband. They won't shift. Nothing I can say will budge them. I'm at my wits' end. I mean we were glad to take them in, only too glad — and they could stay, except it isn't safe. People talk round here. You know what I mean?'

Rosa nodded.

'If you'll just——'

'Oh. Yes. This way. I hope you can talk some sense into them.'

Rosa followed her down a short passage. She opened a door and Rosa walked past her into a tiny room cluttered with beds and tables and chairs. Sitting side by side at a table, dressed in their best hats and coats, were Mr Cohn, the little barber from Toldbodvej, and an equally diminutive woman whom Rosa assumed was his wife. Mr Cohn was clutching a framed photograph of King Christian and Mrs Cohn was knitting.

'Mr Cohn! It's you!'

Mr Cohn looked up, his sad eyes brightening just a little.

'Miss Rosa! Fancy!' he turned to his wife, 'Becca, look, here's Miss Abrahamsen you've heard me talk about.'

Mrs Cohn smiled timidly. Rosa went forward and shook Mr Cohn's hand, and his wife's, but neither made a move to stand up.

'I've come to take you to a safe place – from where we can get you to Sweden,' she said.

Mr Cohn shook his head. 'It's very good of you, Miss Rosa, very good of you, I'm sure, but Mrs Cohn and I are not going to Sweden, or anywhere else – are we dear?'

Mrs Cohn shook her head. Her needles clicked and clacked.

Rosa heard their hostess mutter: 'They've been sitting here like this, all dressed up, for three days. They won't listen to reason. I can't shift them.'

'But you can't stay here, Mr Cohn,' Rosa said gently.

'We don't wish to stay here, Miss Rosa,' Mr Cohn said, 'we wish to return to our own home. No disrespect to you, Mrs Johansen – you've been very kind, most attentive – it's just that we prefer to be in our own home. But Mrs Johansen won't let us go.'

'Of course I won't let you go, you silly old man,' said Mrs Johansen. 'You'd be picked up by the first German patrol, you're that daft both of you.'

Rosa saw that the situation required tact. 'Mrs Johansen, perhaps we could all have a cup of something?'

'I've got some cocoa – at least that's what it says on the packet. My husband tells me it's made out of acorns.'

'That would be very nice, thank you.'

When Mrs Johansen had gone Rosa drew up a chair by Mr Cohn.

'Now Mr Cohn please listen to me. I want to take you to a

house where you'll be safe and comfortable. From there we will get you both on a boat to Sweden and once you're over the water you'll be well looked after I promise you. You cannot go back to your own home. It really isn't safe.'

Mr Cohn laid a hand on her arm and said, very patiently:

'I know you mean well, Miss Rosa, of course you do. You're very kind and good, like the Johansens. Excellent neighbours, Miss Rosa, always most attentive and kind. But you don't really understand. I happen to know for a fact that the King would never allow any harm to come to his Jewish subjects. I have special knowledge, you see.'

Rosa chose her words carefully. 'I'm sure the King has done everything in his power to help the Jewish community, Mr Cohn, of course he has, but you see the King doesn't have the power any more. The Germans have the power.'

Mr Cohn shook his head. 'You don't understand, Miss Rosa.' He turned to his wife. 'Shall I show her the letter, Becca?'

Mrs Cohn nodded and unravelled some more wool from her knitting bag. Mr Cohn fumbled in an inside pocket and brought out a sheet of paper, a photographic reproduction. Rosa could see the Royal crest and the letter heading of the Amalienborg Palace. Mr Cohn held the letter close to his chest.

'Before I show you this, I must explain something,' he said. 'Every year on the King's birthday, September the twenty-sixth, Becca and I send His Majesty a gift, like every loyal subject should. Perhaps it's a little something that Becca has knitted — sometimes I see a thing in a shop I think His Majesty would like——'

Mrs Cohn interrupted him. 'Tell her about Rabbi Melchior's book, dear.'

'I'm coming to that, dear, but I must explain about the telegrams.' He turned to Rosa. 'You see, Miss Rosa, His Majesty always acknowledges his birthday gifts in the same way, with a telegram — here — like this.'

He produced a carefully folded telegram form and opened it out to show to Rosa. Rosa recognized it at once as a standard Royal message of thanks — she had seen dozens like it — the text of which never varied: *My best thanks. Christian Rex.*

'What you must understand, Miss Rosa, is that His Majesty treats everybody the same. Whether it's Becca and myself sending him a modest gift, or somebody very important sending him a magnificent present, the response is always the same – a telegram from the Palace.'

Rosa knew this but let Mr Cohn develop his thesis.

'Now last year the Rabbi Melchior and a colleague sent the King a copy of a book they had written, for his birthday. The King also received a long birthday greeting from Hitler – you remember? To Hitler, the King replied in the usual way: My best thanks. Christian Rex. But to the Rabbi he wrote a personal letter, in his own hand. Look, here is a copy of the letter. Read what the King says.'

Rosa glanced through the letter. After politely thanking Rabbi Melchior and his colleagues for the gift of their book, King Christian went on to ask them to convey to all his Jewish subjects his very best wishes, adding that they were constantly in his thoughts and prayers.

'You understand the significance of it?' Mr Cohn said, taking back the letter and putting it tenderly in his pocket. 'Hitler, the dictator of Germany, gets an ordinary telegram, but the Rabbi gets a letter in the King's own hand. It was His Majesty's way of telling us Jews that he will never desert us, that he will never let any harm come to us. So you see when you ask Mrs Cohn and me to run away to Sweden, you are asking us to be disloyal to our King – and that we will not do.'

'Mr Cohn has shaken the King's hand and talked to him many times,' Mrs Cohn said suddenly.

'He often rides past my little shop,' Mr Cohn explained, 'its being so near to the Palace. He'll lean down from his saddle and shake my hand. "Good morning to you, Mr Cohn," he'll say. "Good morning to you, Your Majesty." "I trust the world is treating you well?" he'll say. "Very well, thank you, sir," I'll say, like we were two old friends passing the time of day.'

'Like old friends,' Mrs Cohn added.

Rosa was baffled. It was clear that argument was useless. She stood up.

'I think I'll just see how Mrs Johansen is getting on with the cocoa,' she said.

She found Mrs Johansen in a bleak but spotless kitchen. Mrs Johansen raised her eyes and shrugged.

'You see what I mean? Daft – both of them. A sweet old

couple, mind, but stubborn. What's to be done?'

'Something drastic I'm afraid. Do you know of a doctor in the neighbourhood?'

'A doctor? What good will a doctor do? It's not a doctor we need, it's the King himself to come along and tell 'em not to be so bloody daft.'

Rosa smiled. 'I agree. But failing that – well, don't you think a doctor might give us a little something——'

'To put in their cocoa?' Mrs Johansen looked shocked. 'Well, I don't know about that,' she said.

'It's been done before, Mrs Johansen. I can't think of any other way.'

'Well, I don't know.' Then: 'There's Doctor Jepsen at number fifty-two – that's four doors down.'

'Is he – reliable?'

'Doctor Jepsen? Oh yes. But are you sure it's the right thing to do? I mean, it seems so, so treacherous somehow.'

'I know – but it's for their own good.'

'Yes, I suppose it is.' She grinned suddenly. 'What a thing!'

It had started to rain, heavy drops splattering on the pavement, and Rosa ran the short distance to the doctor's house. Dr Jepsen was gruff and grumpy at first – he was an elderly man and told Rosa twice that he should really have retired three years ago – but after Rosa had explained the situation he went into his dispensary, and having fussed about among hundreds of bottles and packets, found what he wanted and went back to Mrs Johansen's house with her.

'I'll have to lay on some transport,' Rosa said to Mrs Johansen, 'may I use your telephone?'

She spoke to Niels, then waited for him to ring back. He told her that a taxi would arrive within an hour. She put the telephone down and went into the kitchen. Mrs Johansen and the doctor were smoking.

'Did they drink it?'

Mrs Johansen nodded and the doctor consulted his watch.

'You'd better go and see how they're getting on.'

Rosa went into the little back room, while Mrs Johansen and the doctor waited outside. She found Mr and Mrs Cohn sleeping peacefully, Mr Cohn with his head on the table, Mrs Cohn leaning against him.

221

The doctor came in and examined them both briefly.

'They'll be all right,' he said. 'Keep them warm. They'll sleep for twelve hours and wake up with shocking headaches.'

'With a bit of luck,' Rosa said, 'they'll wake up in Sweden.'

Dr Jepsen shook his head. 'I don't know,' he said, 'I could be de-barred for this.'

'I don't think you need worry about that.'

'They look so sweet together,' Mrs Johansen said. 'It seems such a shame.'

It was cold in the shed, a dank cold that crept into your bones. The rain was thundering on the tin roof and one of the babies was crying. Its mother was trying to hush it, rocking it in her arms and cooing softly into its ear. Two of the men were talking to each other in a low murmur, but the others just sat, hugging themselves, their faces yellowy-white in the light of the single kerosene lamp.

They look as if they are hypnotized, Isak thought, hypnotized by fear and by the utter unreality of what is happening to them. I suppose I look just the same to them. I am just the same, I am on the same level.

It was a curious idea. Here was a group of people – a garage mechanic and his family, a tailor, a factory worker's wife with a brood of children – with whom normally he would have had no contact. They were representatives not only of a different caste but of a different world – the world of Orthodox Jewry – a strange world, with its own rituals, its own internal loyalties, its own traits of speech and dress and looks, and suddenly he was part of it, a member of the tribe, one of the Children of Israel. They deferred to him, of course, all of them, because they knew he was rich and important, yet at the same time they accepted him as one of themselves. He could think of no reason why they should look up to him: he was as frightened and as bewildered as they were. He, who had spent his life making decisions and giving orders, was content to obey every clipped command from the Resistance men on whose courage and skill his life now depended; he was happy to be herded hither and thither with the other sheep, passive and unthinking.

One of the boys, bored and fidgety, was tugging at his mother's sleeve, whining at her. The woman was hollow-eyed and helpless. Her husband had been arrested on the First. He had been working on a night-shift and one of his mates had informed on him. The woman had told Isak the story: how her man had stubbornly refused to believe that anything bad could happen to a Jew in Denmark, how he had gone to his work with that faith in his heart.

'Here, Benny, come here,' he said. 'I've got something to show you.'

The little boy came over to him, glowering suspiciously. Isak took out his pocket watch – it was gold, and it played a tinkling little Mozart tune when you opened it – and it had never failed to fascinate Johannes. It had the same magical effect on Benny. His dark brown eyes grew round.

'Is there a fairy inside?'

Isak, speaking very quietly, began a story. A poor young musician fell in love with a Princess and wrote a love-song for her. But the Princess cared only for gold and jewels and ordered her servants to throw the musician into the street. So he went to a watchmaker and with the last of his money he paid the man to make a tiny musical box, which played the song, and put it into a shiny gold watch. On the way to the palace the poor musician was set upon by bandits and robbed.

His inspiration as to the fate of the watch, the musician, and the Princess, was failing under Benny's perspicacious questions, when the door of the shed opened and Stig, their courier, came in with a big man in boots, sweater and cap, whom he introduced as Captain Andersen.

Andersen, it quickly transpired, was a man of succinct speech and basic preoccupations.

'How many?' He said.

'Fifteen,' Stig said.

'Have they got the money? It's three thousand a head.'

'We agreed on two.'

'Look – the Sound's swarming with patrols and there's a swell on as steep as a house. I shouldn't be going out at all.'

'All right, all right.'

Stig began going round collecting wads of currency and Benny's mother began to cry.

'I haven't enough. I've only six thousand. That's all I could raise.'

223

Stig turned to Andersen.

'Look, she's got three children. They took her husband. I'll see you get the money.'

Andersen shook his head.

'I'm sorry. Cash in advance. I told you those were my terms. Everybody asks the same. Cash in advance.'

'I can guarantee you'll get your money.'

'This isn't a pleasure cruise. I'm risking everything I've got. I'm sorry.'

Isak was suddenly cold with rage. They were being haggled over like a kilo of apples in a market. He stepped forward and began counting out banknotes to Andersen.

'There – five, six, seven, eight, nine, ten, eleven, twelve thousand.'

He turned to Benny's mother, who was staring at him.

'You hang on to your money, Mrs Kleber,' he said. He turned back to Andersen.

'Here, there's another thousand.'

Andersen looked at him.

'What's that for?'

'It's to encourage you to keep well away from me during the crossing.'

Andersen looked away.

'I'm sorry – but you can't expect me to do it for nothing.'

'I don't. You've got your money. Now, can we go?'

They followed Andersen down through a dripping, unkempt garden, past a shuttered holiday house, to a jetty, where a squat, stub-prowed fishing smack was moored. The baby began to cry again as Andersen, and another man, herded them through a rickety deck-house and down into a narrow hold where even little Benny had to stoop and there was a sickening smell of fish.

'The Fritzies have already searched me once,' Andersen said. 'I don't expect to be stopped again. If I am, you just have to sit tight and not make a sound of any kind. Understand? I'm going to have to lock you in. Don't worry. There's plenty of air. And for the love of God stop that damned baby howling.'

A metal hatch clanged shut and they were left in complete darkness. Several of the children began to whine and complain. Isak sat against the cold metal side of the ship. There were bodies all round him, shifting and jostling, and he, who had always

224

hated any kind of physical contact with strangers and had always avoided travelling on crowded trams and buses, found a curious comfort in the warmth and nearness of them. For a moment he felt that they were all like a litter of puppies squirming in a basket. Then the enormity of it all, the indignity, struck him and he wished he had stayed with Rosa and faced whatever it was that had to be faced. Why was he running like this, why was he allowing himself to be locked up in this stinking sardine can? Why? He should have defied the Germans.

The ship was rolling. The vibrations from her screw, magnified in the confined space of the hold, were a steady torture. The baby was crying again, and Benny and the other children were crying too. Isak suddenly thought: I must be strong. I must protect these people and their children. They are my own.

28

The No. 9 tram clattered down Jagtvej and Rosa clung to her strap, swaying a little with the motion of the car, staring, past the pale, washed-out faces of the people pressed closest to her, towards the window. It was dark outside and she could see her own reflection in the glass, opaquely, as in a photographic negative. She avoided her neighbours' eyes, just as they avoided hers, obeying the unwritten etiquette of the late-afternoon scramble for home. The tram drew up at the stop by the cemetery and there was some discreet pushing and jostling as people got off and on. Rosa shifted slightly to make more space round her and she heard a woman mutter: 'Oh God, not again.'

She twisted her head round and looked down the car, through the restlessly moving forest of heads and shoulders, to the far end. There were two of them. Wehrmacht thank God, not Gestapo; even so she felt a premonition of disaster. This was all part of the new campaign in the hunt for Jews – random checks on trains and buses and trams, and in cinemas and restaurants.

The two soldiers were moving slowly up the car towards her, checking identity papers. One of them looked middle-aged, a sergeant probably, and the other was little more than a boy. He appeared tense and nervy.

She turned her face away. What could she do? Impossible to

make a run for it, madness, in fact, to display any sign of distress. There was nothing wrong with her papers, but what about her appearance? All round her were grey-white faces, light blue eyes, and corn-coloured hair. She caught a glimpse of herself in the window: dark complexion, black hair, black eyes. Suddenly she felt as conspicuous as an olive on a white table-cloth. Gradually, as the two soldiers moved nearer and nearer, she became aware that the etiquette of the tram was being abandoned. People standing or sitting near her were covertly looking at her. They know, she thought, they know what I am.

And then she became aware of something else. The people in front of her, between her and the Germans, were bunching together. The man next to her was pushing her arm, gently but firmly. She began to shuffle towards the back of the car, people making way for her, standing aside, helping her, encouraging her with little nudges.

There was a wall of bodies now between her and the Germans and the sergeant had noticed it. The young one too, he knew, he had sensed it − a Jew on the tram.

A strange silence descended. The sergeant was staring at the people and the people were staring back, steady stares − without hostility, without fear. The sergeant seemed to decide.

'Enough,' she heard him say. 'Come on.'

But the young one hesitated. He was fingering his gun, peering down the car. Rosa averted her face. She heard the sergeant rap: 'Come on. Move yourself.'

She looked up. They were moving back down the car, they were getting out. As the tram jerked forward there was an outburst of talk and some laughter. The man standing beside Rosa said:

'Bloody animals.' Then: 'You should be in hiding. You shouldn't be on the streets.'

A woman behind her said:

'Here, take my seat dear. You look as pale as a ghost.'

Rosa sat down. Another man said:

'I can help you. I'll give you somewhere to hide. I know people who can help you.'

'No, no,' she said. 'You're very kind. I − I have a place.'

The tram stopped again. Suddenly she knew she had to get out, get away from all the staring faces − she felt that the whole world

226

was gazing at her. She pushed her way down the car. People stood back to let her pass. There was babble all round her, strangers exchanging Jew-stories. She jumped off the tram and began to walk. There was no strength in her legs. She stopped to rest for a moment in the doorway of a shop. She found she was sweating, as if she had been running. She walked on, grateful for the darkness. If only it would rain, then people would scurry by, their heads bowed against the wind, or masked by umbrellas, and they wouldn't be able to look at her. She didn't want anyone to look at her.

She found the address in Nylandsvej, a block of flats near the hospital. What would she find this time? Poignant stubbornness like the Cohns? Pig-headedness like that old man yesterday who had been convinced that it was all a plot to rob him of the stock of jewellery in his shop? How could she help anyone, anyway? She was herself marked. She felt it in her bones. She mounted two flights of stairs and found the right door. She pressed the bell. The door opened immediately and after an instant, during which everything in her life seemed finally incomprehensible, she threw herself into Valdemar's arms.

Val had given her some *snaps* and it had helped her to compose herself. She had told him everything – about Grandmamma, about Abel and her father, and about the two Germans on the tram.

'That's why I want you to get out, Rosa,' he said. 'Tomorrow. They're stepping up the hunt, putting more and more Gestapo on it. God knows why Father hasn't been raided. He seems to lead a charmed life. But I can't have you running around as you do. It's insanity.'

'But, Val, there are so many, so many who need help.'

'There are fewer every day. The system's running smoothly now. We're getting hundreds out every night. You've been wonderful, Rosa, really wonderful – but I can't do my own work if I'm constantly worrying about you. You and Johannes must go tomorrow.'

'All right, Val, we will.' She laughed. 'I'm just about played out anyway. That business on the tram – I nearly died.'

'I've arranged everything. You're going Pullman class, I can tell you, a route normally reserved for the Resistance.'

'I shall never forget those people on the tram, never. Nobody said a word, you know, nobody even looked at anyone else, but they acted as if they had been practising for weeks – just moved and formed a barrier between me and those Germans.'

'I know.' He had stood up and was pacing up and down. 'It's happening all over the country. It's a revolution, an uprising. This action against the Jews – it's set the country alight. It's the great turning point.'

She stared at him. He was completely the new Valdemar now and there was something cold and cruel about him. She held out her arms.

'Come here – come and sit beside me.'

He did, but then when she bent forward to kiss him he turned away.

'Don't Rosa, we can't. There isn't time.'

'Just kiss me, Val,' she said.

He did, but there was no real intimacy in it.

'Spare a thought for the poor Jews,' she said with a little laugh. 'I think you'd find that most of them would be much happier without your popular revolution.'

'It's the great beginning we've all been working for.'

'Val, you're talking like a street-corner demagogue. Anyway Genesis comes before Exodus – and an exodus is not a very pleasant experience for the people involved. Uncle Abel, for instance.'

He took her hand. 'I'm sorry, darling. I didn't mean to sound callous.'

'Don't become too much of a fanatic, Val. Remember people.'

He stood up.

'Rosa, you've got to go. There's a man outside. He's waiting to take you back to Hellerup. You're not to go out again, not until they come for you tomorrow. Will you promise me?'

'Yes, I promise.'

She stood up and put her arms round him.

'It's all goodbyes now, isn't it?'

'Rosa, I can't promise you anything but there's a chance I'll have to come to Sweden myself soon.'

'Oh Val – really? When?

'I don't know. Four or five months perhaps. I don't know. But it's bound to come.'

'If they want you to get out, you will, won't you Val? You won't try to be heroic?'

He laughed.

'Oh no. I'm getting tired of heroics. I'm not such a fanatic, Rosa.'

They kissed for a long time and now Rosa did feel the old tenderness, the old gentleness. His eyes were bright. He looked like Valdemar, her Valdemar, for a moment.

'You go first,' he said. 'We mustn't be seen together.' His eyes clouded. 'You remember that first time, up at Skagen, when I went and you didn't want to say goodbye? I understand that now.'

She touched his face, once, very lightly, then turned and left the room, closing the door behind her.

29

Rosa and her mother-in-law were sitting in the morning-room. Now that the torrent of refugees had slowed to a trickle – no more than ten or twelve a day – the room had been restored to its usual order. Christina was knitting a sweater for Johannes, trying to get it finished in time, and, outside in the hall, Rosa could hear Niels on the telephone.

'It's you I'm worried about,' Rosa said. 'You and Niels.'

Christina smiled cheerfully – she was perpetually cheerful these days – and said: 'Don't fret about us, my dear. The Germans are concentrating on the coasts and ports. They'd have raided us by now if they were going to – and anyway our job is almost done.'

'You sound as if you're sorry.'

'Well I am in a way.'

'You've enjoyed it all, haven't you?'

Christina glanced up at her.

'I wouldn't say "enjoyed" exactly.'

'Wouldn't you? It's been a happy time for you – for most people. The nation finding its soul and all that sort of thing.'

'Well, the nation *has* found it's soul, I suppose.'

'Yes – but at a price.'

She was about to go on when Niels came in. Christina looked round.

'You look worried, Niels,' she said. 'What's happened?'

'It's those wretched Cohns,' Niels replied and immediately regretted it. Rosa was staring at him.

'The Cohns? Aren't they safely in Sweden?'

'They're on their way. Don't worry.'

'But they should have gone days ago. What's happened?'

'The night they were supposed to go there was a raid – they had to be moved. It's taken time to make new arrangements. But don't worry, they'll be on their way tonight.'

Rosa wasn't convinced.

'I suppose they're refusing to go,' she said.

'Well, yes, they are proving rather difficult.'

'You'll just have to knock them out again.'

'I know, I know. We will, don't worry.'

'There's something else. Tell me.'

Niels hesitated for a moment and then said: 'The thing is they're refusing to eat or drink. Apparently they're very nice about it – quite apologetic – but absolutely adamant.'

'I must go and see them,' Rosa said flatly.

'That's out of the question.'

Christina added: 'Rosa you're going yourself this evening. There isn't time.'

Rosa ignored her and continued to look at Niels.

'Where are they?'

'Rosa you're not leaving this house until Stig comes for you this evening.'

'Just tell me where the Cohns are.'

'I – I don't know. Not exactly.'

'Of course you know.'

Niels shrugged helplessly.

'Very well, I'll find out for myself,' Rosa said.

She began to move towards the door.

'Rosa,' Niels said, 'There's nothing you can do for them. We'll think of a way. I can't allow you to run any more risks. The Cohns are my responsibility now, not yours.'

Rosa turned away from the door and faced her father-in-law. There was something formidable about her and Niels felt it.

'That's what everybody told me when they took

230

Grandmamma,' she said. "Don't blame yourself. It wasn't your responsibility." But it *was*, it *was* – and I failed. Well I'm not going to fail the Cohns. If you want me to leave Denmark tonight tell me where they are. Otherwise I stay – and you'll find me a great deal more intractable than Mr and Mrs Cohn.'

Niels and Christina exchanged helpless looks.

'Tell me, Niels.'

Niels capitulated.

'They're in a house at Vedbæk.'

'Well that's only a few kilometres up the coast. I can go up in the van and be back in under two hours.'

'Rosa it's absolute madness.'

'It's nothing of the sort. It's a routine run. There's no danger attached at all.'

'But even if you see them, what can you do?'

'Talk to them.'

'We've been talking to them for days. They just don't listen.'

'They'll listen to me. Mr Cohn has known me since I was a baby. I'm going to put a verbal rocket under them and if that doesn't shift them I shall personally chloroform both of them.'

'Chloroform – that's an idea. Why don't I just ring Vedbæk and get them to do it.'

'Because it's a last resort. I must try it my way first.'

She looked at her watch. 'The van'll be here in a few minutes. I'll get my coat.'

When she had left the room Christina said: 'Niels, we shouldn't allow her to go.'

Niels was angry, mainly with himself. 'What do you suggest? Chloroform?'

Christina ignored this. 'Is she right, Niels? Is it routine? Is there really no danger?'

'Very little, I have to admit. I just don't like the idea of her going out.'

'Nor do I.'

'Well, I can't think of any way to stop her. She's her father's daughter.'

Rosa sat beside Stig in the front of the van. In the back was a family of refugees due to be dropped off at Nivaa. It had been arranged that Stig would leave Rosa at Vedbæk, make his

231

delivery, then pick her up on the return trip to Copenhagen. Rosa was rather enjoying the drive. In between little bouts of cheery conversation with Stig she rehearsed what she was going to say to Mr Cohn. She was going to invoke the name of the King and point out that His Majesty would be most displeased if he heard that the Cohns were putting the lives of his loyal Resistance workers at risk by their obstinacy. She was going to tell him – and it was not far from the truth – that the King had asked his friend the King of Sweden to look after the Danish Jews and that if the Cohns didn't agree to be put on a boat that night, they would have *two* furious monarchs to contend with. Stig glanced at her.

'Thought of a way of shifting the old buggers?'

Rosa smiled.

'I think so. I'm going to terrify them with the prospect of *lèse-majesté.*'

'Sounds good – whatever it means. What if it doesn't work?'

'Then you can hold them down while I apply the chloroform.'

'That sounds more like it to me.'

He glanced at her.

'What's up? You've gone white.'

'Look, look up ahead.'

Three hundred metres ahead there were barriers, and German soldiers flagging down a lorry. Stig laughed.

'Don't worry,' he said. 'It's only routine. They do it once or twice a week and they all know me. We're old friends. In fact,' he fumbled under his seat and pulled out a bottle of *snaps*, 'I always keep a little present for the sergeant in charge.'

They were slowing down. The tension in Rosa eased as she saw the Germans waving Stig on and pulling the barrier aside. They were moving at a walking pace and Stig was winding down the window. A burly Wehrmacht sergeant was coming towards the van. Stig brought the van to a halt. The sergeant smiled.

'Hello,' he said.

'Hello.' Stig held up the bottle of *snaps*. The sergeant's grin broadened. He looked round quickly, took the bottle from Stig, and slipped it into the capacious pocket of his greatcoat.

'Sheer nectar that,' Stig said. 'Put lead in your pencil.'

The sergeant chuckled and shot a look at Rosa. Stig winked.

'Not a word to the wife.'

The sergeant chuckled again and bent forward to get a better view of Rosa. Rosa turned away to avoid his appraising eyes.

'Shy one, eh?'

'Oh, she's not as shy as that, I can tell you,' said Stig with another wink. The sergeant laughed.

'You're a lucky bastard, and no mistake. Oh well. Be seeing you.'

He straightened and stepped away from the van with a wave. Stig engaged first gear and reached for the handbrake.

'A moment.'

The voice was crisp and curiously high-pitched. Rosa saw Stig's head whip round and she peered over his shoulder. An immensely tall, white-haired man was standing by the sergeant. The man was a civilian, in suit and overcoat, but all the sergeant's jauntiness seemed to have deserted him. He said nervously:

'It's all right. I know this fellow. He delivers for Sandager – the chandlers.'

'Ah,' the other said, 'not a wine merchant then?' He looked at the sergeant's bulging pocket.

'I think I would like to see what goods your friend is carrying today.'

The sergeant was sweating now.

'Of course, Herr Kleist.'

Rosa saw Stig release the handbrake. The van shot forward, whipping her head back.

'Get down,' Stig yelled.

She crouched on the floor. She heard shots stutter and glass explode above her head. She felt fragments of glass dropping onto her hair. She was flung violently onto the floor as the van suddenly stopped dead with a crump of metal on metal. She opened her eyes and struggled to her knees. Stig was lolling over the wheel, his body half-turned towards her. Blood was pumping from his neck in regular spurts.

Then there were hands on her, dragging her out of the van, and shouts, shouts – the yapping of dogs – and she was in Skagen, in that arctic sea, with every cell in her body paralysed, and Valdemar swimming away, away out to sea. But this time there was no coming alive, no crackle or tingle of energy. She was frozen. Only one particle of her seemed to function. It was a minute nerve in the brain and it screamed:

'*Johannes.*'

233

30

There was a Christmas tree in the front room of the house. Lynx could see it through the uncurtained window. Even in the grey early-morning light there were little glints and sparkles from the decorations. In the room next door there was the strong yellow light of an electric bulb. This window was uncurtained too and Lynx could see the man clearly; he was sitting at the table, smoking a cigarette, while his wife busied herself with bread and butter and plates and cups and tended the kettle on the stove. Lynx wondered if the man had children; was the Christmas tree for his children? Were there presents heaped under the tree? There should be. This daddy could afford to buy his children lots and lots of presents. The man was drinking his coffee. He tilted his head back then held out his cup for more. He was arguing with his wife. She was making angry gestures at him, shrugging and turning away.

Lynx shifted his feet. The snow was seeping through the cardboard soles of his shoes. His toes were numb. Melting snow was dripping onto his head and neck from the branches of the thick tree which hid him from the view of the house opposite. Behind him, the garden of the burned-out villa was a white web of snow-laden branches and boughs. Occasionally a pat of snow slipped and fell with a thump. The cold was bitter, but Lynx was not cold – at least the cold made no difference to him. The pain in his feet was merely a pain, and he had become a connoisseur of pain, pain suffered and pain inflicted. There had been a moment when pain had almost obliterated Lynx and had left Valdemar Larsen sobbing on a bed, sobbing for his wife. But Lynx had survived, Lynx had fought the pain, conquered it, turned it to his own use. He had found a new vocation.

Dragonfly had cabled from Stockholm ordering him to pull out; and Dragonfly had been overruled. Lynx was a danger to the organization – so he operated alone. He saw no one but Sven, who gave him the names and addresses.

Lynx looked back towards the house. The man was smoking another cigarette and he was still arguing with his wife. He finished the cigarette and said something that made his wife laugh. He kissed her and they both moved out of view. Lynx

234

pulled the gun from under his coat. It was a home-made weapon, clumsy in shape, but accurate, amazingly accurate. He imagined the man getting into his overcoat, his wife helping him. He imagined him picking up his briefcase and walking to the door. The front door of the house opened and the man was framed in the oblong of light. And not just the man but the stocky little figure of a boy. The man picked the boy up and kissed him, then bounced him a few times and put him down. The man closed his front door – Lynx was glad of that – and walked down his garden path. As he shut the gate behind him, Lynx emerged from cover. The man was walking briskly down the street. Lynx's stride was brisker – and silent.

Lynx noticed the thick fur collar on the man's coat. An expensive coat. How many good men had died to provide him with that luxurious coat?

He opened up at medium close range. Two body shots to fell him – six rapid steps forward – then two head shots, at close range, to make sure of him. All done in a few seconds – a sprint to the end of the road – round the corner and out of sight before the first door was opened or the first curious head poked out of a window – a brisk stroll to the main road – a passing tram – incurious crowds – so simple, so right.

31

Karen heard steps on the stairway and climbed quickly onto the chair. Through the glass panel over Mrs Pilegaard's front door she had a direct view of Gunther's front door – or her own as she had to think of it, since she and Kleist were virtually living together. The panel over Gunther's door was brightly lit. She could imagine Gunther in his shirt-sleeves in the sitting-room, probably pacing up and down, waiting, or perhaps rifling through the wads of currency he would by now have taken from their hiding-place in the bedroom.

A figure came into view and her excitement died. She recognized the man as the elderly lawyer who lived in the flat above. He passed out of sight, up the stairs, and Karen was struck by the strangeness of what she was doing: spying on her own front door from the darkened hall of her neighbour's flat. She stared at the yellow square of glass opposite. She suddenly felt that Gunther must sense that she was near. He had that kind of instinct. Or, worse, was Drewsen, the caretaker, in Gunther's pay? Would he tell Gunther about his girlfriend's curious request to borrow Mrs Pilegaard's key while she was visiting her sister in the country?

She jumped lightly off the chair and sat down on it. She felt sure that the Hot Potato would come tonight. The presence of so much money in the flat, and Gunther's suggestion that she should go home for a few days, almost constituted a guarantee. If it were not tonight, then it would be tomorrow night. She could wait. It was worth waiting for, the culmination of so many months of delicate probing into Gunther's secrets. He had been getting careless lately, and took her devotion to him for granted. His physical demands on her had seemed to increase with the mounting tension in the city, not because he himself required any special release, rather because as the terror grew so his personal power grew, and as his personal power grew so did his appetites. The loose talk had started with boastful stories of shady deals, of lucrative 'expropriations' carried out under the noses of his rivals in the Gestapo, and the cunning ways in which he was converting his gains into hard foreign currencies, stashing his money away in Swedish banks. The curious thing was that as his own affluence increased, and her inherited wealth became less of an affront to him, he became more palatable as a man. Gangster though he was, he still retained one human quality: the need to see the tawdry lustre of his achievements reflected in the admiration of another.

Life was easier in another way: she no longer had to dissemble to her father. Father was something of a power in Resistance circles these days, and he was one of the few who knew about her work. He wasn't exactly proud of her, in fact she knew he had been wounded by the realization that she was capable of handling Gunther Kleist mainly because she had served such a long apprenticeship in deception with him as the dupe; but his anti-German feelings were now as hot as they had once been tepid, his belief in extremes as fervent as his former faith in compromise, so he condoned, even admired, what she was doing.

She heard footsteps again and stood on the chair. A figure passed below her door and stopped by Gunther's. The man –

236

medium height, medium build, in a soft hat and overcoat – had his back to her. She heard the ring of the bell, faint but familiar, and imagined Gunther slipping into his jacket (he had an idea that 'gentlemen' didn't appear in their shirtsleeves) and striding into the hall. The door opposite opened. Gunther appeared and ushered his visitor inside. Before he closed the door he put his head out and looked up and down the stairs and Karen instinctively ducked.

She heard the door shut and stepped off the chair. She picked up the camera Christian had provided – it was loaded with special film and its exposure was pre-set – and climbed back onto the chair. There was no proof yet, but she somehow knew that Gunther's guest was the Hot Potato, Gunther's ace of trumps, the super-informer about whom he had not been able to resist boasting to her.

She waited. Time crawled by and then Gunther's door began opening. She put the camera to her eye. A figure appeared in the view-finder. Her finger was poised on the shutter-release. She could see Gunther too, his great height fore-shortened in the distorting lens of the camera.

She lowered the camera and sank very slowly below the level of the glass panel. The face of the man beside Gunther was a trigger to memory as the lever on the camera was a trigger to the shutter; for a moment she looked through a lens in her mind at the past. She saw ice-strewn streets and four tipsy people cavorting among the crowds after a wedding, and she carefully laid the camera down on the seat of the chair. There was no need to photograph the Hot Potato. She knew him.

32

Lynx scented the trap seconds before he consciously analysed the fact that a truck was being unloaded in a place where a truck had never been unloaded before. He slid into a doorway and waited. A man strolled out of the building opposite his lodgings, conferred casually with the two men by the truck, then sauntered away again. Lynx waited, observing the men by the truck. They were dressed in blue overalls and they were slowly piling crates onto the pavement. Lynx smiled to himself. You only had to look at the amateurish way in which they were lifting the crates, bending down stiffly and putting all the strain into their backs, to see that they were fakes.

Lynx walked away and found a telephone box. He pressed a ten-øre piece into the slot and dialled his own number. He heard the telephone ring and then a voice. The voice, slightly hesitant, said:

'Lynx.'

Lynx put down the receiver. Christ! This was serious. Dragonfly had always said it would happen one day. 'They're getting close to you, Lynx, they're getting very close to you,' he'd said. Close? They were breathing down his fucking neck.

Dusk was coming and he had to be off the streets by nightfall. There was another safe house – he hadn't used it for a couple of weeks – it was only fifteen-minutes' walk away. He'd have to try it.

Valdemar had been visiting Lynx more and more frequently in the past few nights, visiting him in his dreams, showing him glimpses of their shared past. Worse, he had felt the presence of Valdemar in his waking hours, had felt him standing at his shoulder. He had gone by train to Roskilde the day before yesterday to pay a call on a certain lady of Hungarian origins in whose flat in Copenhagen little Birdie had lodged for a time. Birdie had died under torture in Dagmarhus and his lady friend had been traced to an opulent house on the edge of Roskilde Fjord. He had found the house, checked that it was empty, and waited in the garden for the woman. She had returned, at noon, alone. She had not even bothered to lock her front door behind her. He had simply walked in. He'd found her in the kitchen. The sleeves of her blouse had been rolled up. She had been kneading dough. For a moment she'd looked like dear old Cook at home in Hellerup – plump, pink fingers sunk in dough. Then she'd screamed, horrible screams like a snared rabbit. And suddenly it had been Valdemar holding the gun, Valdemar firing, once, twice – wild shots – Valdemar gaping at the blood on those plump, pink arms, and Valdemar crashing blindly out of that sweet-smelling kitchen. They'd rung later and told him that the woman hadn't died.

He stopped at a corner. The light was bad now and he peered down the street. He felt his stomach tighten – a sensation that had been alien to him for a long time. Two cars parked in a slum street where nobody could afford a car. A man strolling up and down, pretending that he was waiting for somebody, looking at his watch all the time – a ham performance. Lynx turned and walked back the way he had come. The light was failing fast and the situation was beginning to be desperate. He found a telephone box and dialled one of Sven's numbers. There was no answer. He tried another and felt a surge of relief – another alien sensation – when he heard Sven's voice.

Sven was in the old headquarters of L Group, in Hillerødgade. He caught a No. 20 tram up Fasanvej. All the way he felt people were staring at him. Sven's firm hand-clasp was reassuring, and it was wonderful to sink into a familiar chair with a bottle of Tuborg and a real cigarette, and leave it to Sven to contact the Controller.

Sven put down the telephone and slumped into the sofa opposite.

'It's a big one,' he said. 'The bastards are staking out half a dozen places.'

'Are we all right here?

'God knows. Anyway, you're getting out tomorrow morning – the *Lise* route, my boy. No argument this time.'

'What about you?'

'I can stay for the time being but——' he shrugged.

'Damn it all, things are beginning to hot up, Sven. They can't put me into cold storage now.'

'It won't be for long. They'll soon have you back in harness. You could do with a rest anyway.'

'I suppose I could.'

'And some company. You've been out on a limb for too long.'

Lynx sipped his beer and smiled. It was true. Loneliness! He hadn't thought about it. Empty rooms, empty flats, empty streets, they'd been his world for so long that he'd forgotten what it was like to sit in a warm room with a friend, to drink and smoke with another man, to talk.

Suddenly he had an overwhelming desire to reveal himself to Sven, to tell him that he was Valdemar, to reminisce and laugh. He sighed.

'I'm all in,' he said.

Sven smiled.

'Get as much sleep as you can. We'll move out at dawn.'

But Lynx couldn't sleep. The prospect of Sweden was agony. He had imagined it so often – before. He had imagined a little house in a steep forest with mountains all round and the sea glinting in the distance. He had imagined sheer cliffs enclosing water that was like molten emeralds, water whose arctic purity washed away the years, cleansed and restored him so that when he emerged, his skin afire, he was Valdemar again. But always there had been Rosa there, Rosa and Johannes, laughing and playing in the white snow as they had laughed and played in the white dunes of Skagen.

Lynx shifted and turned in the bed. It was as if there was another body beside him, a hot, alien body, repulsive to the touch – Valdemar's body. But Valdemar was *inside* him, Valdemar's tears were pricking at his eyes, Valdemar's sobs were curdled in his throat. He fought, but he saw Rosa standing in the sea, standing where he had dropped her, the water lapping her breasts, the look of outrage and shock on her lovely face slowly turning into a vigorous joy. He fought, but he saw Rosa swimming towards him, diamonds cascading from her arms. She dived and he felt her hands on his thighs. She darted away like a silvery fish and he dived after her. It was all light and salt and laughter. He fought, but he saw her there in the shallows, saw the perfection of her body magnified by sun and sea. He saw the sand on her skin like breadcrumbs as they lay down together. He tasted the salt as he kissed her. But the salt he could taste was the salt of his own tears. He could not fight any more. Lynx was at bay, Lynx was down. And it was Valdemar who sobbed himself to sleep at last, like a child.

Lynx woke soon after dawn to find Sven standing by the bed with a cup of coffee – real coffee, too. He swallowed the scalding brew and scrambled into his clothes. They left the flat and clattered down the stone stairs to the basement. It had thawed overnight, and a thin rain was falling. They unchained two bicycles and heaved them up the area steps onto the pavement. They pedalled away towards Nørrebrogade, Sven cursing the rain.

It was Lynx's instinct that told him that the car they passed and the car they could see ahead, moving slowly in the same direction, were linked. It was Valdemar who seemed to whisper to him:

240

'This was inevitable. This was meant to be.'

The traffic light was red. Lynx and Sven pulled up and waited. Lynx's voice was terse.

'Do you see them?'

Sven nodded. His face was chalky. Rain dripped off the brim of his hat.

'Are you sure?' he said.

'Pretty sure. Let's test them.'

They turned their bicycles round and began pedalling back towards the parked car. They passed it and Lynx twisted his head round. The driver of the parked car had started his engine. Beyond, the other car was making a three-point turn.

'Case proven,' Lynx said.

'Separate?'

'Yes.'

'Enghavevej 63. Ask for Thorkild.'

'I'll see you there.'

Sven wheeled left, down a side street, and disappeared. Lynx speeded up, pumping the pedals hard. The bicycle was heavy and clumsy, the wheels seemed to snag every bump and lump in the road. He glanced back over his shoulder. One of the cars was following him, keeping its distance. The other had vanished.

He slewed to the right, increasing his pace. There was an alley ahead, too narrow for a car. He skidded into it, one foot grazing the ground. The alley twisted left and right: he was out of sight of the road behind. He dismounted and tipped the bicycle into some dustbins. It was a liability. He'd be better off on foot. He ran to the end of the alley and looked left and right. Empty. No, not quite. There were a few people about, three of them waiting for a tram.

He pulled into a doorway and lit a cigarette. What would the car be doing? Circling round, obviously. Yes, there it was, coming down the street. He moved further back into the doorway, well out of sight, and watched it go by. There were three men inside. Was there a fourth, patrolling on foot? Unlikely. The rain was falling steadily now and even the Gestapo were human enough to dislike getting their feet wet. What were they playing at? Concentrating on getting Sven?

The car had disappeared. Lynx turned up his collar against the rain and emerged from his doorway. He decided to cut through the maze of streets behind the Forum and try to pick up a No. 3.

241

He glanced left and right. Nobody much about. Two workers pedalling slowly towards him on bicycles, a dairy cart delivering milk. But – Christ – there was the car again – God – and the other one. One of Valdemar's memories came to him. A street in Hamburg. *Your only chance is to cross the road, now, and run like hell.*

As he started to run he saw the two workmen, who had just passed him, jump off their bicycles, drawing guns. He fled along the pavement, zig-zagging. No shots. *They want me alive.* There was a turning ahead, just past the milk van. He could make it. He could hear feet pounding behind him. There were men piling out of the cars. The milkman had put down his cans. Lynx tore past him. There were two shots, three. He stumbled into the side street. His blood was hissing in his ears. The pavement was like thick earth, hugging his feet and calves. Agony exploded in his knee. His legs buckled and he rolled. It was like before – the black night, the bobbing lights, twigs and thorns and barbs.

Lynx struggled to pull his gun out of his pocket. Valdemar began to sob at the pain in his knee. Lynx saw the milkman running towards him, a gun in his hand. Valdemar tried to get to his feet, make his paralysed leg work. Lynx took cool aim at the milkman, pumped two shots at him and watched him stagger. Valdemar saw the others coming and began to whimper. Lynx put his gun to his temples, saying *not alive, never alive.*

But it was Valdemar who curled up on the pavement, like a child asleep, with the drip, drip of the rain around him; and it was Valdemar's voice in Valdemar's head that cried, when they tore the gun from his hands, and their boots thudded into his back and chest and groin: *it's over, it's over, thank God, thank God, it's over.*

Christian said: 'Let's get out of the rain,' and they pushed their way into the Guldæblet Automat and secured a table at the back. Christian fought his way to the counter and bought them coffees. Karen thought he looked ill; there was a quiver in his hand that made the cup rattle in its saucer.

'They got Lynx this morning,' he said. He misinterpreted the bleached look on Karen's face. 'Don't worry. They'll never make him talk. Not Lynx.'

But Karen wasn't thinking of that, she was thinking that she could not even tell her mother and father. She and Johannes had played together that morning, after breakfast, and he'd said: 'Are you my mummy now?'

'His friend got away,' Christian was saying. 'He had to shoot his way out. It was a well-laid trap.'

Karen stared at him. She said:

'I've got the information you want.'

Christian looked awed.

'You've got the photograph?'

'I didn't need a photograph. I know him.'

'I don't understand.'

'He's an old friend of my family. He's probably using a different name now, but his real name is Sven Carlsen.'

Now Christian's face was bleached, and his voice was hoarse.

'Are you sure about this?'

'Absolutely sure. I saw him with Kleist last night.'

'My God——'

'Do you know him?'

'Yes – yes I do. He hasn't changed his name. He, he was Lynx's friend – the one who got away.'

They stared at each other. There was talk and clatter and laughter all round them.

'Then it's not surprising is it,' Karen said, 'that Sven got away?'

As he became aware of light in the cell, he became aware of pain. The light was an orange glow in his eyes, the pain crawled and throbbed and stabbed throughout his body. He tried to open his eyes but it was difficult because the flesh of his face was puffed and swollen. He could taste blood in his mouth and when he moved his tongue there were unfamiliar gaps in his teeth. It wasn't his own mouth any more. At last he forced his eyes open and tried to move his arms. Fire seared through his shoulders, the same fire that had burned him when they'd hung him by his wrists from the ceiling.

Slowly he sat up. He was back in the cell, back within those four welcoming walls, alone, wonderfully alone. How long would they give him? How long before the door would open again? He examined himself. His wrists were swollen with pus where the steel had bitten and the flesh had festered. There was

243

caked blood on his chest. His testicles were dark purple, swollen to three times their size. His left knee, through which the bullet had passed, was simply not a knee any more.

Lynx was dead – killed by Valdemar in the street. It was Valdemar who had to endure the pain now, Valdemar who had to hold out against the questions, the dazing catechism that went on and on. And Valdemar knew that he would break, he knew it.

He heard the rattle of the bolts and shut his eyes. He heard two or three men come into the cell and waited. Nothing happened. He opened his eyes. There was a man standing in the door, an immensely tall man with white hair. The white giant took a step towards him, took a step across a few centimetres of cracked tiling and across four years of time, from the barrier at Flensburg station into this cell. Valdemar stared up at him, remembering that panic, remembering Becker in the street in Hamburg, with the clerks and shop-girls averting their eyes, remembering the mud of Germany dragging at him as he fled across the fields, remembering the dawn at the old ruined tower, the peace of the fields and woods, his rage.

The white giant stared at him, then turned to one of the others. There was a brief conversation and Valdemar heard the word Kleist. *Kleist.*

'Bring him,' the white giant – Kleist – said.

Their hands gripped his shoulders and he groaned. They pulled him to his feet. But this time he knew he wouldn't break, not ever.

Part Four

In Limbo

33

'I want some milk, Lipinsky,' she said, 'fresh cow's milk.'

'You want I should bring the cow to your place so you can milk it yourself?'

She smiled and said: 'I'm serious. It's important.'

Lipinsky shrugged. 'Why don't you send home for some? You Danes get letters, clothes. Soon they'll be sending you boxes of caviare.'

She stared at the little man, trying to gauge whether his remarks were a genuine reflection of general anti-Danish feeling, or whether they were simply part of his bargaining technique. After all Lipinsky was a businessman, the most successful scrounger and fixer in the place.

'When you get your caviare, come see me again,' Lipinsky said, 'maybe we can do business.'

'We can do business now. Look.'

She showed him the pills. He picked one up and examined it like a jeweller appraising a stone. Lipinsky had been a jeweller.

'What is it?' he said.

'It's a vitamin pill. I've got——' she hesitated, 'two boxes of them.'

Lipinsky darted a shrewd look at her – the first time she had ever known him look her in the eye.

'Vitamins, eh? What sort of vitamins?'

'All sorts.'

Lipinsky put the pill to his mouth and touched it with his tongue.

'It could be chalk,' he said.

'Come on Lipinsky, you know it's not chalk.'

'How many boxes you got?'

'Two.'

She had five. She had received two in the parcel from Niels and had traded her good woollen coat which had come in the same parcel, for a further three. She had calculated that Lipinsky's price would be three boxes. Vitamin pills would soon be hard cash. Lipinsky sighed.

'To get milk,' he said, 'I have to bribe one of the Czechs and he has to bribe the cook at the SS barracks. Also I have to give my

246

friend in the Ghetto Watch a little present. It's a very costly affair.'

'Vitamin pills are a very valuable commodity. And I only want a little milk, a glassful, that's all.'

'Maybe for four boxes——' Lipinsky said.

'I've only got two.'

Lipinsky shrugged. He can't possibly know that I've got more, Rosa thought, yet somehow he does.

'All right. Four.'

'You give me two now, two when I have the milk.'

Rosa handed over the boxes and Lipinsky said:

'I like you, but you're crazy. All this for a little milk. Why milk?'

'How long will it take you?'

'Come back tomorrow, around this time.'

'All right. Tomorrow. Thank you, Lipinsky.'

'Why thank me? Thank me for what?'

Rosa smiled. 'Tomorrow,' she said.

It was three hours after curfew but by special arrangement – a further expenditure of vitamin pills – Rosa was permitted to sit by her grandmother's bunk in the so-called hospital. There were over a hundred women, crammed into wooden bunks, in the ward. Rosa had become accustomed to the stench, she had learned not to hear the moans of the dying and the ravings of prisoners in the grip of typhoid; she had even come to terms with the hopelessness of it, the mockery of a hospital without medicines or any facilities that could conceivably aid the recovery of its patients.

What she found hard to bear were the elements of the familiar that intruded into this utterly alien world: the nurses with their meaningless routines, reminiscent of some well-ordered clinic, the professional cheerfulness of the doctors, and above all the daily visits of Dr Blum himself.

Dr Blum had been the victim of his own dedication to duty. On the night of October the First he had come out of hiding in order to perform an emergency operation at his clinic. They'd arrested him as he was scrubbing up after the operation. Now he was one of the most respected doctors in the camp, being especially in demand at the SS barracks where he traded his expertise for drugs and medicines. Although it had been a comfort to Hannah to have

247

her old friend attending her, to Rosa Dr Blum's visits were a reminder of her grandfather's death, and his kindly eagerness to talk about old times was almost more than her fortitude could withstand.

On the morning of her arrest, after she had watched them drag Stig from the wreck of the van, the blood still pumping from his neck, after she had seen them haul the family out of the back of the van, watched them beat the man while his wife and children wailed and screamed, she had felt power return to her limbs and purpose to her mind. She had said to herself: unimaginable things will happen to me. My only duty is to survive and my only means of survival is to blot out the past, blot out the future, and contend with each moment as it comes.

In the truck that took them back into the city she had told herself: I am being transported into limbo. I must survive because I have a son. I must not imagine a future, I must live in the present and I must kill memory now. She had discovered a reservoir of fortitude inside her, a reservoir that grew as she faced and outfaced each new degradation. When they'd reached this place there had been an official welcoming ceremony during which members of the Independent Jewish Administration had made gushing little speeches, and the SS Commandant had looked on, nodding and smiling, and the leader of their party had moved a vote of thanks. Someone had whispered to her: 'I think it's going to be all right. I don't think it is going to be so bad here.' But after the farce reality had quickly reimposed itself as they were stripped, searched, herded through showers, and finally issued with yellow stars to sew onto their clothes. One of the men had broken down and sobbed. 'It burns,' he had moaned, 'I can feel it burning through my jacket and my skin to my heart.' Rosa had thought: it's nothing. It's a scrap of cloth.

But then she had found Hannah, lying in the hospital, dying of dysentery. Memories had flooded back, draining the reservoir inside her, creating a drought of courage. Hannah had retreated almost wholly into the past. Sometimes she was back at her father's estate at Rungsted, an elegant young lady in a long ball gown filling in her programme with a tiny tasselled pencil. Sometimes she was the châtelaine of the apartment in Copenhagen. She would wake in the stinking sty of her bunk and ask Rosa to fetch her little knife. 'You know the one I mean, my dear. You will find it in my sitting-room.' She would talk of Reuben and Isak and dinner parties at the Micheelsens, and once she told Rosa all about Rosa's marriage and what a dreadful business it was.

But it was Hannah's lucid moments that tried Rosa most sorely. Then her grandmother would talk very quietly. She would say: 'I don't want you to worry about me, Rosa. I am an old woman. I have had a long life and it doesn't matter so very much what happens to me. But you, you are young. You must not lose hope. Somehow you will get out of this terrible place. You must believe that. You must have faith.' How could Rosa tell her that faith had to be confined to the space within a moment?

Letters and parcels from home were another test of fortitude. Everyone else seemed to receive them with a kind of ecstasy. The man who had felt the yellow star burn his skin told her: 'Just to know they're thinking about me, praying for me, at home, gives me strength.' Rosa had felt strength trickling away from her as she fingered her old woollen coat and read Niels and Christina's letter. It was a wonderful letter, practical, intelligent, understanding, but the very word *Johannes* on the page made her feel helpless and lost. She sought distraction in a challenge to her ingenuity, in securing for Grandmamma a glass of milk.

Three nights ago Dr Blum had told her that Hannah would not live another week. She had sat by the bunk, watching Grandmamma for once enjoying an untroubled sleep, and she had suddenly seen such a look of Grandpapa about her, it had been like a revelation. She burned to procure for Grandmamma some tiny comfort, and she remembered standing in the door of Reuben's room, watching him exert the last of his strength to drink a sip of milk. Lipinsky had obtained the milk. She had collected it from him that afternoon, a small medicine bottle, filled with the mystical substance. He had even given her a glass, rather a fine one too, a Bohemian goblet with the arms of some defunct nobleman etched into the bowl. Now she was waiting for Grandmamma to wake from a shallow, muttering sleep before giving her the milk.

Hannah did wake at last, weak but lucid. Rosa bathed her temples and wrists with cold water and Hannah asked her what time it was.

'It's just after eleven, Grandmamma.'

249

'You shouldn't be sitting up with me like this. You need your rest.'

'How are you feeling?'

'I wish you wouldn't sit up with me. If you don't get your rest you will become ill.'

Rosa lowered her voice. 'I've brought you something, Grandmamma. Some milk.'

Hannah stared at her.

'Would you like some? Shall I pour you some?'

She glanced round, to make sure nobody was watching, then took the little bottle, and the glass, from her pocket. She pulled the cork out of the bottle and tipped a little of the milk into the glass.

'Look, Grandmamma, the best Bohemian crystal.'

Hannah stared at the glass.

'Where did you get the milk?' she said.

'Never mind. Now see if you can sit up a little.'

But Hannah continued to stare at her.

'You take it,' she said. 'It's of no use to me.'

'It'll help you sleep. Come on now, see if you can sit up.'

She helped Hannah raise herself and put the glass to her lips, her arm round her shoulders. Slowly and painfully Hannah drained the glass, then lay back with a sigh.

'I will sleep now,' she said. 'And you too, you must get some rest.'

Rosa put the cool cloth to Hannah's temples again but was suddenly aware of a curious intensity in her eyes.

'I don't want you to see me die in this place,' Hannah said.

She took Hannah's hand – spidery, like Reuben's – and held it. A tear formed in Hannah's eye. The drop of water welled in her red eyelid and then rolled over the deep furrows and cavities of her cheek, breaking up into tiny trickles. More tears came and Rosa wiped them away with the cloth. She bent over and kissed the damp, wasted cheeks. Hannah began to speak, her voice almost a whisper.

'When Reuben died,' she said, 'I went into his room. He looked so peaceful, so beautiful – and I wanted to lie down by his side and take his hand in mine. But I didn't. I couldn't bring myself to do it. I thought there was something unclean about his body. How could I have thought that?'

Fresh tears came and Rosa wiped them. When at last the eyes

closed she took both Hannah's hands in hers. She waited. Hannah was sleeping peacefully. There was a curious stillness in the ward. For once the moans and cries were muted. Hunger and exhaustion dragged at Rosa. She thought about taking some of the remaining milk for herself; but she did not want to let go of Grandmamma's hands.

Only when she awoke did she become aware that she had slept. She awoke to find herself half lying across Hannah's body. There was a grey light in the room, like the grey of stone. Her hands were no longer in Hannah's hands and when she reached out to take them again she found that they were absolutely cold and stiff, like claws. She put her head close to Hannah's head but there was no breath on her lips. She drew away and gazed down at Hannah's face. The deep lines were smoothed and softened and there was an extraordinary quality in the features which Rosa hardly recognized as those of her grandmamma. It was more than peace, more than beauty, it was dignity, Reuben's dignity, smiling there on lips that Rosa had only ever seen pursed and humourless.

Rosa suddenly knew that something miraculous had happened while she slept, that Hannah, in her dying, had overcome everything that, in life, had set her apart. And she knew, as clearly as if she had seen it, that it was Hannah who had gently detached her hands from Rosa's, gently so as not to waken her, that Hannah had died with Rosa's warm body close to her own slowly freezing flesh, and that the smile on Hannah's lips was the smile of someone who at the last, and not too late, has let love in.

34

From the window of the office in Hälsingborg Isak could look directly across the Sound to the roofs and spires of Elsinore and the sixteenth-century towers of Kronborg castle on the other side. At this point Sweden and Denmark were separated by a few metres of grey water; yet what a fundamental divide that little strip of sea represented. He sometimes thought it was as profound and impassable as the vast barrier of history that locked the Jews out of their Promised Land. In a melancholy mood – and his mood was invariably melancholy whenever he visited Hälsingborg – he would see himself as a figure out of history, the Wandering Jew, standing on the banks of Jordan, gazing with a two-thousand-year-old hunger at the plains of Israel. Once he had pointed out the parallel to Simeon, now pursuing his scholarly studies in Stockholm after escaping by boat from South Jutland, and his uncle had been delighted. 'You're beginning to think like a Jew,' he'd said.

Was it true? Was this the lesson he was supposed to learn – to embrace what his father had rejected? He turned away from the window, away from the tantalizing view of home, and sat down at his desk. He wished to God he didn't have to come to Hälsingborg – at least in Stockholm there were distractions – but it was part of the job and he was grateful for the job. Old Per Janson had been very decent about it, given him a seat on the board and a free hand to re-organize his company's financial structure, had made a place for him, in fact, as the Swedish Government, already over-burdened with refugees from all over Europe, had made a place for the Danish Jews. If it wasn't for the thought of Rosa, and the necessity of visiting Hälsingborg, he could almost be content.

The internal telephone rang and he picked it up.

The secretary said: 'There's a young man to see you – a Peter Jørgensen.'

'Who? I don't know anyone of that name. Has he an appointment?'

There was a brief hiatus and then the girl's voice came back: 'He says he was a friend of your brother.'

'Is he a Dane?'

'Yes.'

'You'd better send him in.'

Isak was puzzled and slightly irritated. He didn't like to think about Abel, it aroused too many feelings of guilt. In a way he felt more responsible for Abel's death even than for his mother's arrest.

He recognised Peter Jørgensen the minute he slouched into the room. It was The Viking.

'So you're Peter Jørgensen,' he said. 'I'm sorry, I didn't recognize the name.'

He shook the boy's hand and offered him a chair.

252

'Well now, what are you doing in Sweden? What can I do for you?'

'I escaped,' The Viking said. 'I had to get away. I have been here for six months. I tried to find you in Stockholm and they told me you were here. I have a holiday – three days. I had to see you.'

Isak's original suspicion, that this interview was going to cost him money, now became a certainty.

'And why is it so important for you to see me?' he asked.

'I want you to help me.'

'You mean you need money?'

'I want you to find me a job.'

'Haven't you got a job?'

'Yes. But they make me work in lumber camps up in the north. Look at my hands.'

He spread his hands and Isak saw that the palms were scarred and calloused. It was a rough, bleak life in those camps, he knew; but what other work was there for boys like The Viking?

'It's hard, I know – but at least you do have work. And it won't be for ever.'

'You don't know what it's like up there. It's so cold. I want a job like yours, in an office. I have always worked indoors.'

'I'm sorry, but jobs like that just don't exist.'

'You don't work in a camp.'

Isak smiled.

'I'm afraid I'm rather too old.'

'That's not the reason. You have influence, you have rich friends. You could help me.'

'I've been very fortunate – but you exaggerate my influence. I'm a refugee, just like you.'

'Because I'm not a Jew they make me work in the camps. The Jews don't work in the camps, they all have good jobs in offices and factories.'

'It has nothing to do with whether you're Jewish or not,' Isak said sharply. 'There are no distinctions of that sort made here.'

He pulled his wallet out of his inside pocket.

'I can give you some money, but that's all I can do. You will just have to put up with hardship the way we all have to.'

The Viking made no attempt to take the banknotes.

'That's easy for you to say sitting warm and comfortable here,' he said. 'You Jews don't suffer. It is the Danes who suffer.'

253

Isak was angry now.

'I have offered you money. I can do no more.'

'You have an obligation to me. I was your brother's friend. He told me he would leave the shop to me in his will. He told me I would be a rich man one day. But he left me nothing. Nothing.'

So that's it, is it? Isak thought. Had Abel promised any such thing? He doubted it. He'd made his will years before. Everything to Rosa. This was a crude attempt at blackmail.

'What my brother said, or didn't say, is no business of mine,' he said. 'Now take your money and go.'

'Do you know what kind of man your brother was?'

Isak noticed a tremor of anger in the boy's voice even though his face remained expressionless.

'He was a pervert.' The Viking said. 'He perverted me.'

Isak rose.

'Look. I've given you money. Now please leave.'

But The Viking did not stir.

'Do you know what happened to me when the Germans came for him? They took me instead. They took me to a prison and they raped me.'

Isak stared at him. He didn't understand what the boy was saying. Raped him?

'They called me a Jew's whore and they beat me. I had to escape. I had to come to Sweden or they would have killed me.'

'I'm sorry,' Isak said rather feebly. 'I'm sorry for you. I would help you if I could – but I can do nothing.'

Now The Viking stood up and there was a hint of an expression – anger – in his face.

'You have an obligation to me. It is your fault. It is the Jews' fault that all these things have happened in Denmark. But the Jews don't suffer. Oh no, the Jews sit comfortably in their offices and it is the Danes who suffer.'

Very quietly Isak said: 'Both my mother and my daughter are in a concentration camp. They may be dead. My brother shot himself. Don't talk to me about suffering.'

'Your brother was a coward and a cheat.'

Isak picked up the money and held it out.

'Take it – and go.'

The Viking glared balefully at him. For a second Isak thought the boy would attack him, but then The Viking snatched the banknotes from him. He looked Isak in the eye for a moment then deliberately spat on the carpet.

When he had gone Isak sat down in his chair and wiped his face with his handkerchief. Abel, Abel, he thought, what kind of legacy is this?

Even in limbo spring came. With the budding of the trees in the ghetto there came a spate of new rumours and a frenzy of curious activity.

The old Bohemian fortress town, built for five thousand free citizens, and now a prison for forty thousand, began to take on the appearance of a town again. Gangs of prisoners were set to white-washing the walls and painting the shutters of the houses. The streets were swept and washed. Teams of hastily recruited gardeners planted bulbs and shrubs, and signs went up – 'To the Park', 'To The Hospital', 'To The Post Office' – as if a flood of merry tourists was about to descend on the place. Even in the houses, where the Jews lived like ants in a nest, the pressure on space eased as thousands were transported away to the East; curtains went up in windows, pictures appeared on walls.

Prisoners who had paid large sums to the Gestapo for the privilege of being allowed to live in the model *Judenseidlung*, and who had very soon discovered that the conditions were little better than those of the charnel houses in the East, were suddenly inclined to take a more optimistic view of their investment. Rosa took no notice of rumours. She was beginning to believe that she could survive. Danes were privileged. The Red Cross parcels they received kept starvation at bay and left them only hunger to contend with; the vitamins fought off disease. Above all, no Danes were sent East.

One evening in June, when there was a scent of balsam in the air from the poplars in the park, and the daffodils and late crocus made a brave display along Sydstrasse, the Danish community was summoned to a meeting with senior representatives of the Jewish Administration. The Danes were informed that on the following day the camp would be visited by representatives of their Government and the International Red Cross. They were given clear instructions on how the Germans expected them to behave: no criticism of the *Judenseidlung* or the way it was run; no mention of starvation or contagious diseases; a cheerful demeanour at all times. The penalty for disobeying any of these orders would be loss of all privileges for the Danish section and deportation to the East for the transgressor.

For the first time in eight months Rosa found herself wanting to laugh. Now she saw the significance of all those buckets of paint, all those bulbs and shrubs and sign-posts. The sepulchre had been well and truly whited and the stage dressed for a gigantic farce in which she and her compatriots were expected to perform their roles for the benefit of—— well, of whom?

That night as she lay on her truckle bed in the room to which she had been newly assigned – she shared it with only four other women, there were plants in pots, and a row of plates on the wall – she tried to determine what the Germans could possibly gain from such a performance. Was it possible that the Danish delegation would be bamboozled into believing that this was a typical camp? Would they believe that daffodils nodded their yellow heads in Auschwitz, that a scent of balsam wafted across the heaped corpses at Belsen? There were people here who had seen both those places. She had spoken to them. One man, who had bought himself out of Belsen, had said to her: 'I cannot describe it because it is indescribable.' No, no; surely they knew that the Germans had converted half Europe into an abattoir; they could not be blind to it. Yet would the Germans have permitted this visit unless they were sure that the delegation would unwittingly perpetrate some such lie? One of the Elders had warned them: 'If you are asked about the death of any relative here, you must say that he or she died of natural causes.' What if they asked her about Grandmamma? Could she lie?

In the morning she rose early. Soon after six she went to the park. She knew of a place where some wild primroses were growing. She made sure that nobody was looking as she picked them. She took them back to her room and tied them into a posy. Then she sat down, and hoping that her room-mates would assume that she was keeping up her diary, she wrote on a piece of flimsy paper, in pencil: 'Believe the opposite of everything you are told. Thousands have died here and thousands more will die. For their sakes tell the world that you were not deceived.'

256

When no one was looking she wrapped the paper round the stems of the primroses, folding it so that it formed a natural frill round the blooms. Her plan was very simple. She would present the bouquet to the leader of the Danish delegation and make sure he understood that the paper contained a message. She was sure she could handle it safely. Everyone would think it a touching gesture. She made sure there was water in the old Bohemian wine glass, then put the flowers in it.

At seven she went off to her work in the grotesquely named 'Old People's Rest Home'. Any 'old people' who showed obvious symptoms of the various endemic camp diseases, or who were simply so emaciated as to cause distress, had been locked away in upper rooms. Only the halest and heartiest of the camp's septuagenarians and octogenarians were to be on display.

At noon the rumour began to circulate that the delegation had arrived. As she made her way back to her quarters Rosa saw them by the Children's Pavilion. There were three of them, smartly dressed, smiling and nodding. The senior Elders were dancing attendance and five or six SS, also dressed in suits for the special occasion, were pointing out the sand-pit, the slides, and other hastily manufactured items.

A delicious smell of cooking made her nose flare as she went into her house. The idea was that when the delegation inspected the Danish section they should find their fellow countrymen sitting down to a substantial luncheon. She passed the kitchen, pushed through a knot of gossiping prisoners in the passage, and went into her room.

Birgit, the eldest of her room-mates, was there, but she was not alone. There were two men in the room. They were dressed in plain clothes but Rosa recognized them immediately as SS guards. One of them was holding the posy of primroses.

257

—36—

44692 stood by the trip-wire and stared through the heavy mesh of the perimeter fence towards the women's camp. The bitter north wind, blowing off the frozen Silesian plain, cut through the cloth of his striped jacket and trousers. The wind shunted great banks of smoke, thick and black as crude oil, across the pale sun, laying a shroud of darkness over the huts and towers, the bunkers and cell-blocks. He moved along the trip-wire, keeping his eyes to the ground, and pulled off his forage cap as two guards strolled by. He forced his damaged leg to perform in case the Germans should notice how he limped and arbitrarily decide to put his name on the extermination list, or, as had happened before, beat him up with pick-axe handles.

When the Germans had gone he stopped again to stare, wondering why he had bothered to disguise his limp, wondering why he still clung to any belief that he could survive. Was it instinct? Or was it just that having reached this final stage of his journey, having discovered this ultimate territory, the abode of pure fear, he wanted to go back to a world in which fear could never touch him again? There was perhaps a chance for him, after all. Because he was a Dane, rather than a Jew or a Russian, they gave him easy work and the Red Cross parcels kept him alive. He did not have to grovel and claw in the sand for scraps of potato peel. There again, he probably had less to fear from the Germans than from his fellow prisoners — especially the Communists — who'd cheerfully cut his throat on ideological grounds, let alone for his store of bread. Would it matter very much if it happened? Better that perhaps than slow strangulation on the hook or the unimaginable communal death by gas. And what was he anyway now? Only a number — 44692 — nothing else.

But not quite. That morning he had watched the general *Appell* in the main square, from which he, as a Dane, was exempted. In that throng of barely animated skeletons he had seen a figure that, in spite of its extreme emaciation, he had recognized. It had been supported on either side by two equally wasted men and all three had worn the pink triangle on their sleeves. As the interminable count had proceeded, the SS guards floundering in a bog of mental arithmetic while their semi-naked victims shivered in the wind, it had slowly dawned on him that the figure he had recognized was dead and that his friends were holding up his corpse to be counted, according to the regulations.

At last one of the friends had reached the end of his endurance and had collapsed, with the corpse, onto the ground. 44692 had turned away from the sight of the guards' boots thudding into the quick and the dead alike, with a wave of pity and memory washing through him. He had felt arms round him, a sweet smell of scent, then he had heard a voice. 'I'm so sorry,' the voice had said, then: 'Go home to your wife. Get out of this hateful country.'

He had turned back, to watch them drag Becker's body away and fling it onto the heap, and, for a moment, he had ceased to be a number and had remembered what it had been like to be a man.

Now, as he looked out through the mesh towards the women's compound where dim figures moved about like shadows on a wall, he felt the man in him stir; and as he moved away he forced himself into walking like a whole man, and did not allow his crippled leg to trail in the sand.

Through the wire-mesh she watched the stick figure move away and merge into the hundreds, the thousands of other mussulmen who shuffled endlessly back and forth in the men's compound, the permanent chorus in this vast tragedy.

She recognized Reuben in each one of them, Reuben as she had seen him on that last day, skeletally thin, his striped pyjamas hanging on him in drapes. Reuben's dream had filled her thoughts as never before because she was finally living in it. Yet still she knew that she would survive. It wasn't just the certainty that the kapo in her block would protect her, as she protected all her favourites, it was something more powerful. In the worst moments, when her body raged for food, when the kapo murmured loathsomely to her in the dark, when, as each month turned and she remained arid inside and remembered that starvation had dried out her very womanhood, then she would reach out for the strap in the swaying tram and she would see the people, those pale, tired, unflinching people, her people, gather round her and form a human barrier between her and extinction. Their spirit sustained her, the memory of their unspoken unity

259

with her gave her the strength to survive the moment, and the next, and the next.

Between her finger and her thumb she kneaded a little ball of bread. Every week she kept back a morsel of bread which she rolled and fashioned into the shape of a petal or a leaf. She dyed the petals red with the rust from a pipe at the back of the hut. The green, for the leaves, came from a bottle of ink the *kapo* had. She found odd scraps of wire for the stem and branches and over the months her artificial flower had grown. The bread hardened until it was like clay. It was brittle, she had to handle it carefully. At night she would hold the flower close to her face. During the day she kept it well hidden. The first person who found it would eat it.

Part Five

1945

37

'A wolf at bay,' Squire Tøller boomed, 'is the most dangerous creature in the forest.'

There was a murmur of assent round the table and Bolm, the Gestapo chief of Sønderborg, added, with a sidelong look at fat old Possel:

'Now that it is simply a matter of defending the Fatherland, victory is assured. The Führer's hands are no longer tied.'

Kleist sipped his wine and said nothing. He looked at his host, whose shaggy bulk and blustering voice dominated his end of the table, and thought: You idiotic buffoon, I wouldn't like to be in your shoes. In France, so he had heard, many of the prominent collaborators had shot themselves, as the German armies retreated, rather than face the vengeance of the Resistance. Was that what this bumbling idiot would do?

Old Possel was trying to change the subject but Bolm was determined to demonstrate his loyalty for the benefit of Kleist.

'By concentrating the issue in this way,' Bolm said, 'the Führer has produced yet another master-stroke.'

Yes, what a master-stroke, Kleist thought: the Red Army entrenched on the west bank of the Oder, seventy kilometres from the Brandenburg Gate; the British advancing on the Rhine; Berlin in ashes. He said, and it still pleased him to notice how his voice produced an uneasy hush over the candle-lit, extravagantly loaded table: 'There is one factor which could yet rob the Führer of the victory he has planned. Defeatist attitudes.'

He left Bolm to develop this theme and let his eyes rest for a moment on Possel, who avoided them, then on various members of Possel's staff. He knew exactly what they were thinking; they were praying that the defeat would come swiftly and that they would, at last, be safe from the Nazi fanatics who, even at this stage, even with Germany blazing round their ears, were capable of punishing disloyalty with death. They wanted to survive did these plump soldiers. They could smell an armistice, but they could also smell a firing-squad.

Kleist appreciated the irony of the situation. Here were these fools jabbering about the Führer's strategic genius and the spirit of Colberg, not one word of which did any of them believe, except possibly Bolm who was ex-Hitler Youth, and their host who was evidently an eccentric, all for the benefit of the one man in the room who had decided, months ago, to extricate himself from the mess before it was too late.

Kleist was getting out. This was, in fact, the first stage of his journey to safety. Ostensibly he had visited Sønderborg to confer with Bolm about the increase in Resistance activity in South Jutland; in reality he intended, with a new identity and a money-belt, to disappear to Sweden the following night.

He had the whole thing meticulously planned. He would sail from Stockholm to Cadiz as a Swedish businessman. In Spain the Swede would disappear and a few weeks later a Brazilian merchant of German origins would board a ship bound for his native port of Rio Grande do Sul. In Brazil the final vanishing trick would be performed. Eichmann's friend Pfitzer had talked of an island off the Chilean coast, called Chiloé, where a man could buy many hundreds of hectares, many houses and shops, and the entire police force and judiciary, for a small valise full of gold.

It was all going to cost a great deal of money, of course, but there would be enough left over for that farm and that ultimate form of protection: the silence of well-bribed officialdom. It was hardly the fulfilment of his dream, no; he had always dreamed of a place like this – rooms with gilded mirrors, a table glistening with silver, a park and a lake and a great estate: still, if Chiloé was any sort of pond, he would be the biggest fish in it.

His one regret was Karen. She would have come with him, he was sure of it. Her devotion to him was obsessional. But naturally the risk was too great. Poor little Karen. He wondered what would happen to her. When he failed to return she'd no doubt become frantic. His former colleagues in Dagmarhus might give her a rough time. And after? In France the lucky ones had their heads shaved and were paraded through the streets. The unlucky ones got a knife in their bellies or a bullet in their necks.

He turned to look at the end of the table where the Squire was rising and holding up a hand for silence.

'Gentlemen,' he said, 'there will now be a short lull in the proceedings.'

Possel and his friends began clapping; the old eccentric bowed and walked away from the table. Kleist turned to Bolm and asked:

'What is this?'

Bolm grinned.

'It's a tradition. On his birthday the Squire always roasts a whole goose himself, carves it, and serves it. In a minute he'll come back in a chef's hat.'

'A very stange man,' Kleist said.

'A great character – and a very good friend of the Reich.'

Kleist felt suddenly tired out. The last few weeks had been one hell of a strain. He rather wished he hadn't agreed to come. But Bolm had persuaded him that this man Tøller set the best table in Denmark and it would have seemed curious if he had refused. He rolled a little wine round his tongue. He'd asked Pfitzer about the level of civilization on Chiloé. 'Well,' Pfitzer had said, 'it's the end of the world, but the climate's European and a man with money can make himself comfortable anywhere.'

That was true, Kleist thought, and, in any case, perhaps one would not have to spend the rest of one's life at the end of the world. An opportunity to return would no doubt arise. He turned to Bolm.

'Our host is taking a long time to put on a hat.'

'Ah – our host is a perfectionist,' Bolm said.

Squire Tøller had walked down the long passage to the hall where Willem had been waiting. He and the poacher had exchanged a nod, then the Squire had pushed through the green baize door and walked into the kitchen. Mrs Hansen had been struggling into her overcoat and the Squire had helped her. Then Mrs Hansen had held up the Squire's coat so that he could slip into it. Now the Squire buttoned up his coat and smiled at Mrs Hansen.

On the kitchen table were two objects. One was the roast goose on its salver, the other was a small black box from which a wooden plunger protruded. The Squire placed his hand on the plunger.

'I feel the honour should go to you, Mrs Hansen; you've had to cook for them all these years.'

'No, no, sir,' Mrs Hansen replied, 'you have a better right.'

'I'll tell you what. We'll do it together. Put your hand on top of mine.'

Rather hesitantly – she was nervous of electrical things – Mrs Hansen obeyed.

'It's been worth waiting for, this moment, eh, Mrs Hansen?'

'It has, sir.'

The Squire smiled, Mrs Hansen closed her eyes tight, and together they pushed down the plunger.

The explosion lifted the roof off the fake seventeenth-century dining-room. One of the German chauffeurs, who had been strolling in the drive, smoking a cigarette, was cut down instantly by a horizontal hail of glass. The others, five of them, died seconds later as Willem led his men out of the bushes, their machine guns stuttering out an even deadlier hail.

Then a strange silence fell on Vidlund, broken only by odd crashes and crackles from the ruins of the dining-room.

The Squire and Mrs Hansen crunched across the gravel. Mrs Hansen carried a small suitcase and the Squire a couple of bottles of *snaps* and a case of crystal nips. With the tiny glasses brimming they all drank a toast to freedom, then moved cautiously forward to view the remnants of the dining-room in which a few little fires were flickering.

'Most neat and scientific, Willem,' the Squire said. 'Those fires won't spread?'

'On no, sir,' said Willem.

'I've been waiting for thirty years to get rid of that damned excrescence.'

He rubbed his hands together. 'Ah well,' he said, 'can't stand here gloating all night. Ready Mrs Hansen?'

He went round the circle of men shaking each one by the hand. He said to Willem:

'Wonder how long it'll take 'em to work out that my august carcass is not among the assembled bits and pieces?'

'Doubt if they will, Squire,' the poacher said.

'Hope not. Bastards'd probably burn the whole damned place to the ground. Keep an eye, eh?'

'I will, Squire.'

'Ah well, good night to you all and – dammit – God bless you. Come along Mrs Hansen.'

The Squire and Mrs Hansen took the path through the spinney and then the track to Christiansen's farm, where they would spend the night before crossing to Sweden. The Squire carried Mrs Hansen's case for her. It was a clear, frosty February night. The Squire sniffed the air and said:

'Exit The Rhino, eh, Mrs Hansen?'

'Yes, sir.'

'Couldn't have done it all without your help, you know.'

'I didn't do very much, sir.'

He stopped by a stile and looked up at the stars.

'Seems a curious way to end it all, just walking away like this,' he said.

He took out one of his fat cigars and lit it.

'I'd imagined − I don't know − columns of Allied troops streaming across the border − flowers, champagne, victory parades. Let me help you.'

He handed her over the stile, then followed, and they continued their unhurried walk.

'On the other hand perhaps this is the better way. A bit of dignity to it. No nonsense.'

He was silent for some moments, then he said:

'Remember that day when young Valdemar arrived − eyes like a madman, gibbering like a baboon?'

'I do, sir.'

'We were two of the very first, Mrs Hansen. We should be proud of that.'

'And we've won, sir, haven't we?'

The Squire stopped.

'By God we have, Mrs Hansen. By God we have.'

He threw away the butt of his cigar.

'Mrs Hansen,' he said, 'I'm going to kiss you!'

And so he did, once on each cheek; and then he took her arm and they walked together down towards the farm.

38

Light flurries of April rain were spattering against the windows of Poul Larsen's office and Poul was pacing the room, twisting and rubbing his hands together, in a series of gestures which his closer associates, accustomed to the almost inhuman sang-froid of the Permanent Extra Secretary, would have recognized as evidence of extreme anxiety.

But Poul was more than anxious, he was haunted. He was haunted by the memory of a girl, a dark and vibrant young creature moving towards him through the throng in his brother's drawing-room, a baby in her arms, and then talking to him so easily and unaffectedly. Rosa and her little son had come to occupy a very special place in his limited affections, especially after Valdemar's disappearance. She called him Uncle Poul and sought him out at family gatherings and seemed to display a genuine fascination for the discreet and dusty anecdotes of Court and political life which the majority of his friends, he knew, considered a bore.

The news of her arrest had shocked him more profoundly than almost anything else in his career. He had mobilized every person of influence in the capital to persuade the Germans to release her, but it had been hopeless. The fact that she had been married to a non-Jew, and a Larsen moreover, might have saved her had it not been for the fact that she had been caught in the act of aiding and abetting the escape of proscribed persons, in the company of a notorious Resistance worker. From the Gestapo's point of view the case had been unarguable yet Poul had felt his inability to sway them as the culminating failure in a series of gross misjudgements which were inextricably bound up in his mind with the disasters that had befallen the Abrahamsen and Mendez families. He had not been able to rid himself of the idea that Abel Abrahamsen's suicide, Hannah Abrahamsen's arrest, Isak's flight, and Rosa's deportation were his personal responsibility. The catalogue of his errors appalled him: he had failed to see the inevitability of the invasion; he had failed to grasp the obvious fact that the German occupation must inevitably end in something like civil war; he had totally misread the political complexities that had led to the German action against the Jews (he still cringed at the memory of the verbal pap he had fed Simeon Mendez); finally, when little Rosa had needed him, he had been impotent.

Outwardly he had remained calm and in control, inwardly he had shivered, stripped as he was of his major defence: confidence in his own judgement. The result had been an uncharacteristically passionate concern with the fate of Danish prisoners in Nazi hands. He had fought for, and obtained, extraordinary concessions from the Germans: Red Cross food parcels, clothes parcels, personal mail. For months he had worked behind the scenes with friends in the Swedish Government, making several trips to Stockholm, to bring about the early release of Scandinavians. He claimed no personal credit but the result of Scandinavian pressure on the Germans had been a meeting between Count Bernadotte and Himmler at Hohen-Luchen in early February. Himmler had agreed to a phased release of Scandinavian prisoners and the Swedes had organized convoys of buses to transport Danes and Norwegians from the death-camps to the comparative safety of Neuengamme.

Yesterday Himmler had agreed to the unconditional release of all Scandinavian prisoners and the day before the white buses had carried the Danish Jews out of Theresienstadt; but Rosa Larsen had not been among them. Rosa Larsen had disappeared.

All Poul knew was that she had been sent East ten months ago and all his efforts to trace her through his German sources had been frustrated by the utter chaos that now reigned in the Third Reich. He was tortured by the thought that Rosa would die horribly in one of the Polish camps with peace and safety only a few weeks, perhaps only a few days away.

The internal 'phone rang and his secretary announced Major Aksel Olsen. When Olsen came into the office Poul was sitting at his desk as usual. He rose and shook the officer's hand. Olsen smiled and the spring inside Poul's belly, which had been taut for days, ruining both his sleep and his digestion, very slightly uncoiled.

'I think we've located her, sir,' Olsen said. 'We have an agent — a woman who works as an interpreter for the Gestapo — who has kept files on the movements of Danish prisoners. She's not one hundred per cent sure but she thinks she has tracked Mrs Larsen down.'

'Where?'

'Auschwitz.'

Poul stared at him.

'Why? Why did they send her there?'

'I don't know, sir. I'm trying to find out. But in the meantime?'

'Yes, yes, of course. You may leave it to me. I will speak to the Commander of the South Jutland corps immediately.'

'There are other Danes in Auschwitz, sir. In particular a man the Resistance are anxious about. I have a list here.'

Poul took the paper.

'I will see to it, Olsen. I'm very grateful, really very grateful. I just hope to God we're in time.'

If there was one thing Karen hated more than the country it was a small country town; and Randers, in Jutland, had always seemed to her the quintessence of a grey, dull, smug, ugly, little country town, exactly the sort of place, in fact, where a grey, dull, smug, ugly, little woman like her Aunt Gertrud could be relied upon to settle.

Aunt Gertrud's house was on the eastern fringe of the town, and in spite of its views over Randers Fjord, was somehow always dark inside, even on the sunniest day. On a drizzling April afternoon it had the atmosphere of a sarcophagus and even the damp streets, mercantile architecture, empty shops, and dismal people of Randers seemed preferable by contrast.

As she walked down the hill, past the glove factory where Aunt Gertrud's late husband had piled up a tidy fortune (or so it was alleged by the widows who frequented her aunt's dreary card parties), Karen could not help reflecting that to be exiled in this provincial dump was a curious reward for two years' service in the Resistance. But her father had thought it prudent to get her out of Copenhagen for a time, and after that four-hour interrogation at Dagmarhus, she had been frightened enough to agree with him.

They had suspected her of complicity in Kleist's death because it had been engineered by her uncle Henrik. It had taken all her histrionic powers to convince them that she had been helplessly in love with Kleist and that his death had genuinely shattered her. They had been suspicious and angry – the anger of frightened men – but in the end they had let her go.

269

She went to the public library, exchanged two or three books, and chatted briefly to the librarian. The war news was inspiring: the Russians were pounding Berlin to dust, the Americans were thrusting into Czechoslovakia. She went out of the library and wandered somewhat aimlessly about the centre of the town. The sky had cleared and there was a hint of warmth in the wind. As she strolled past St Morten's church she wondered about Fritz. Fritz had been transferred to France in early 1944. He'd actually come to say goodbye to her. She'd been touched. But where was he now? A prisoner? Dead? Fighting in the rubble of Berlin?

She was passing the railway station, on the way back to Aunt Gertrud's, when she saw, ahead, a faintly familiar figure. Her heart began to thump a little as she increased her pace to catch up with him. He was dressed like a workman, in blue jacket and cap, but something about the way he walked, something about his narrow shoulders and sandy hair made her sure she was right.

The man turned into the station. She saw him join the queue at the ticket office. There weren't many people about and she hung back by the magazine stall. A couple of old women joined the queue behind him, and he looked round for a moment. She caught only a brief glimpse of his face but it was enough. Sven Carlsen. Three or four other people had joined the queue now. Could she risk joining it herself? If he saw her ... No, he must not see her. The Resistance had been hunting him for a year but he had vanished. If he saw her now he would vanish again. On the other hand, if only she could find out for what town he took his ticket. She walked slowly over and stood in the queue. Carlsen was only a few paces away. He had his back to her. He leaned forward to speak to the ticket-clerk and Karen heard him say:

'Aalbaek. A single, please.'

As he was fumbling in his pocket for his money, she turned and walked quickly out of the station.

Aalbaek! It was on the coast, a little way south of Skagen. Was Carlsen hiding somewhere in the marshes? What an incredible piece of luck, seeing him like that − in Randers of all places. Sven Carlsen! He'd disappeared the same day they took Val. Somehow he must have found out that the Resistance were on to him; or more likely, given the way he'd disappeared so completely, he had always planned to fade out once he had delivered Lynx to the Gestapo.

She passed a telephone box and stopped. Yes, safer to 'phone Father from here. Sven Carlsen! Father would be delighted. She might even be able to persuade him to let her return home. It would be dangerous after all if she and Carlsen accidentally met again.

39

The bus swayed and juddered as the wheels bounced in and out of pot-holes. Some of the prisoners were waltzing and singing in the aisles, even the Gestapo guard was smiling. But Rosa remained in her seat, her face pressed against the window, in her hand the red and green flower, made of bread. Ahead she could see the long column of white buses and ambulances wheel right over a bridge. One of the motor-cycle outriders buzzed past and by the side of the road a little group of dirty, hollow-eyed children were staring at the buses as they passed, staring at white ghost buses flitting through the dawn.

It had been the same in every town and village: pale, bewildered people staring at the buses with their white, white paint and their bold red crosses. They'd driven through bombed-out towns, they'd seen packs of starving dogs snarling and barking in the rubble. They'd seen great smudges on the horizon where whole cities were burning. Once, when they'd stopped in open country, they'd seen formations of Allied bombers growling towards Berlin. The worst spectacle had been that endless, straggling, struggling line of refugees, hundreds and hundreds of dazed women and children fleeing from nowhere to nowhere. The Gestapo guard had fallen silent. Rosa had detected tears in his eyes and she had found herself pitying him.

She knew that she should have felt exultant. She had been magically transported out of hell; she was being wafted through the devastated heartland of Germany, a privileged witness to the destruction of the nation that had created the hell, that had heaped the world with corpses – yes, she should have felt exultant. But she did not. She slept and woke, slept and woke, the white buses swimming in and out of her sight as they ate up the twisting miles towards Denmark, swimming in and out of her dreams.

271

When they crossed the border at Flensburg everyone fell silent. Then people began to weep and hug each other. Rosa felt them kiss her and embrace her, but she kept her face pressed to the window, kept her eyes on the white buses weaving and swaying ahead of her.

When at last they halted, in a great square of asphalt, surrounded by school buildings and filled with Red Cross lorries and vans, there were hysterical cries and wild caperings and a rush for the door. Rosa remained in her seat. She could see the burly driver helping people off the bus. Even the Gestapo guard was helping, lifting down ancient, roughly corded cases, and grey bundles. Still Rosa did not move. The driver came down the aisle towards her. He peered at her.

'Are you all right? Are you ill?'

Rosa withdrew her face from the cold glass.

'You're home,' the driver said, 'you're safe. Come along, I'll help you.'

He reached out to take her arm. She put a hand up and grasped the leather strap over the seat.

'That's right,' the driver said. 'Easy does it. Can you walk?'

Rosa nodded. They walked together down the bus, between the seats, the driver slightly behind Rosa, supporting her. When they came to the door, Rosa detached herself.

'I think I can manage now,' she said.

She looked down: two steps, metal steps, with strips of grey rubber, between her and the soil of Denmark. She took them slowly, carefully, gripping the handrail. Two Red Cross women came towards her. One of them was crying. She put her arms round Rosa and said:

'Welcome home. Welcome home.'

The other pointed to a line of trestle tables. The tables were draped with white cloths. There were pyramids of fresh loaves, mounds of cheeses, fat china pots full of butter, jugs steaming with hot chocolate, and little posies of wild flowers among the heaps of plates and cups.

'Let's get some food inside you,' the Red Cross woman said. 'Come along.'

Already crowds of released prisoners were clustering round the tables, laughing and crying and tearing at the food. Rosa began to move towards them, the Red Cross women flanking her.

272

Suddenly she stopped. She had heard a voice. The voice was saying:

'I know you.'

It was a dry croak of a voice but she recognized it. She turned. There was no one near, no one addressing her. She could see only the driver of their bus and one of the released prisoners, a ghost of a man, gaunt and cadaverous. It was the man who had spoken. He was staring at the driver.

'I know you.'

The driver was staring back.

'Your name is Lund. I know you.'

The man's eyes were fever-bright. His whole body was quivering and twitching. The driver was gaping at him, half-smiling.

'That's right. That's my name. But——'

'I know you. You are Lund — you are Sergeant Lund.'

'Yes — I am — but, I'm sorry, I don't recognize you——'

'You don't know who I am?'

Lund shook his head. One of the Red Cross women tugged gently at Rosa's arm.

'Come along dear. You must have something to eat. You'll feel better when you've got something inside you.'

But Rosa was oblivious. She was staring, staring at the man. He was smiling but his mouth was a dark hole, toothless.

'I'm Larsen,' the man said, 'Lieutenant Larsen. Valdemar Larsen.'

Lund was ashen. He was hardened to the sight of the mussulmen by now, and this one was better covered than many, yet there was something appallingly corpse-like about him.

'Larsen — do you hear? I'm Larsen, Larsen, Larsen, Larsen.'

Lund suddenly remembered. Larsen. Lieutenant Larsen. The ammo truck. But it couldn't be him. It couldn't be. He put an arm round the man — there were tears glistening on his yellow-grey cheeks.

'It's all right, old chap,' he said, 'you're safe now. You're home.'

'I'm Larsen,' the man said. 'Do you understand? I'm Larsen.'

Lund looked up. Two of the Red Cross women were walking towards them. Thank God. They'd be able to cope.

'I – look, I think I know this chap. He's in a pretty bad way. I think we'd better get him to the doctor.'

'Yes,' one of them said, then to the man: 'Come along. We'll get you some food. Some nice hot chocolate.'

Her voice was crisp and competent. But the man clung to Lund. 'I'm Larsen. I am. I'm Larsen.'

Then came another voice. Lund gaped. It was the strange, silent girl from Auschwitz.

'I knew you, Val,' she said. 'I knew your voice.'

She moved closer and held out her hand. The weight on Lund's shoulder lifted as the man stood straight. The man took the girl's hand and held it.

'I knew you,' she said again.

On the night of the Liberation Niels Larsen primed and lit the semi-circle of braziers in his drive. Candles glowed in every window of the house; the dusk danced with fire. Earlier Niels and Christina had strolled together through the quiet streets of Hellerup and had seen candles flickering in the windows of every house they passed. They had realized that the whole city, probably the whole country, was illuminated in this way. 'It's over, Niels,' Christina had said; and at that moment a truck had clattered by, a truck loaded with Resistance men brandishing guns. 'Not quite over, I suspect,' Niels had said. Now, he was glad to be alone for a moment, glad to be alone with the brilliant, crackling fire of the braziers, alone with the warm breeze, the peace of the night.

He felt no joy; rather an overpowering emptiness and a sense of apprehension. For over two years a single issue had filled his life; now there was nothing. There was still work to do, of course, routing out the collaborators, stool-pigeons, and Nazis; but that was mere refuse disposal. The main task, the great task, had been accomplished. And what of the future? Business again? Yes, inevitably; what else? But the thought of it frightened him. The war had shattered the economy of Europe, and Denmark had not escaped. The prospect of rebuilding was daunting. Had he the energy, had he the will?

He thought of Valdemar, asleep in the house, strange, silent, unrecognizable Valdemar who seemed to be able to communicate only with Rosa. Rosa! What a woman – what strength. When she'd first seen Johannes the little boy had burst into tears and shouted: 'Go away, go away, I don't like you.' He'd flung himself at Christina and sobbed. 'She isn't my mummy, she's a witch.' Rosa had been so calm, so completely understanding. Very patiently she had allowed Johannes to get used to her presence in the house and one afternoon he'd overheard them talking in the garden. Rosa had been telling him the story of her arrest and imprisonment. Johannes had been mesmerized – he adored stories – and had listened with wide eyes, hardly interrupting at all. Niels had gone quietly away, as moved as he had ever been in his life, and with a feeling of deep content in the certainty that Rosa would be able to reunite this little family, split apart by war; that she would be able to lead Valdemar gently back into the world and lead Johannes gently to the father he hardly knew.

I too must rebuild, Niels told himself, rebuild for Valdemar and Rosa and Johannes. He walked round the corner of the house and onto the lawn, which was rough and lumpy now, after years of neglect. The flag was flying from the old mast – he had hoisted it that morning and Christina had cried. He'd been near to tears himself.

He stopped suddenly. There was a figure moving across the lawn, a figure like a wraith, a pale, limping wraith. Valdemar. Niels watched his son step painfully onto the jetty. As Valdemar threw off the old towelling bath-robe that Christina had for some reason preserved along with his school photographs and pennants and old toys, Niels moved nearer. The moon was up. Its creamy light seemed to accentuate the deformities of Valdemar's body. His ears and hands and feet seemed abnormally large and his left leg was wasted and scarred. Niels gazed at this travesty and it did not occur to him that Valdemar would dive into the sea until he did so.

Niels ran onto the jetty. This was madness. The sea was ice cold and the doctors had said warmth, rest, and plenty of food. But Valdemar was striking out strongly, his arms cleaving the water with something of their old grace and power. He dived and turned and began to swim back towards the jetty. Niels knelt down, gripped his arm, and helped him out of the water. As he wrapped the bath-robe round the shivering frame he said:

'Have you gone mad?'

But Valdemar was gasping and laughing.

'I feel clean,' he said. 'I feel clean for the first time in years.'

'Back to the house and straight into a hot bath,' Niels said firmly. 'Rosa will be furious with you.'

'The last thing I need is a bath, Father.'

Niels almost started. The life was back in Valdemar's voice. It was the old Valdemar, crisp and confident.

'Well a *snaps* then,' Niels said.

'Ah yes. A *snaps*.'

They walked together across the lawn and through the French windows into the morning room where a good fire was burning. Valdemar sat by the fire, rubbing himself dry, while Niels fetched a bottle and glasses. They toasted each other and then Valdemar said:

'Father, I've got so much to tell and so much to ask.'

And for Niels twenty years were wiped away and Valdemar was a boy like Johannes, thrilling at the prospect of a story, and bursting to tell a story of his own.

41

On a brilliant morning in June Rosa walked through the Citadel gardens on her way to Niels's office in Bredgade. The day before her father had come home from Sweden, to the flat in Fridtjof Nansens Plads which Niels and Jensine, between them, had defended from expropriation and damage. Valdemar was in hospital, undergoing surgery on his damaged leg, and Rosa had slept in her old bed, in her old room. It had been a short night, for she and Isak had sat up talking until the early hours. When Jensine woke her, at half-past ten, Isak had already left for a meeting with Niels.

She was eager to get to the office and collect the keys to Uncle Abel's shop which had been her property since early 1944 when, again thanks to Niels, the legal complications over Abel's will had been sorted out and a caretaker manager appointed; but she decided to sit for a while on her old bench by the duck pond and collect herself, as she had done so many times before in her life.

For weeks she had felt as if she was walking on the edge of a void. She had kept steadfastly to the path on the lip of the void for Johannes's sake, for Valdemar's sake. She had been strong and cheerful, she had concentrated every bit of her energy on rebuilding a life for her husband and son, and they had suckled themselves on her strength and grown healthy again. But most nights she cried herself to sleep, feeling that she must fail, that she could not go on, that she must have rest; and every morning there was the fight against the temptation to give up the struggle, to let herself topple into the void, to let the sand slither and heap over her.

The gardens had never looked so beautiful and serene. The dazzling sun imparted a vigour to the green leaves of the trees, and the air, sea-fresh but tinged with summer spices, seemed to carry the very essence of life and health into her blood. Outside the gardens, she knew, the city was sick, debilitated after five years of war, poisoned with hate and fear, as old scores were settled and bitter accusations traded; but here its heart beat strongly. She stood up at last, refreshed and renewed, the darkness retreating, and continued her walk.

In Toldbodvej the first person she saw was Mr Cohn. He was dressed in a threadbare double-breasted suit and he was standing outside his old barber's shop, which was closed and padlocked, looking like a child lost on the beach.

'Mr Cohn!' she said, taking his hand in both of hers, 'I'm so glad to see you, so very glad. How are you and how is Mrs Cohn?'

'Ah – Miss Rosa,' Mr Cohn said dully. Added to his normal expression of profound mourning was a look of bewilderment. Rosa bubbled with questions.

'My father-in-law told me you had both got to Sweden safely. When did you get back?'

'I don't know,' Mr Cohn said. 'A week, two weeks – I don't know.'

'What's the matter, Mr Cohn? Aren't you well?'

'We should never have gone away,' Mr Cohn said with a little more animation. 'That I do know. We should never have gone away. We should have known what would happen.'

'But what has happened?'

'We've lost everything,' Mr Cohn said with a helpless gesture

277

of his arms. 'I knew how it would be. Everything, Miss Rosa. I don't know what's to become of us.'

'I don't understand – how have you lost everything?'

'I don't understand either, Miss Rosa. When Becca and I came back we found people in our house – a whole family. They'd been living there for two years, they said, paying the rent. I told them it was my house but they said no, they were paying the rent to the landlord. All our furniture was gone, everything; I don't know who took it. I can't find out.' He gestured towards the little shop. 'I don't even have a business any more. I signed it away to a friend. I had to do that, you understand. Now he says that – I don't know – it was a legal transaction, that the business is his.'

'But that's nonsense, Mr Cohn. He can't do that. You must go to a lawyer.'

Mr Cohn blinked.

'I went to a lawyer. He says I must fight the case – but it may take months, years. What am I to do in the meantime? How am I to live?'

'Where are you staying?'

'In a hostel, Miss Rosa. The Government people are very kind, most kind – but we only have one room and Mrs Cohn is not well, not well at all. It's the worry.'

'I'll speak to my father-in-law. He will help you, I know. It's monstrous that you should be treated this way. You'll get your house back and your business, don't you worry.'

Now Mr Cohn looked at her almost accusingly.

'We shouldn't have gone. I *said* we shouldn't have gone. I blame myself.'

'You'd better come with me now and we'll see my father-in-law. He'll know what to do.'

'I have to see my lawyer now.'

'Very well – give me his address, and give me your address, and I'll ask my father-in-law to contact you today.'

Rosa scribbled down the addresses.

'Don't worry any more, Mr Cohn, we'll get it sorted out I promise you.'

'You know what they said? The people who've taken my house? They said I should be grateful. I should be grateful that the Danes saved my life. But I *am* a Dane, aren't I? I *am* a Dane.'

278

'Of course you are. And nobody can take your property away from you. Don't worry. We'll sort it out, I promise.'

She left Mr Cohn still standing by the door of his shop and walked briskly down Bredgade. She collected the key from Niels's secretary – Niels and her father were closeted and she didn't want to disturb them – and caught a tram. As she went towards an empty seat she stumbled against one of the other passengers, but she did not hear him mutter 'Bloody Jew' or notice the looks he exchanged with the people nearest to him. Inside the shop it was damp and musty. She went into the back room and turned on a light. Nothing had changed. There was still the same profusion and confusion of books and pictures and papers.

She walked along the bookshelves, running a finger over the spines, like a child trailing a stick along a paling. It was all there, all bound up in leather and cloth – poetry, history, philosophy, science. She remembered one of her uncle's favourite dicta. 'The search for a meaning in life has filled a million books and has been called the parent of Reason. But in fact it has been nothing but a gigantic flight from Reason.' He would smile and shrug in that provocative way of his. 'All these volumes,' he would say, 'amount to no more than the log-book of a voyage to nowhere.' He would grin and scratch his head and puff away at his limp, crinkled cigarettes while five or six voices eloquently defended the intellectual achievements of mankind. Then he would suddenly break into the discussion with another of his cherished statements. 'By and large mankind has learned absolutely nothing from its artists and philosophers. Why? Because fundamentally, there is nothing to learn from them.'

She came to the end of the line of books and stopped. Between the tops of the books and the base of the shelf above someone had put an object that was not a book. It was a rectangular mahogany box inlaid with silver and ivory. She pulled it out and carried it to the table. She opened the lid. Inside lay a pistol, a pistol with a long, elegantly chased barrel, and beside it was an empty recess where its twin had lain. She picked up the pistol and weighed it in her hand.

She stood for a long time, holding the pistol, remembering Abel, remembering his relish for a good argument, his talent for defending the opposite of what he believed purely for the sake of debate.

279

Gradually she became aware of a commotion in the street outside – shouts and feet shuffling on the pavement. Still carrying the pistol, she wandered into the shop. There was a figure kneeling at the window, on the other side of the glass; behind and around him were the legs and feet of other people. The man was daubing white paint on the window – letters; a slogan – she couldn't read it.

She could hear shouts – chanting, slogans – what were they saying? Something about Jews. She moved closer to the window and looked up. Through the dribbling white paint and the dusty glass she saw a face. The face was mouthing something at her, there was hatred in the eyes. She knew the face. It was The Viking's. She saw The Viking straighten, step back, and pick up a can of paint. She saw him draw back his arm, heard the can strike the glass. A great stain of paint spread over the window. She heard her grandfather's voice: 'I know that I should talk to them, reason with them, but I cannot move, I cannot speak.'

Rosa could not move, could not speak. She could hear the boys running away and their footfalls seemed to echo through catacombs walled and roofed with sandstone.

42

There was a hush over the world as Valdemar waded out of the shallows. There were no bird-cries; the crickets in the dunes were silent; even the sea's ceaseless washing of the sand was a lisp. The sun was climbing into the sky and it seemed as if all nature was still, awaiting the fire of noon. He walked slowly up to the cottage, his stride strong and even, with hardly a trace of the limp left. His body was bronzed and although it had a lean look, which the doctors said it would always have, there was flesh on it again, firm, healthy flesh. He went into the bedroom.

Rosa was still asleep, curled round her pillow. She always slept like that now. He opened the shutters and let the light stream in and Rosa stirred and blinked. He sat on the edge of the bed and held out the mug. She sat up and took it and he kissed her lightly on the temples.

'Sleep well?'

She nodded.

'No bad dreams?'

She shook her head and smiled nervously, then took another sip of coffee. He looked at her body. She too had put on flesh and the sunshine of Skagen had tanned new bloom into her skin; yet the look of fragility was still there.

The police had found her wandering along Strøget, clutching a pistol, tears streaming down her face. She had been unable to answer any of their questions and they had identified her, in the end, from the number tattooed on her wrist.

'It's going to be a scorcher today,' he said, 'what would you like to do?'

She smiled. 'Read, eat, swim, read, eat, and sleep. What else *is* there to do?'

'Nothing, thank God.'

He reached for a cigarette and lit it, then lay beside her on the bed.

'In the camps,' he said, 'I used to spend hours day-dreaming about this place. When it was bitterly cold – you remember the incredible cold of those north winds? – I used to pretend that I was swimming in the sea, that the cold was washing me clean and toning me up. Ridiculous.'

'It was brave of you – to remember like that. I never dared. I wouldn't allow myself.'

He had been idly, almost unconsciously, stroking her upper arm and he was suddenly overwhelmed by his love for her. Yet for a moment he made no move.

When he had discussed their mutual impotence with Blum the doctor had said: 'This is where you must exercise the greatest patience of all. Time will do it, I promise you. Don't force it. Be as loving as you can, and wait. Remember what a precious thing it is.'

His sudden silence and the quickening of his breath alerted Rosa. She turned to him and looked down at his body. Then his arms were round her, his face was on her breast. An appalling sense of desolation filled her as her body failed to respond to his murmurs and caresses. Her mind reeled with love and tenderness for him, but her senses were dead. She was cold, dry, shut. When she closed her eyes, to block her tears, she seemed to look out onto a devastated landscape, a place of craters and rubble, where nothing could grow. A sorrow greater than any she had ever

281

known, greater than the hopelessness of the catacombs, greater even than the hunger of the camps, possessed her utterly. A wave of water swept across her landscape, as if a dam had burst.

Valdemar held her as her body shook and heaved with sobs. All desire had gone but tenderness remained. He stroked her hair and her streaming cheeks and then he released her and let her lie down to sleep and stayed beside her as she slept.

For the next few days Rosa was very quiet but Valdemar noticed that the fragile look had gone. Together they taught Johannes to swim and helped him to build sand castles on the beach. They went for walks through the marshes and forests and Rosa cooked gigantic meals.

Desire for her filled Valdemar's every waking moment but he kept himself in check. His instinct told him that until she came to him he must restrain himself. Yet the light and air acted on him as elixir: he craved the act of love.

One morning they saw a car bumping and rattling across the marsh towards the cottage and Johannes ran out to meet it. The car pulled up at the back of the house and a man got out whom Rosa immediately recognized as Christian. Valdemar and Christian greeted each other heartily but Rosa remained distant. She felt Christian's presence in the house as an intrusion and, in some way, a threat to their future. She was glad when he and Valdemar set off for a walk along the beach; but when they came back an hour later and she saw the chilled, in-turned look in Valdemar's eye, she was suddenly frightened. When Christian and Johannes were playing on the beach she asked him:

'Why has he come here, Val? What's happened?'

'Nothing's happened, darling. He, he was on holiday in the area and thought he'd look us up. That's all.'

'You're lying.'

He was. Why?

'Tell me, Val,' she said. 'For God's sake don't let's start having secrets again.'

'It's Sven Carlsen,' he said after a moment. 'They've found him.'

She stared at him and looked away.

'And Christian has come all this way to tell you that?'

'They had to tell me. Damn it all Rosa, the man betrayed the whole Resistance movement, and specifically me.'

'You're going to kill him, aren't you?'

'Of course not.'

'Which means you are.'

It was the old, formidable Rosa who had spoken, and for a second Valdemar was thrilled. Then, as she sat down at the table by the front door, he was apprehensive. He said to himself: I can't put her through any more. Damn Christian for coming openly like that. But he also heard a voice whispering to him that justice must be done. It was a voice he had almost forgotten, a voice from a remote past – Lynx's voice.

'Why, Val?' Rosa said. 'Can't you see that it's over?'

He sat down beside her. He must be gentle, choose his words.

'Rosa,' he said, 'surely you of all people must see that Carlsen should pay for what he did.'

'Of course he must pay. But not by lynch-law. The war's over, Val. If you kill Sven Carlsen you are just a murderer.'

'What do you suggest – that Carlsen should be handed over to the police?'

'What else? What did we fight the Germans for if it wasn't for justice – proper justice under the law?'

He laughed harshly.

'Justice? He'd hire the smartest lawyers in Denmark, get his trial postponed and postponed again. People are sick of hearing about the war already. In a year or two everyone will have forgotten. Let's forgive, let's pretend it never happened, they'll all be saying. Let's be compassionate. Carlsen would spend a couple of years in gaol and then he'd go free.'

Rosa stood up. 'I thought,' she said, 'I really thought that – after everything – you had learned about compassion.'

'Rosa, for God's sake——'

'Why don't you track down The Viking? Why don't you kill him? Doesn't he deserve to die for the poison he tried to spread? But no. You've told me a hundred times that all that was an aberration, the aftermath of war and occupation, the product of resentment and fear and confusion. How many times have you told me that? Are you saying it isn't true?'

'Of course it's true.'

'Yes it is. And because I understand it I can forgive. If I don't, if I don't have compassion, I just perpetuate it all.'

'It isn't the same.'

'It is, Valdemar. It is the same.'

She turned and walked into the house. She was almost silent for the rest of the day and at dinner hardly looked at Christian, who was staying the night. Valdemar and Christian sat up talking and she was asleep when Valdemar came to bed.

She awoke before dawn and found herself alone. She got up and went into the living-room, then into Johannes's room. Valdemar was not there. She went out to the shed and found that his bicycle was gone. She went to the spare room and woke Christian. Christian was dazed and blinking.

'Where has he gone?' she demanded. 'Tell me where he's gone. He's gone to kill Carlsen, hasn't he? *Hasn't he?*'

'I – I didn't know he was going to do it tonight. We were going to do it together.'

'Where is Carlsen? Tell me.'

Christian was groggy and frightened by Rosa's intensity. She said more gently:

'You must tell me, Christian. I cannot let him do this thing. You can do it, or someone else, I don't care. But not Valdemar.'

Lynx stood in the little spinny of stunted pines and looked down towards the cottage. It was an ancient, thatched building, rather like Valdemar's, with sheds and outhouses. He hefted Christian's gun in his hand, and looked at his watch, then up at the sky where the first hint of dawn was flushing the clouds yellow and red. As he had done so many times before, Lynx coolly reviewed the facts. Carlsen worked on the night-shift of a fish processing factory outside Frederikshavn, six or seven kilometres away. In fifteen or twenty minutes Lynx would see him cycling along the lane towards his house. He would see him turn into the stony track, ride up to the front door, dismount, and lean his cycle against the wall. Lynx would move out of cover the minute Carlsen entered the house. Carlsen would be brewing up coffee on the stove in the kitchen and Lynx would fire through the open window – three body shots. Then he would go into the house and pump two more shots into his head. Then he would ride away and it would be over.

According to Christian, Dragonfly had said: 'If he wants to, Lynx should do it. He has the right.' Yes, he did have the right. He waited, thinking of nothing.

When he saw the cyclist come, when he saw him turn onto the track, he cocked his gun. Carlsen pedalled right up to the house, jumped off his cycle, and leaned it against the wall. It was getting light now. Lynx could see him clearly. Carlsen bent down to remove the clips from his ankles and as he straightened, he hesitated. He had heard something. Lynx had heard it too. Lynx looked towards the road. There was a car approaching. He recognized it – it was Christian's car.

He cursed to himself but remained cool. He raised the gun. Could he be sure of hitting Carlsen at this range? His finger tightened on the trigger – then relaxed again. Carlsen was coming towards him, running. Lynx dropped to his knees. Carlsen was going to hide in the spinney. He was going to run right into his arms.

As the car turned into the track and Carlsen came panting up the incline towards the spinney, Lynx saw the door of the house open and a dark figure emerge. There was a long stutter of machine-gun fire. Carlsen spun and stumbled, fell and jerked and rolled. Lynx saw the car pull up. He saw the dark figure with the machine-gun walking towards Carlsen's body. Then everything became crazy. He recognized the slight figure who stepped out of the car as Rosa and he recognized the other figure, the figure bending over Carlsen's corpse, as his own father.

At last he moved and walked down towards Niels. Niels looked up and Lynx stopped dead. They were not his father's eyes staring at him over the bloodied huddle of Sven Carlsen's body, they were Lynx's eyes. Then he saw the horror of it. If Lynx could exist in Niels then he could exist in any man. There could be a whole world of Lynxes.

43

'Trust Simeon to turn the whole thing into a public spectacle,' Isak said.

Rosa smiled. 'Well, after all, the Bar Mitzvah of someone your age is quite an event, I imagine.'

'Quite an event for me, perhaps,' Isak said, 'but did Simeon have to invite the entire Jewish community of Copenhagen to his house?'

Rosa laughed. Great Uncle Simeon's modest drawing-room

was certainly full; there were even some faces she recognized from Theresienstadt.

'Rosa.'

It was a young man's voice. She turned and there was a figure in a neat new suit whom she vaguely recognized. She couldn't put a name to him, however.

'You don't remember me.'

'I do but ...'

Isak came to her rescue.

'How are you, Arne?' he said.

'Arne Katz,' Rosa said. 'How marvellous.'

Isak smiled and moved away. Arne blushed.

'You didn't recognize me,' he said.

'I did but − oh, so much has happened. How are you? What have you been doing? It's been years.'

'Oh, I was in Sweden. I'm working for my father now.'

'Arne! Working for a capitalist?'

Arne blushed again − he was still a blusher.

'The last time I saw you was at The Citadel, before the war. You remember?'

'You were off to Moscow, I seem to recall. Did you ever make it?'

'Hardly. I was arrested in '41, you know, after the Nazis invaded Russia. It rather cured me of communism.'

'I'm sorry to hear that. You were always such a man of principle.'

'And you always laughed at me.'

'How did you get out of prison? How did you get to Sweden?'

'Oh, you don't want to hear yet another escape story, do you? My father got me out of prison.'

'The power of capitalism.'

'Exactly.'

'And Sweden?'

'Oh, the usual thing.'

The usual thing. Rosa looked away for a moment, remembering Stig and the blood pumping out of his neck. She was suddenly bored with Arne, so smug and clean in his beautifully tailored suit.

'What happened to you, Rosa?' he was saying.

'Oh, nothing very much. I must go and rescue my husband

from Uncle Simeon. After his triumph with my father, he sees a potential proselyte in the unlikeliest people.'

Arne looked crestfallen and Rosa felt sorry for him.

'You must come and see us,' she said and he brightened. 'Goodbye for now.'

She and Valdemar walked back to the flat in Grønningen. Isak had let it to a doctor after Reuben's death and Hannah's removal to Rosenhus. The doctor had left a few months after the Liberation and Isak had made it over to Rosa. Half the rooms were empty, but they were furnishing it gradually, both Niels and Isak contributing pieces.

They slept in what had been Reuben's room. The two tall windows overlooked the Citadel gardens and the English church and got the morning sun. Rosa had missed her period. She wondered if she was pregnant. She told Valdemar as they lay in bed and he hugged her.

She had waited for desire to return suddenly and of course it had returned gradually. She could not even remember now the first time they had been able to make love, it was merged into nights and days of love-making in the cottage, after Johannes had gone back to Copenhagen and they had decided to stay on for a few weeks in Skagen.

'I saw Father talking to you earnestly,' Valdemar said. 'I suppose it was the usual thing?'

'He's very keen for you to make up your mind.'

'I know. But I just feel like drifting.'

'I suppose we've got to do *something* for the rest of our lives?'

'I suppose so. I've been thinking – about building at Skagen – a house we could live in.'

'But what could you do up there?'

'I don't know. Fish. Farm. Could you live there, city girl?'

She didn't answer for a moment. She thought of Arne Katz in his suit, a young stockbroker with a bright future.

'I think it would be wonderful, Val,' she said.

'Father will be appalled.'

'I don't think so,' she said after a moment, 'I think he'll understand.'

287

Epilogue

A reception in Copenhagen, 1947

The merger of the Larsen Shipping Company with R. Abrahamsen caused a considerable stir in business circles, especially when the Mendez Bank announced that shares in the new company, Consolidated Shipping, were to be offered to the public. The opening of Consolidated's rebuilt yards was almost a state event. As Christina Larsen put it, 'Le tout Copenhagen' flocked to the reception afterwards: Royalties, Ministers – and rival shipowners slightly uneasy about the christening of this baby giant. The one missing face was Isak's. He had written to Rosa from Palestine: 'I fear that it is impossible for a midwife to desert his post during the delivery of a new nation. Tell your revered father-in-law that he must exert himself to keep me rich. Rearing this child, Israel, is going to be an expensive business.'

But Baron Hans Mendez was there, of course, looking a little stouter and greyer, and boring everybody with the tale of his arrest by the Germans and how he had protested so vigorously that they had not dared touch him in October '43. To the Baron's credit it should be said that he did not mention the fact that he had donated five hundred thousand kroner to the Jewish escape fund.

Squire Tøller happened to be in town and went to the party. He was collecting yet another decoration ('I've got a chest like a pawnbroker's window,' he declared) and buying clothes for his dazzling Swedish bride. ('I thought it was time to start propping up the family tree.') The Squire, who was now by way of being a national hero, was courted and fawned on, and startled his admirers by stating loudly that the only real satisfaction he had got out of the war was the utter obliteration of his grandmother's dining-room. Karen was there, but Fritz Brenner, to whom she had become engaged a few weeks before, tactfully declined his invitation.

Valdemar wandered about, looking bored and lost, as he invariably did at parties, and Rosa kept an anxious eye on Johannes who was being plied with champagne by, of all people, his great uncle Poul. At the height of the rout Niels drew his son to one side.

'There's still a future for you here, Val,' he said with a smile. Valdemar shook his head.

'No thank you, father. I'm cultivating my garden, remember.'

Niels sighed and was about to protest when the Minister stood up and began to make a speech.

He talked about the legacy of war, by which he meant the economic legacy of war, and the challenge that faced the nation. He spoke of the future in rosy terms. He spoke of wealth and prosperity for all, of the good life that it was the right of every Dane to enjoy.

As the Minister moved towards his peroration Valdemar caught Rosa's eye. She grinned and he whispered:

'Shall we go?'